MAUNA KEA

Ua Mau Ke Ea O Kaʻaina I Ka Pono

"The Life of the Land is Perpetuated in Righteousness"

—King Kamehameha III,
Royal Coat of Arms, 1843

HAWAII THE BIG ISLAND TRAILBLAZER
Where to Hike, Snorkel, Surf, Bike, Drive

first edition
text by Jerry Sprout
photographs, design, production by Janine Sprout

For: John and Patty Brissenden, Paula Pennington and Jimmy Dunn,
John and Suzanne Barr, Greg Hayes, and Ellen Scott

Diamond Valley Company, Publisher
89 Lower Manzanita Drive
Markleeville, CA 96120
www.trailblazertravelbooks.com
trailblazer@gbis.com

ISBN 0-9670072-5-9
Library of Congress Catalog Card Number 2002096351

Printed in the United States of America.
Copyright © 2003 by Jerry and Janine Sprout

Proofreaders: Greg Hayes, Ellen Scott

Mahalo Nui!

Les, Loraine, and Freckles Miller; Barbara and Gary Anderson, Shipman House; Lorna and Albert Jeyte, and Janet, Kilauea Lodge; Dave Griffin and Chris Kaluau, Blue Hawaiian; Doug Arnott and Susan Keris at Arnott's Lodge; Michael Tuttle, Hawaii's Best Bed & Breakfast; Donna Saiki, Pacific Tsunami Museum; Daniel Kaniela Akaka, Jr., Mana Lani Resort; Luana A. B. Neff, Hawaiian Force; Laura Aquino, Current Events; Sharon Sakai, Kohala Coast Resorts; David Nardin and Paul Fukumura-Sanada, Mauna Loa Observatory; Keoki Pa'aoao, Mauna Lani; Laura Craft, Barbara Bower, Keck Observatory; Longboarder T. J. Street; Mountain biker Rick Solomon, Kamuela; Gary Rothfus; Roz Roy, Bayview Farms; Albert Kehaulani Solomon, Jr., Kamuela Museum; Gil Kaheli at Miloli'i;

Chris at Hapuna Beach; Marsha Hee, Fia Mattice and Alison, Volcano Art Center; Doris Komomua, Alamo; Shannon and Rene, Jaggar Museum; Kawika and Enoka at Wawaioli Beach Park; Arnold at Hawaii Volcanoes Observatory; Larry at White Sands Beach; Tom Dequiar, Pu'uhonua O Honaunau; Janet, Sean, Paul, and Bento, Hawaii Tropical Botanical Gardens; Caleb Nazara and Keahi, Kaupulehu Cultural Center; Staff at the Department of Land and Natural Resource; Kumu Nani Lim Yap, Hula Halai; Hiko'ula Hanpai, Storyteller; Beau at Kalopa State Park; Lorrie at the Hilton; Vivian Steeley, Randilyn Juan, Big Island Visitors Bureau; Chef James Cassidy at the Four Seasons; Susan Rice and Tomoe Nimori, Kona Historical Society; Jeff at Kona Village; Steve at Ahalanui Beach Park; Sailors Koca and Casey;

Jan and Tim Gillespie; Michelle Murray and Christine at Hawaii Volcanoes National Park; Patty McCarthy, Waipio Valley; Dave McRobbie, Marmot Mountain; Auntie at Keauhou Beach Hotel; Paul Gephart at Hawaii Artifacts; Marie at Kealakekua Bay; Jana and Jevon Ka'aloa and Jarren Moeoge, Super J's; Kamuela Moraes, Richardson Ocean Park; Tony and Bonnie Foote; Nancy at Akaka Noodle Shop; Reed Harmon, Kohala Divers; Debbie at World's Best Gardens; Lynne Kreinberg, Kealia Ranch Store; Momi Subiono, Greenwell Ethnobotanical Garden; County of Hawaii, Parks Department; Dr. Jeffrey B. McDevitt; Fanny Au Hoy, Hulihe'e Palace; Laurie Beers and Tailiko Scarbrough at Kahalu'u Beach; Christopher Smith, Kilauea Military Camp; James Kimo Pihana and Kelani, Mauna Kea; Rob Ely, Nancy Reilly, Kathy Hollingstworth, and Andrea Ka'awaloa, Hawaii Volcanoes National Park; Ken Pacchio at Kihilo Bay; Joann Bragalone, Ululani Gallery; Suga' Daddy; and to everyone else whose name we didn't get!

PUʻUHONUA O HONAUNAU, A PLACE OF REFUGE

HAWAII TRAILBLAZER is an offering to the strong and beautiful and intelligent people of the Big Island. May your message of Aloha spread to the farthest reaches of the earth and live on forever.

HAWAII
THE BIG ISLAND

WHERE TO
HIKE, SNORKEL, SURF, BIKE, DRIVE

JERRY AND JANINE SPROUT

DIAMOND VALLEY COMPANY

MARKLEEVILLE, CALIFORNIA

PUBLISHERS

TABLE OF CONTENTS

ALOHA AND WELCOME
TO THE BIG ISLAND OF HAWAII

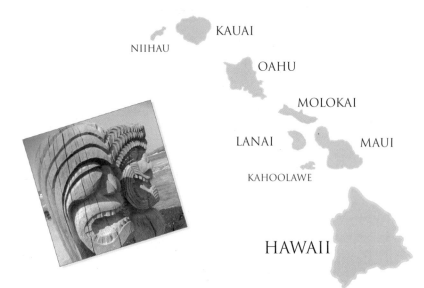

KAUAI

NIIHAU

OAHU

MOLOKAI

LANAI   MAUI

KAHOOLAWE

HAWAII

Forget the movie version of Hawaii and prepare yourself to see another planet altogether when you journey to the Big Island. Yes, you'll find white-sand beaches arranged
around turquoise coves, whose warm, clear waters are packed with fish and coral as
colorful as a bag of gum drops, and, yes, deep green valleys are laced with waterfalls,
and birds as colorful as the fish will flitter through exotic forests. Even so, these are just
a few predictable elements of this strange and wonderful new land.

Usually, after taking an initial spin around the island, visitors are struck by its diver-
sity—and for good reason. The Big Island is comprised of five separate volcanoes that
have joined together over a million years, making it about twice as large as the rest of
the Hawaiian Islands combined. On the slopes and shores of these oceanic peaks you
will find 11 of the world's 13 climatic environments. No place is more diverse. Yet, after
taking another spin or two, visitors begin to appreciate the singular nature of this land,
and to realize that the notion of island-as-planet is more than just a metaphor.

Creation enfolds here, right before your eyes. Enough new lava—molten earth batter—has erupted in the last twenty years alone to pave five round-trip roads to the
moon. The newest of earth is nearly barren, fields of rock glistening smooth or heaped
in jagged piles. At the coastline of these barren fields, coconut palms sprout after just
years. At other eruption sites, just a century into the light of day, new trees and shrubs
take hold. And at older flows, exposed to the elements for thousands of years, full
forests have established. On the island's oldest eruptions sites in the north are tropical
jungles with beaches and valleys that hardly hint of their fiery origins. Recipe for Eden:

Squirt a zillion tons of molten earth into the sea, add rain, air, and time—*et voila!*

The new-planet idea is most apparent from a perspective atop the Big Island's mammoth twin peaks, Mauna Kea and Mauna Loa. Although both stand *only* about 14,000 feet above sea level (at 13,796 feet Mauna Kea bests its sister by 119 feet) the real story is below the waterline, where the mountains descend another 40,000 feet to the seafloor, making them easily the largest on earth. Surrounding these unearthly bodies is a universe of water, about 2,500 miles of open sea in every direction, the most-isolated landmass on the planet. This was the last land discovered by human beings, the Polynesian argonauts some 2,000 years ago. Western culture didn't set foot here until nearly 1800.

If history can foretell the future, then the fate of this new planet is sealed. All the Hawaiian Islands in the archipelago—130 of them, stretching over 1,600 miles—are moving with the earth's crust in a northwesterly direction, like the shell of an egg turning around its magma yolk. As they move, erosion and sea action wear away the land, and the highest peaks are submerged into the ocean. Some 5-million years ago, Kauai, the farthest north of the eight major islands, was where the

THURSTON LAVA TUBE, WAIPIO VALLEY

KOHALA FOREST RESERVE, PUʻU OʻO STEAM PLUME, KAUPULEHU PETROGLYPHS

Big Island is now, sitting over the molten Hot Spot. Maui, just north, used to be one huge island, but is now eroded away to four separate islands. The Big Island will slowly be worn down, its joined volcanoes becoming separate islands, and, finally, sea-washed coral atolls. Unless, of course, history is not a predictor, and the Hot Spot changes its nature and volume so that Loihi, the seamount brewing 20-miles offshore the Big Island today, does not simply herald a new island, but the beginning of a new Pacific continent.

Fortunately, NASA technology is not required to explore this planet—just a car, a swimsuit, and some flip-flops. In the north are the Kohala Mountains, whose high green pastures are home to Parker Ranch, the largest ranch in the U.S. On the seaward slopes of Kohala, the Big Island's oldest land, are the lush valleys of Waipio and Pololu

KAMAKAHONU BEACH, PU'UHONUA BEACH PARK

that call forth romantic images of the South Pacific. Sightseers will be attracted to the quaint plantation towns and history parks in Kohala, and hikers will love walking on some of the state's best tropical trails.

South from Kohala, on the west side of the island, are vast, barren lava fields. This is land only a lizard would love at first sight. But drive toward the ocean a mile or two along the almost-always-sunny coastline and you'll discover Hawaii's best beaches. Hidden in the wild sections, and well marked on resort grounds, are ancient petroglyphs and village ruins that speak of an earlier time. Trails connect long stretches of coastline, both through the gardenscapes of the resorts and the natural lands.

The Kona coast, the Big Island's most recognizable place name, covers the southwest side of the island. While rightly known for sunshine, Kona gets enough moisture at its 1,000- to 2,000-foot level to yield its famous coffee and macadamia orchards. Kailua-Kona, just south of the airport, is a strip of modest resorts and condos, a few miles long. Snorkeling and surfing spots are interspersed along this coast, where Kamehameha the Great chose to live his final decade.

Midway on the Kona coast is Kealakekua Bay, where Captain James Cook made landfall and was heralded as a god, only to be slain later along its shores. Some of the best snorkeling in the Hawaiian Islands is in this bay. The coast gets steep in the south of Kona, but you can duck down at Hoʻokena and Miloliʻi for snorkeling and remote coastal hiking. At Manuka State Park, farther south just before forests give way to desert lava fields, are native forests with both nature trails and wilderness treks.

At South Point, Mauna Loa's 60-mile-long southwest rift zone slopes gently into the sea. This most-southerly land in the United States was the most northerly for the Polynesians, who are thought to have made first landfall here. Going northward along the east side, the land rises steadily to the 4,000-foot level, 30 miles away, at Hawaii Volcanoes National Park. On the way up, you pass the rain forests of the Kau Forest Reserve, which are home to Hawaii's sixth volcano, Ninole. Within the forest, Wood Valley is a botanical wonderland that most visitors miss.

One of America's treasures, the quarter-million acre national park is centered around Kilauea Caldera, where volcanology became a science. Eruptions of this "lava lake," have occurred as recently as the 1970s. Puʻu Oʻo, where current flows meet the sea in a towering plume of toxic steam, is a short drive from park headquarters, down Chain of Craters Road. The upcountry of the park and its adjoining state lands are hardly volcano-like, with ferns the size of trees in thousands of acres of native rain forests.

A half-hour down the mountain to the north of the park, is Hilo, which gets a bum rap because of its yearly rainfall. With many square blocks of vintage storefronts that survived two tsunamis—set in an arboretum of banyans and beach trees, and enveloped by a greenbelt of bay-front parks—Hilo is the Hawaiian Island's best-kept secret. It does get monsoon rains, feeding the Wailuku River that rushes down from the saddle of the island's twin peaks and through the town. Then after the rains comes the preternatural brilliance of the tropical sun. Within a few miles of the historic part of town are two state parks, Waiola and Wailuku, with a large lake and waterfalls. Also near Hilo is a run of four beach parks that offer snorkeling lagoons and surfing waves.

The Puna coast is a short trip from Hilo, but too far away for a reasonable day trip from Kona. Many visitors miss this coast which features views of the current eruption at the national park and the unheralded but fantastic Kehena-Poihiki Scenic Coastal Drive. In Puna, you'll also find several excellent snorkeling tide pools and natural thermal ponds in which to take a soak. Cape Kumukahi gets practically no play, in spite of being the island's dramatic east point, where you can breathe the freshest sea-level air in the world. This coastline was moved a half-mile seaward by a 1960 eruption of Kilauea's east rift zone. On the uplands of Puna grow most of the exotic flowers exported around the world.

The center of the island is Mauna Kea—Ka Piko Kaulana o Ka Aina, "The Famous Summit of the Land." Near the summit, in the Mauna Kea Ice Natural Area Reserve, is one of the highest lakes in America, Lake Waiau, which the ancients considered the "umbilical cord to the heavens." Fittingly, also near the summit, are a dozen of the world's most powerful celestial observatories, including the Keck and the Subaru. Tours take people to the top, or you can make the trip in your own four-wheel drive vehicle.

Hamakua is Mauna Kea's east coast, going north from Hilo. Dozens of streams cleave this windward side, issuing forth in waterfalls at Akaka State Park and Umauma. The old highway intertwines with the new, creating a scenic drive through wild tree tunnels and the fanciful Hawaii Tropical Botanical Gardens. Hamakua's rolling shoulders were former sugar cane fields, a history that is told by the plantation towns tucked away along the coast. Above the former fields are a run of forest reserves, with old-growth Koa and other trees, most easily seen at Kalopa Native Forest State Park.

The high plains of Mauna Kea are reachable through Mana Road, a cowboy trail, as well as several trailheads off the notorious Saddle Road. Set above 6,000 feet between the two big mountains, these locales will have you asking, Where am I? Saskatchewan? Africa? No, you're on the Big Island of Hawaii, a planet unto itself in the middle of the Pacific. If you can find the time to at least hit the highlights, hither and yon, the place will leave your head spinning in sync with the earth.

PAHOEHOE LAVA FIELD, HAWAII VOLCANOES NATIONAL PARK

GETTING TO AND AROUND ON THE BIG ISLAND

AIRLINES

Most flights to either the Kona or Hilo airports include a stopover and change of terminals in Honolulu. Most international airlines service Honolulu. Some airlines have non-stop flights to the Big Island (unless schedules have changed): United flies from San Francisco and Los Angeles, American from Los Angeles, and Aloha Airlines has direct flights from Oakland and other western cities.

CAR RENTAL

All the major companies, plus a few local companies, service the Big Island. Book early and phone around to get the best deals. Some companies offer mini-leases, if you're planning to stay longer. Tour companies and shuttle taxis are widely available. Public buses are also available. For independent travelers, a car is essential. Numbers for car rental agencies and bus companies are in *Resource Links*. See *Free Advice & Opinion*, page 214 for driving conditions and advice on renting a four wheel drive vehicle.

WHEN TO COME

High season on the Big Island is when school's out during the summer, and also briefly around Christmas and New Year's. Visitation doesn't drop off much during any month. Unlike the other Hawaiian Islands, the Big Island's tourists are spread over lots of country, and you will not feel the crush at any time—except for traffic snarls either side of Kailua-Kona. But if you'd like a slack time, early autumn and mid-to-late winter are the best bets. Room occupancy rates vary from 60 to 80 percent. See *Strategies for Visiting the Big Island* on page 198 for trip planning help.

DRIVING TIMES ON THE BIG ISLAND

See *Driving Tours,* page 183 for specific road descriptions and routes.

KAILUA-KONA TO:

Kona Airport, 7 mi. (15 min.)
Kawaihae, 32 mi. (35 min.)
Hawi, 52 mi. (1.25 hr.)
Pololu Lookout, 61 mi., (1.5 hrs.)
Waimea, 40 mi. (50 min.)
Waipio Valley, 63 mi. (1.5 hrs.)
Middle Saddle Rd., 58 mi. (1.25 hr.)
Hilo via Hwy. 19, 94 mi. (2 hrs.)

Captain Cook, 15 mi. (30 min.)
Miloli'i, 42 mi. (1 hr.)
South Point, 68 mi. (1.5 hrs.)
Volcanoes National Park, 98 mi. (2 hrs.)
Hilo via Hwy. 11, 124 mi. (2.5 hrs.)
Puna Coast via Hwy. 11, 143 mi. (3 hrs.)

HILO TO:

Volcanoes National Park, 28 mi. (35 min.)
South Point, 78 mi. (1.5 hrs.)
Middle Saddle Rd., 30 mi. (40 min.)
Waipio Valley, 41 mi. (1 hr.)
Waimea, 55 mi. (1.25 hrs.)

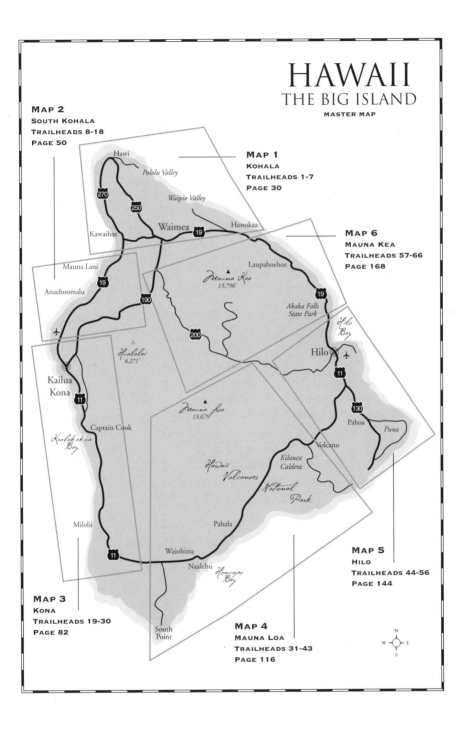

HAWAII
THE BIG ISLAND
MASTER MAP

MAP 2
SOUTH KOHALA
TRAILHEADS 8-18
PAGE 50

Hawi

Pololu Valley

270

250

Waipio Valley

MAP 1
KOHALA
TRAILHEADS 1-7
PAGE 30

Kawaihae

Waimea 19 Honokaa

MAP 6
MAUNA KEA
TRAILHEADS 57-66
PAGE 168

Mauna Lani

Laupahoehoe

Mauna Kea
13,796'

Anaehoomalu 19

190

Akaka Falls
State Park

19

200

Hilo
Bay

Hualalai
8,271'

Hilo

11

Kailua
Kona

11

Mauna Loa
13,679'

130

Captain Cook

Pahoa

Puna

Kealakekua
Bay

Volcano

Kilauea
Caldera

Hawaii
Volcanoes

National
Park

Milolii

Pahala

MAP 5
HILO
TRAILHEADS 44-56
PAGE 144

Waiohinu

11

Naalehu

Honuapo
Bay

MAP 3
KONA
TRAILHEADS 19-30
PAGE 82

South
Point

MAP 4
MAUNA LOA
TRAILHEADS 31-43
PAGE 116

N
W — E
S

HOW TO USE THIS BOOK

Use the INDEX to locate a trail or place that you've already heard about. Use the TABLE OF CONTENTS and MASTER MAP to find a part of the island you'd like to explore. Then use the TRAILHEAD MAP for each region to focus on a particular spot, and go to the trailhead descriptions to pick out a hike or other activity that sounds good. Trailheads include hikes of varying lengths, as well as snorkeling and surfing spots.

Use the ACTIVITIES BANNER in the TRAILHEAD DIRECTORY to see which recreational opportunities are available and where. Go to the BEST OF section to locate a hike or other activity that suits your interests, mood, and the day.

Use RESOURCE LINKS to find listings and phone numbers for public agencies and organizations, museums and attractions, tours and outfitters, accommodations and restaurants, and all other visitor information. Also see STRATEGIES FOR VISITING THE BIG ISLAND, which will aid in planning your trip.

CALCULATING HIKE TIMES

Hikers in average condition will cover about 2 mph, including stops. Groups and slower-movers will make about 1.5 mph, or less. Well-conditioned hikers can cover 3-to-3.5 mph. Everyone should add about 30 minutes for each 800 feet of elevation gain. Also add 60 minutes or longer to daylong hikes, for a margin of error, and just because this is Hawaii—trails are not generally easy and people tend to look around more.

To check your rate of speed: 65 average-length steps per minute, equals about 2 mph; 80 steps per minute is about 2.5 mph; 95 average steps per minute comes to about 3 mph.

---

23. TRAILHEAD NAME   ACTIVITIES BANNER

What's Best:
Parking:

HIKE: Hike Destination (distance, elevation)
            Hike descriptions.   (S A M P L E)
Be Aware:
More Stuff:

SNORKEL: SURF: Snorkeling and surfing descriptions.

KEY TO READING TRAILHEAD DESCRIPTIONS

"23." **Trailhead Number:** These correspond to the numbers shown on the six Trailhead Maps. Numbers begin with Map 1, Kohala and continue to Map 6, Mauna Kea. In most cases, trailhead numbers that are close together numerically will be close geographically. There are 66 trailheads, listed sequentially in the text of the book, divided into six sections. When looking for a particular trailhead, "TH23" for example, you may find it easier to flip through the text rather than look up the page number in the Trailhead Directory.

Trailhead Name: Each trailhead offers one or more recreational activities—hiking, snorkeling, and surfing. (Mountain biking is mapped and described in a separate section.) Some trailheads offer one parking place and a single activity. Other trailheads have several parking places, all close together, and several recreational activities. Some trailheads take a whole day, or more, to explore, while others can be combined with nearby trailheads to fill out a day of adventuring.

Activities Banner: This shows which of the three recreational activities are available at this trailhead. Included are one or more of the following, always listed in the same order:

HIKE: Hikes, ranging from long treks to easy strolls.

SNORKEL: Snorkeling and swimming, including freshwater pools.

SURF: Surfing with boards, bodyboards, and bodies.

What's Best: A thumbnail description of what to expect when visiting this trailhead.

Parking: Gives specific directions from the nearest highway to the parking spot for the trailhead's primary hike destination. Secondary parking directions are also given, for nearby hikes. Directions usually include the nearest mile-marker, which is abbreviated as "mm." For the island's main highways, the mile markers start at "0" in Hilo and increase as you drive around toward Kona. Roadside signs mark every mile.

HIKE: The first paragraph after the Hike: symbol lists each Hike Destination available at the trailhead, followed by the (distance, and elevation gain) for each hike in parentheses. Distances are given to the nearest .25-mile. Only elevation gains of 100 feet or greater are noted. All hiking distances in parentheses are ROUND TRIP.

The second paragraph after the **HIKE:** symbol often gives background and history for the trailhead. Following paragraphs give trail descriptions. The first reference to a **Hike Destination** is boldfaced. Trail descriptions include junctions with other trails, the type of terrain and walking surface, as well as elevation changes and landmarks along the way. **Second Destinations** follow in subsequent paragraphs, boldfaced and described in the order they are listed in the first Hike paragraph.

Mauka means to turn or head inland, toward the mountains. *Makai* means to go seaward, toward the coast. These are island-style directions.

Be Aware: Notes special precautions and difficulties associated with a hike or other activity. Also read *Free Advice & Opinion* for listings of rules and hazards that apply to adventuring on the Big Island.

More Stuff: Gives other hikes and activities available at this trailhead that are not among the primary listings. Normally these are out-of-the-way spots, sometimes with difficult access and terrain. Fewer visitors will be at these places. A hike for "trailblazers" means, in general, you're on your own.

SNORKEL: SURF: Descriptions for snorkeling and surfing follow, in order, after the hike paragraphs. Descriptions include where to go for these water sports, as well as notations for precautions. Parking directions for these activities will be included in the descriptions—unless they have already been listed in the parking directions or hike descriptions above. For example, parking directions for a snorkel or surf spot will most often be among those already given for a beach walk. **Snorkel** and **Surf** locations are boldfaced. One trailhead may describe several nearby locations for each activity.

okay, you now have your feet wet, time to jump in . . . .

Best Of
THE
BIG
ISLAND

WHAT DO YOU WANT TO DO TODAY?

Best Of lets you pick an activity to suit your whims and the weather. The picks are listed by trailhead number, with the lowest number first.

TH = TRAILHEAD
DT = DRIVING TOUR

BEST OF THE BEST

HIKING

TROPICAL CLIFFS AND VALLEYS

VOLCANO AND CRATER HIKES

HISTORICAL PARKS & PLACES

GARDENS

PETROGLYPHS

NATIVE FORESTS FOR THE BIRDS

RAIN FOREST

FOR SEASONED TREKKERS ONLY

SNORKELING & SWIMMING

BEST OF THE BEST

GOOD IF CONDITIONS ARE RIGHT

FOR ADVANCED

HIKE-TO BEAUTIES

TURTLES GALORE

Puako, TH10, page 56

Wainanali'i Lagoon, TH14, page 67

Aiopio Fishtrap, TH20, page 186

Kahalu'u Beach Park, TH24, page 92

Honaunau Bay, TH27, page 104

Punalu'u Beach Park, TH33, page 121

WARM POOLS

Pohoiki Warm Spring, TH51, page 158

Ahalanui Hot Pond, TH52, page 158

Kapoho Bay Sea Pool, TH54, page 161

LOCALS BEACHES

Wawaioli Beach Park, TH19, page 83

Alula Beach, TH20, page 84

Kailua Pier-Kanuha Beach,
TH22, page 90

Ke'ei Beach, TH26, page 98

Lihikai Beach, TH48, page 153

Kehena Black Sand Beach,
TH49, page 156

BEACHES WITH KEIKI
(KIDS') PONDS

Nanuku Inlet, TH11, page 58

Makalawena, TH18, page 75

Old Airport Beach, Kukailimoku Point,
TH21, page 87

Kailua Pier, TH22, page 90

Riviera Pool, TH23, page 91

Pu'uhonua O Honauna,
TH 27, page 105

Onekahakaha Beach Park,
TH48, page 153

Carlsmith Beach Park, TH48, page 153

CLASSIC BEACH & SWIM

Kaunaoa Bay, TH8, page 52

Hapuna Beach State Park, TH9, page 54

Anaeho'omalu Beach Park,
TH12, page 62

CALM & PRETTY COVES TO TAKE A DIP

Pauoa Bay, TH10, page 56

Kikaua Park, TH16, page 71

Aiopio Fishtrap, TH20, page 86

Kamakahonu Beach, TH22, page 89

Keauhou Bay, TH25, page 96

Moku Ola, TH47, page 151

SURFING

PLACES TO WATCH SURFERS

Kawaihae Cultural Surf Park,
TH7, page 45

Ka'aha Point, TH8, page 52

Holualoa Bay, TH23, page 91

Kuemanu Heiau, TH24, page 92

Honoli'i Beach Park, TH56, page 163

LEGENDARY FAVORITES

Waipio Beach, TH1, page 34

Lyman's, TH23, page 91

Kahalu'u Bay, TH24, page 93

Ke'ei Beach, TH26, page 100

BODYBOARDERS

Kaunaoa Beach, TH8, page 52

Hapuna Beach, TH9, page 54

Spinners-Oneo Bay, TH22, page 90

White Sands Beach Park,
TH24, page 93

POINT BREAKS

CARRY THE BOARD

OFFSHORE BAY BREAKS

REEF BREAKS

PICNIC PLACES

RAINBOW FALLS

TRAILHEAD DIRECTORY

MAUNA LOA

HILO

MAUNA KEA

Kohala

POLOLU VALLEY LOOKOUT

TRAILHEAD PREVIEWS

That the Big Island actually is made up of five volcanoes mashed together is evidenced most clearly in Kohala, the green nub in the north that points toward Maui. The mile-high Kohala Mountains are long-since-dormant volcanoes, about a million years older than other parts of the island. They have reached the erosion stage, beginning their losing battle with waves and rain. The topographical result is what many visitors come to Hawaii to see: The northeast coast, which receives the trade wind's wet weather, is creased by three dozen streams, creating valleys one- to two-thousand-feet deep, adorned with tropical greenery and ribbony waterfalls.

No roads travel the entire coast. But hikers can explore the valleys and beaches on several trails that are among the most exhilarating in the state. Waipio Valley is the best-known, accessible via a four-wheel-road—or a 20-minute walk. The beach and lagoon, also known as Valley of the Kings, was young Kamehameha's favorite surfing hangout. Kaluahine and Hiʻilawe falls, as well as others, rain down from jungly cliffs, and the Miliwai Trail climbs from Waipio to Waimanu Valley, a wilderness to the north. You can explore the upper part of Waipio on an easy walk into the Kohala Forest Reserve, on a trail that leads from near Waimea to a spectacular diving-board lookout. To see the other end of Kohala's fissured coast, you need to drive around to the other side, to the Pololu Valley—another fabulous foray into a deep green crease with a wild beach.

WAIPIO BEACH

ALAKAHI FALLS, LAPAKAHI HISTORICAL PARK

The south end of Kohala is a reminder that it is not a separate island. Here, instead of beaches, are rolling plains at 3,000-feet and higher, the sprawling pasturelands of the Parker Ranch, which is the largest privately held cattle ranch in America. Flows from Mauna Kea, none more recent than 4,000 years ago, have piled up against the Kohala Mountains to create these pastoral ranchlands.

The west side of Kohala is another story altogether. In the 25-mile drive from Waipio on the east to Kawaihae on the west coast, you go from forest getting nearly 200 inches of rain yearly to kiawe deserts receiving less than 15 inches. You can experience a similar shift in climate by driving the 20 miles north from Kawaihae to the end of the road at Pololu Valley. Nature's sprinkling system has provided nicely for outdoor adventurers, since you can always retreat from a storm and find sunshine.

For seekers of Hawaiian history and culture, arid west Kohala is a garden of abundance. Start with the Kamehameha Statue, just east of Hawi in Kapa'au, a monument that was lost at sea before finding its home. Then continue west to King Kamehameha Birthplace and the Mo'okini Heiau, on a windswept shore where the echoes of history are palpable—no kidding. Just down the coast from this remarkable site is Mahukona Beach Park, where a decrepit mill and dock tell of more recent history, that of the sugar industry of the late 1800s and early 1900s. The old wharf at Mahukona is Kohala's best snorkeling spot, and among the best on the island.

You can hike a wild coast from Mahukona to Lapakahi State Historical Park (or drive there) to hark back again to ancient times at a village that was Hawaii's first to be preserved. Craft workers ply their trades on-site, further-

ing the traditions of Old Hawaii. A self-guided trail winds through the village, passing a cove that also doubles as a snorkeling venue, in a marine conservation district.

The Big Island's newest temple, the Pu'ukohola Heiau is at the southern end of west Kohala. Now a national historical site, it was built in 1790 by Kamehameha the Great and was where

MAU'UMAE TRAIL, WAIPIO LOOKOUT, MAHUKONA

he vanquished his rivals to gain control of the island. Surfing and snorkeling are popular at several locales nearby, including Kawaihae and Spencer Beach Park. The choice spot around is a short hike down the coast from Spencer to Mau'umae Beach. You might stake out some sand and hang for awhile at this semi-secret snorkelers' cove.

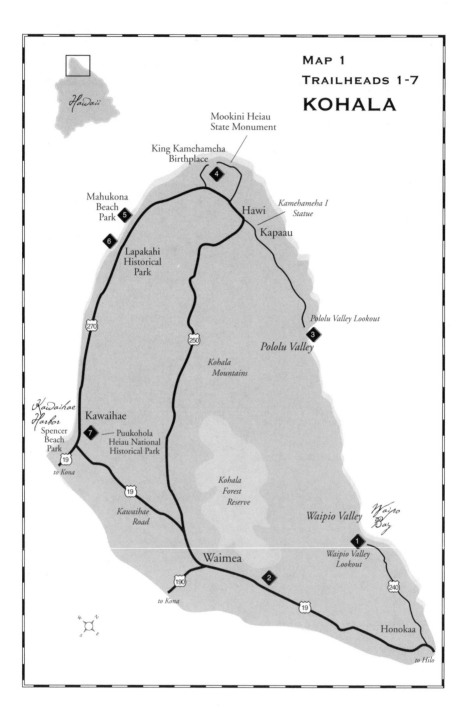

MAP 1
TRAILHEADS 1-7
KOHALA

Hawaii

Mookini Heiau
State Monument

King Kamehameha
Birthplace

4

Mahukona
Beach
Park 5

6

Lapakahi
Historical
Park

Hawi

Kamehameha I
Statue

Kapaau

270

250

Pololu Valley Lookout

3

Pololu Valley

Kohala
Mountains

Kawaihae
Harbor

Kawaihae

Spencer
Beach
Park

7

Puukohola
Heiau National
Historical Park

19

to Kona

19

Kawaihae
Road

Kohala
Forest
Reserve

Waipio Valley

Waipio
Bay

1

Waipio Valley
Lookout

Waimea

2

190

to Kona

19

240

N

Honokaa

to Hilo

T R A I L H E A D S

TH :	TRAILHEAD
HIKE :	HIKES AND STROLLS
SNORKEL :	SNORKELING, SWIMMING
SURF :	BOARD, BODYBOARD, BODYSURF
MM :	MILE MARKER; CORRESPONDS TO HIGHWAY SIGNS
MAKAI :	TOWARD THE OCEAN
MAUKA :	INLAND, TOWARD THE MOUNTAINS

ALL HIKING DISTANCES IN PARENTHESES ARE ROUND TRIP.
ELEVATION GAINS OF 100 FEET OR MORE ARE NOTED. SEE
RESOURCE LINKS FOR CONTACTS AND TELEPHONE NUMBERS.

1.   WAIPIO VALLEY   HIKE, SURF

WHAT'S BEST: Picture a tropical fantasyland with cliffs spewing waterfalls into a lush valley, and calm lagoons just inshore of a surfer's beach. Waipio is a marquee attraction. Spend the day and you'll get swallowed up by the beauty. At the very least, take the 15-minute drive from the highway to the lookout.

PARKING: Take Hwy. 19, the Mamalahoa Hwy., east from Waimea. Near mm44, take Hwy. 240 toward Honoka'a. Continue for 9 mi., following signs for Waipio Valley. Parking is at the end of the road. *Be Aware:* Four-wheel drive vehicles are permitted to take the steep and narrow road down to unimproved parking at the beach. Normal rental cars are sacrificial lambs on this 25-percent grade.

HIKE: Waipio Valley Lookout (.25-mi.); Waipio Beach and Kaluahine Falls (3 mi., 525 ft.); Muliwai Trail Halfway Vista (4.25 mi., 975 ft.)

The ali'i of ancient times favored verdant Waipio for both agriculture and leisure, and it became known as the Valley of the Kings. Taro, bananas, guava, coconuts, and other fruits grow amid exotic and native trees. In 1780, Kamehameha the Great, who had spent much of his youth frolicking and surfing here, chose this valley to receive his commission as guardian of the war god, Kukailimoku. Several heiaus that predated Kamehameha also graced the valley, including the massive Honuaula Heiau. Tunnels are said to have connected some of the heiaus, one of which was the entranceway to the underworld, where souls left the land of the living and ghosts returned for a visit. Today the torch-carrying "Night Warriors," chanting as they go, frequent the valley trails in a clandestine commemoration of this ancient legend. The entire valley used to be protected by a 50-foot high sand dune, called Lalakea, or "white fin," but the 1946 tsunami took out much of the dune, and also damaged the valley's wealth of over-grown archeological sites.

The **Waipio Valley Lookout** is a short stroll down a paved path to a covered pavilion and railed viewing area. This is a postcard shot, taking in about half the beach below and the 1,200-foot cliffs a mile away at its far end. To **continue to the valley**, start down the paved road. The road immediately crosses the stream on its headlong pursuit of the falls. An unofficial trail leaves the road to the top of the falls, but use extreme caution if exploring this area. At the bottom of the main road, turn right. In the shade of a variety of exotic trees, you'll soon reach the fine, black sand of **Waipio Beach**. To your right is **Kaluahine Falls**, making a straight shot down the cliff to the surf.

For the **Muliwai Trail Halfway Vista**, walk to your left through the stand of ironwoods and the rustic campground. You'll see the trail's long switchback etched into the cliff at the far end of the beach; the seaward crook of the trail is your destination. To get there, you need to cross Waipio Stream, which is usually best accomplished where the fresh-water meets the ocean. *Be Aware:* Make sure to wait for a lull in the surf, and don't attempt a crossing if the stream is running swiftly. Take valuables from your pockets and have knapsack in hand to raise over your head if need be.

After crossing the stream, veer left across the sand into the ironwood trees, where you will find a path that skirts the margin of the beach. As you reach the cliff, to the left is a private cottage, with a barbed-wire fence on the cliff side of its driveway. The Muliwai Trail, probably still marked by a tattered and unreadable sign, heads up the hill to the right. You'll make several short switchbacks before beginning the long ramp to the halfway point—which is actually a little more than a third of Muliwai's 1,200-foot climb. A shaded spot affords a penthouse look down at Waipio Beach, as well as an excellent spot to view whales during the winter and spring. On the way back down you'll get fabulous looks up the valley.

More Stuff: The Muliwai Trail is a backpackers' favorite. It ascends another 800 feet from the halfway point and continues another 6 miles to Waimanu Valley, a wilderness version of Waipio. Along its entire course, the rugged Muliwai dips into a half-dozen stream valleys, each about 500 feet deep. Even seasoned packers need to suck it up for this trek.

At the base of the Muliwai Trail—to the right of the driveway and barbed-wire fence that leads to the cottage—is a trail that leads up the valley to two waterfalls. Trailblaz-ers will find the largest falls about a mile in from the beach. But another way to explore inland is to stay left on the road down from the lookout, rather than going right to the beach. Upon taking this road, you'll pass a fishpond, loku pu'uone, its slack waters mirroring the valley's towering cliffs. As you continue, you'll pass rustic homes on the left, set beneath the twin silvery ribbons of 1,200-foot Hi'ilawe Falls, the flows of which are controlled by the agricultural ditch above. A footpath leads to the falls. The

LOKU PUʻUONE FISHPOND, WAIPO VALLEY

road up the six-mile-deep valley becomes a trail, which eventually connects with the waterfall trail mentioned above, although you face the near certainty of getting lost if attempting a loop hike.

SURF: With a many-tiered shore break, **Waipio Beach** is the most popular surfing spot on a rugged coast that has few beaches. Breaks are both left and right. Observe and ask locals before riding the waves. About half of Maui is visible from the beach, and it's easy to imagine the fleet of war canoes that Kamehameha launched here in 1791 to thwart invaders from Oahu and Kaua'i. *Be Aware:* Riptide generated by surf makes Waipio usually unsafe for swimming. The shallow shore break is also a hazard for bodysurfers. Also, be hesitant about encouraging the cute, semi-wild horses that hang around at the beach. Like extremely large squirrels, these beasts can be pests.

2.   KOHALA FOREST RESERVE   HIKE

WHAT'S BEST: Who would suspect that a thrilling precipice and waterfall vista are down the trail from the rural neighborhood trailhead? A lovely forested trail leads to an airborne look down the length of Waipio Valley. Ring the gong: This hike is among the best in the Hawaiian Islands.

PARKING: Take Hwy. 19, the Mamalahoa Hwy., east from Waimea. After mm54, pass in quick succession on your left, Kipahele and Ho'ohoa roads and a paved alley. Then turn left on White Road, a dead end. Continue .6-mi. up White Road and park off-street near a locked metal gate.

HIKE: Kohala Forest Reserve to: Alakahi Falls Lookout (3 mi., 175 ft.), or Waipio Bamboo Altar (5.75 mi., 350 ft.)

For both hikes, squeeze around the gate and follow the road up and to the right around Waimea Reservoir. Then the road curves left, beginning a contour around the green hillock of Pu'u Ka'ala, and you reach a **Kohala Forest Reserve** gate. You'll ascend a short distance in a garden of ferns, flowers, and leafy trees. The route levels off and crosses the Hamakua Ditch, which you will follow intermittently for the remainder of the hike. Bamboo and other exotics buffer the waterway. After about a mile, the trail narrows as you curve to the right through a lush gully and cross a short stretch of boardwalk. Say goodbye to the irrigation ditch for awhile. The trail is shaded by a sparse overstory of huge native trees, plus a few surprises like towering sequoias. And just when you start to marvel at the lovely forest, the trail abruptly reaches the ledge of Waipio Valley. The drop-off is nearly 2,000 feet. Across the half-mile width of the valley, **Alakahi Falls** tumbles in several pitches toward Waipio Stream far below.

For the **Waipio Bamboo Altar**, which is at the head of valley, continue left from the falls lookout. After about 100 feet on the trail you'll see a cave on your left, and a few minutes later reach a viewpoint that will satisfy less ambitious hikers. The trail dips into the ripples of the cliff in a few places and rejoins Hamakua Ditch, flowing at times in raised trestles and into mysterious tunnels. Near the head of the valley, the ditch is unleashed in a waterslide, above which the trail climbs to the plateau.

The plateau is swamplike, with rainfall of more than 200 inches per year. The Kohala Mountains, the oldest volcanic vents on the Big Island, rise inland. Continue several hundred feet on the trail and you'll enter the darkness of a bamboo thicket. Soon, an opening will appear to your right, the Bamboo Altar, where you can stand at a 2,000-foot cliff and look down the green barrel of Waipio Valley to see waves crashing at the black sand beach, 6-miles distant. To your left is Waimanu Gap, a slot in the fissured cliffs. *Be Aware:* Although perfectly safe for the careful hiker, the trail from the lookout to the head of the valley is one-person wide in places and some segments are only a step away from free-fall. Watch your feet when walking and you'll be fine.

More Stuff: Although not well-traveled, the trail continues from the Bamboo Altar. After several miles, you reach a trailhead in Waimea, creating the potential for a car-shuttle hike. But this trail segment is overgrown, so trailblazers should first attempt the hike by beginning at the Waimea access: In the middle of Waimea, at the junction of Highways 19 and 190, go west on Highway 19. Veer right on Lindsey Road, and take your first right on Kapiolani Road. At the end of Kapiolani, jog left on Spencer and then go right on a narrow, paved road, steeply uphill. After two miles, you'll reach a Kohala Forest Reserve gate.

You can also get to the green pu'us of the Kohala Forest Reserve, and the Pu'u O Umi Natural Area Reserve, from Kohala Mountain Road, or Highway 270. Go west on Highway 19 from Waimea, and veer right on Highway 270. As the pastoral road curves down through eucalyptus groves, look for Kahua Ranch on your right, about .25-mile

KOHALA FOREST RESERVE

before mm12. Drive in a short distance and keep right on an unpaved road toward the ranch's wind generators. A little-used access trail is on the right, about a mile in on the wind-farm road. You should ask permission at the ranch office before using this trail.

3.   POLOLU VALLEY   HIKE, SNORKEL, SURF

WHAT'S BEST: Kissing-cousin Waipio Valley gets more attention, but this lush amphitheater and rugged beach is the prime choice for many hikers. No roads or homes detract from a tropical wilderness experience, and the ridge trail out of the far end of the beach is virtually untrod.

PARKING: Take Hwy. 19 north from Kailua and veer left toward Kawaihae on Hwy. 270. Continue through Hawi. The road narrows at several one-lane bridges and comes to an end past mm28. Park off-road at the guardrail.

HIKE: Pololu Valley Lookout to: Pololu Beach (1.25 mi., 425 ft.), or Honokane Valley view (3.75 mi., 900 ft.)

The commanding view of green sea cliffs and pounding surf from the **Pololu Valley Lookout** will sell most visitors on this hike. **For both hikes**, start down the trail at road's end, which is marked by a state Na Ala Hele sign. This steep cobblestone trail was once Old Government Road, making switchbacks to taro farms in the valley. At the bottom of the trail, veer off to the right to get a portrait-quality view of the valley, looking over the surface of the large freshwater pond. Then backtrack through a stand on ironwoods, and cross the stream near shore at **Pololu Beach**. Black sand and jumbles of driftwood front a near-constant shore break. Just inland is a parklike sand dune with a few heliotropes, nicely spaced ironwoods, and makeshift tables.

For the **Honokane Valley view** hike, find a trail that runs toward the far end of the beach, between the base of the sand dune and the driftwood of the beach. Stones mark the trail's edges in places. Nearly at the end of the beach, the soft-dirt trail veers to the right, through lush groundcover and heads toward a crease in the sand dune. You go up this crease and then veer left to begin a series of switchbacks that climb the cliff. *Note:* The trail is easy to follow. If you are unsure of the way, then you are wandering on one of the other trails in the dune, not the real trail.

Under a ceiling of hau, pandanus, and other native trees, the trail jogs out to the sea bluffs, before heading inland for good. Near the top, you'll pass through upright pipes of a gate that will probably be open. A few minutes later the trail pops out to open, low-lying scrub and a big view of the mile-deep Pololu Valley. You continue inland on a moderate climb for another .25-mile or so, penetrating a tunnel of vegetation, before coming to an open area with a chest-pounding look down at Honokane Valley. Turtle-shaped, tiny Paoakalani Island lies just offshore. Beyond this valley is a 12-mile, roadless

POLOLU VALLEY

coast that extends to Waipio Valley, gouged by five other valleys and countless streams. Even in ancient times, this was the least-populated region of the Big Island.

More Stuff: The trail continues inland and joins the Kohala Ditch Trail after about 2 miles; before that junction a spur trail drops down the narrow, jungly valley to Honokane Nui Stream. To access the Kohala Ditch Trail, you're better off taking a road that is just above trailhead parking. The trail meanders along the 24-mile long irrigation channel that was completed in 1906 to bring water to the sugar cane fields of North Kohala. The ditch trail is an exciting, 3-plus-mile hike that gets up close with this engineering marvel, and brings you to a vertigo vista behind Kapoloa Falls. This hike is in *More Stuff* because permission to cross private property is required, although much of the ditch is in the state Kohala Forest Reserve. You can buy a trip from Hawaii Forest & Trail, a private hiking company that is located across from the trailhead.

SNORKEL: Though snorkeling is usually iffy at **Keokea Beach Park**, take a ride down for a picnic and a view of the cove from the park's elevated kiosk. To get there, turn makai at mm27.5, just after the Makapala Filipino Camp. A paved road curves a mile down to rugged Keokea Bay, which faces the trade wind swells. Originally a retreat for sugar cane workers, the 7-acre site was made a county park in 1975. Scope the surf from a kiosk that sits above the bay. To your right is a small keiki pool, created by a boulder breakwater, that is normally safe for swimming.

SURF: Experienced surfers carry their boards down to ride the break at **Pololu Beach**, but conditions are not for beginners. If surf is relatively mild and you feel like playing, avoid the center of the beach, where rip current is notorious. A good place to watch surfers, and to check out the surf conditions, is from an overlook at the outside of the trail's lowest switchback.

4. KING KAMEHAMEHA BIRTHPLACE HIKE

WHAT'S BEST: Listen to the heartbeat of history on these windswept slopes by the sea, where the great king was born and a large heiau remains intact.

PARKING: Take Hwy. 19 north from Kailua and veer left toward Kawaihae on Hwy. 270. Go .75-mi. past mm18 and turn makai on Old Coast Guard Rd., also called Birthplace Rd. It may be unsigned; the road is the first left past the guard station at Puakea Bay Dr. Drive down 1.5 mi. to the coast and park on the left in an unpaved fenced area.

HIKE: King Kamehameha Birthplace (1.25 mi.); Mo'okini Heiau (1.75 mi., 100 ft.)

For both hikes, pass around the fence on the ocean side and go to the right. Stay in the grassy area and then, beyond the first few homes, veer right up to the red-dirt road. You'll pass by abandoned Coast Guard buildings and reach a berm where the road has been closed to vehicles. The road continues along a wild seascape. From a rise in the road you'll be able to see **King Kamehameha Birthplace.** A commemorative sign fronts a double-walled enclosure about 100 yards square. In the center are the birth-stones. During a nighttime storm in the fall of 1758, the infant prophesized to rule the kingdom, "the Lonely One," was born. This isolated spot was chosen to protect the future king from early assassination by High Chief Keawemauhili of Hilo, an uncle who had other ideas about who should rule the island. Some historians believed Kamehameha's birthday to have been 1736 or 1753, but oral chants from the time tell of a mysterious celestial object that passed overhead, which astronomers have since pegged as an appearance of Haley's Comet.

To **Mo'okini Heiau**, continue up the dirt road less than .25-mile, until reaching a signed junction. The heiau, with walls 25-feet high and nearly 100-yards long, is a short walk up the hill. Earliest portions of the heiau date from around 500 AD, constructed of stones carried by early Marquesan settlers in a human chain of some 20,000 workers who transferred the smooth rocks from Pololu Valley, about 12 miles distant. Later portions of the temple were built by the second wave of Polynesians from Tahiti, around 1200 AD. Designated as the state's first national historic site in 1935, the 3-acre site is now part of a state historical park. Although many forms of worship took place here, Mo'okini Heiau is best known for human sacrifices.

Resting on the lawn on the ocean side are large stones, called Pohaku, Holehole, and Kanaka, which were used for stripping flesh from bone as part of the ceremony. The heiau has been presided over continuously by family kahunas, generation by generation, up until present day. If you're reading these words at the site you will be glad to learn that the kapu against visiting here was lifted in 1978 by Kahuna Nui Leimomi Mo'okini Lum.

More Stuff: You also can drive on a marginal dirt road nearly all the way to the heiau and all the way to the birthplace. To do so go north on Highway 270 and turn toward the ocean at mm20 on Upolu Road, which goes to a small airport. Continue almost 2 miles to the airport and turn left on a dirt road. Huge mud puddles after rains will make driving two-wheel-drive vehicles chancy. The sites are about a mile down this road, which is a dead end after 2 miles.

From the primary parking spot, you can also walk a trail south toward Honoipu Landing. Look for a Public Shoreline Access sign just beyond the fence to the left as you face the ocean. A trail leads inland and up, hooks to the right, and reaches a paved easement that passes a couple of high-end homes. A life-sized bronze statue of a breaching whale is to the right as you reach the paved section, and may be the highlight of the hike. Walk down the pavement and follow fishermens access signs down to the right, to a jagged wave-bashed coast.

KAMEHAMEHA BIRTHPLACE, MAHUKONA HARBOR

5.   MAHUKONA BEACH PARK   HIKE, SNORKEL

WHAT'S BEST: Big fish and sunken relics await offshore North Kohala's best snorkeling site. A little-used, scenic coastal trail will attract hikers.

PARKING: Take Hwy. 19 north from Kailua and veer left toward Kawaihae on Hwy. 270. Before mm15, turn makai on Mahukona Beach Park Rd. Continue for about .4-mi. *For hiking:* Keep left at the Shoreline Public Access sign and continue a short distance to the beach park. *For snorkeling:* Go right at the old railway building, toward another Shoreline Public Access parking on the wharf. Don't park on the ocean side of the wide wharf if the surf is up; a saltwater car wash is likely.

HIKE: Coastal trail to Lapakahi Historical Park (2.75mi.)

For the **Coastal trail to Lapakahi Historical Park**, walk by the camping area on the lawn and the metal-roofed pavilion. Behind the pavilion you'll find and unsigned gate and the trail. Within the first .25-mile is a Coast Guard light and a sign marking the northern boundary of a marine conservation district that extends to just south of Lapakahi. Kiawe trees provide most of the shade in this arid region, although coconut palms appear as you get farther south. Also keep an eye out for ruins, as fishing villages once were scattered along miles of the coastline.

More Stuff: A grassy two-track road leads north from Mahukona Beach Park for a mile or so to Kapa'a Beach Park. To find the road, look to your left by a large metal building, just as you leave the wharf, in the direction of the highway. The road goes by a water tank and other defunct workings of the mill, which closed in 1975. Along the road, ruins of an ancient Haena Village can be spotted, overgrown by kiawe. Kapa'a Beach Park is nicely sited on a rugged cove. Driving access is via Kapa'a Park Road, about a mile north of the road to Mahukona.

SNORKEL: Submerged relics, a unique entry, and unusual marine life combine to make **Mahukona Wharf** one of the better snorkeling spots on the Big Island—if conditions are safe. Walk to the channel at the end of the wharf and you'll find a ladder leading to the water. The old sugar mill looms above. Not far offshore, water gets deep, 30- to 60-feet, amid rocks and a few coral heads. Manta rays and octopi have been spotted here, as well as turtles and reef fish, large and small. The propeller and boilers of a 1913 shipwreck lie in about 50 feet of water, while an anchor chain and railroad wheels are closer to shore. A shower is located to the right as you face the entry stairs. At the base of the pier is a historic building, dating from 1930, the Hawaii Railway Co., Ltd. North Kohala's sugar shipped out from this harbor for many decades until the 1950s. *Be Aware:* High surf can make Mahukona treacherous. Waves enter the former loading area with a lethal vengeance. Water on the wharf's surface indicates a high-surf day. If you encounter high swells when in the water, wait for the set to subside and make your way to the ladder during a lull.

6.   LAPAKAHI HISTORICAL PARK   HIKE, SNORKEL

WHAT'S BEST: With the imagination of an anthropological detective, you can roam this village and piece together all elements that were needed to sustain life. Or just sit in the shade of a coco palm and get a feeling for it all before taking a swim.

PARKING: Take Hwy. 19 north from Kailua and veer left toward Kawaihae on Hwy. 270. Just before mm14, turn makai at the signed and gated park entrance. *Note:* Hours are 8 a.m. to 4 p.m., except for state holidays and when they decide not to show up. Don't despair. If the gate is locked, park at the top and take a short path down to the small visitors center.

HIKE: **Koaiʻe Village (1.25 mi., 150 ft.)**

Even if the park is closed, a trail brochure should be available, either at the visitors center or grass shack opposite it. A rocky path circles the **Koaiʻe Village**—you'll prob-ably want to go left, or clockwise. Or take another path that goes through the center of the park to the coast. Whatever, this hike is for wandering around. The partially re-stored village is within the several hundred acres that comprise the state park. In an-cient times, the village was within the 10-square miles of the ahupuaʻa (division of land) of Lapakahi, which included about 4 miles of coastline and extended inland to an elevation of 2,000 feet. This arid area has never been prime real estate. But villagers flourished here until the late 1800s, when grazing cattle and horses gradually made the meager farming lands inhabitable.

As you take the path around to the left, wave-watchers may wish to veer off to the left to reach the southern boundary of the marine district. Then loop back to the trail. At the shore of Koaiʻe Cove is the park's most scenic spot, where you can sit under the shade of a hala tree and admire an old dwelling, sitting under palms and above cobalt waters. Then continue along the coral- and black-rock shore, passing several hollowed-out flat stones that were used to extract salt from ocean water. At the far end of the cove is the former fire pit, where generations of villagers played konane, or Hawaiian check-ers, on a board carved into a rock—all the while keeping an eye on offshore waters for passing fish that would send them rushing to their canoes. From the south bluff, the path winds back to the visitors center.

Aside from the prickly kiawe trees, which dominate the greater area of Koaiʻe, the dozen or so species of trees you see are among those brought centuries ago by migrat-ing Polynesians. All the building materials for their fiber-and-stone culture were de-rived from these plants. The village now is harsh, mostly rock rubble, but in its prime the terraces were green and blond-grass roofs topped the black-stone huts, whose shaded interiors were carpeted with layers of soft matting.

SNORKEL: In the Lapakahi Marine Conservation District, **Koaiʻe Cove** offers excel-lent snorkeling. Huge boulders and ample coral support lots of fish, and the water is clear and strikingly blue. Near shore are depths of about 30 feet. The bad news is that high surf can create treacherous currents, and the entry over coral and stone is not easy. In addition, park people ask that you not enter to the left of the cove below the historic house, the site of ancient graves. For an entry point, go to the right of the little rocky point in the middle of the bay, at the pebble "beach." *Be Aware:* The park people also ask that no towels or clothing be left on the beach, with the exception of hat, sunglasses, and shoes. Since this is a marine district, feeding fish, normally a bad idea, is prohibited. During the winter, wave action is often too high for safe swimming, but on the right day this place is a winner.

7. PU'UKOHOLA HEIAU
HIKE, SNORKEL, SURF

WHAT'S BEST: Now a national historic site, this massive Hawaiian temple is where Kamehameha the Great—by trickery and happenstance—achieved final control of the Big Island. Close by, a garden path leads down the coast to a hidden, fine-sand beach with excellent swimming.

PARKING: Take Hwy. 19 north from Kailua and turn left toward Kawaihae on Hwy. 270. After mm2, turn makai at a sign for Spencer Beach Park and Pu'ukohola Heiau. *For heiau hike:* Turn right immediately into a parking lot for the historic site. *For Spencer Park and Mau'umae Beach hike:* Continue down the hill, go left at the park entrance, and continue to the parking at the far end.

HIKE: **Pu'ukohola Heiau (.75-mi., 150 feet); Spencer Beach Park to Mau'umae Beach (1 mi.)**

The Pu'ukohola Heiau information center is in a trailer, but plans are in the works for a grand complex nearby. The heiau is Hawaii's most recent, built in 1790 as a tribute to the war god Ku by thousands of commoners at the behest of Kamehameha, who toiled alongside them. The future monarch, then aged 32, had waged successful battles against Maui and Molokai, but in his absence had lost some turf on the Big Island to his cousin, Keoua Kuahu'ula. This branch of the family from Hilo was Kamehameha's lifelong nemesis. At a dedication ceremony in 1791, cousin Keoua was the life of the party, or rather death, since he and his small retinue were killed in a scuffle, thereby becoming the heiau's first humans to be sacrificed. Whether Kamehameha planned the attack, or it transpired by unforeseen events, is open to historical interpretation.

For the **Pu'ukohola Heiau hike**, take the path from the information center, which passes to the left of the heiau and continues to the shoreline below it. On the way down you'll also pass the ruins of Mailekini Heiau, a much older site that sits below Pu'ukohola. When in use, both heiau platforms supported several pole structures with thatched roofs. At the water's edge is a junction with a coastal trail that, taken to the left, reaches to Spencer Beach Park, a short distance away. At the junction is a Stone Leaning Post, where you can look just offshore and imagine the shark temple—Hale o Kapuni Heiau—which lies submerged. Silt from flashfloods of Makeahua Gulch have all but buried the shrine, which was last seen at low tide in the 1950s. But the black-tipped reef sharks, the heiau's honorees, still frequent this bay. For the prime Kodak moment at the heiau, head to your right from the Leaning Post and walk across the palm grove that was once the site of the royal courtyard. Then go left, step up to the unpaved road and look back at the king's temple of war, somehow looming larger from this more-distant view.

The superlative trail from **Spencer Beach Park to Mau'umae Beach** begins behind the beautiful stone pavilion that sits on the bluff at the south end of the park. The soft-dirt route penetrates a garden of beach trees alongside crashing surf. It is part of the state's Ala Kahakai Trail, which covers about 10 miles of coastline in a series of disjointed segments. About halfway into the short hike you'll cross a stream bed, from

LAPAKAHI HISTORICAL PARK, PU'UKOHOLA HEIAU

where you'll be able to see the white sand cove, across the water beneath a bluff. Once at the beach, continue on the trail to its south end, which normally has the best sand and swimming. Some of the trail here may be blocked by branches placed by locals who were sued to allow access to the beach. Cheerfully disregard these minor obstacles.

More Stuff: As indicated by Ala Kahakai signposts, the trail continues south from Mau'umae toward a different trailhead near the Mauna Kea Resort. If you're spending some time at Mau'umae, you may wish to take the trail on a 15-minute jaunt to Wai'ulaula Point, a whale watcher's perch. You'll walk up the stairs and pass a few homes before the trail pops out to the point.

SNORKEL: **Mau'umae Beach** is a Big Island jewel, with sloping white sands for easy entry and excellent swimming along the rocks at the south end of the beach out to Keawehala Point. Coco palms and kiawes, as well as other tropical trees, shade the shore. Although the beach is not a secret, it is seldom crowded. *Be Aware:* Heavy surf can bring stronger current to this normally safe beach, and no services are available.

Spencer Beach Park is only fair for snorkeling, with the best spots to the south near the stone pavilion. Water clarity is not the best, due to runoff from two streams. Spencer is best known for children's wave play, and for beach camping. Travelers tend to gather on the grass near the pavilion, while the north knoll appears to be reserved for the alfresco cocktails of longer term campers. You may

KAWAIHAE HARBOR, SPENCER BEACH PARK

CANOE PRACTICE, KAWAIHAE JETTY

also try snorkeling at **Kawaihae**, but the promise of an encounter with a black-tipped reef shark dissuades most. The reef sharks are virtually harmless, but still …

A deep-water snorkeling spot is **Frog Rock**, a few miles up Highway 270 from Spencer Beach Park. Look for an opening in the guardrail at mm5.9—not the Shoreline Public Access which is at mm5.6. The easiest approach is to spot the parking area on the way by and hang a U-turn at Ala Kahua Drive. From the unimproved parking just inside the guardrail, you need to walk about .25-mile down a steep gravel road and veer right at the bottom to a rocky cove. Offshore a few hundred feet are moorings used by scuba boats that frequent this spot. *Be Aware:* High surf means hazardous snorkeling.

SURF: Long boarders ride the rolling tiers off the most-westerly breakwater at the **Pua Kailima o Kawaihae Cultural Surf Park**. To get there, drive up from Spencer to Highway 270 and turn left. Pass two small bridges and turn left toward the Port of Kawaihae. Keep right on an unpaved road, with the container ship harbor to your right. Locals use this part of the harbor as a water park, swimming and diving off two concrete mooring platforms. The surf park is off the breakwater at the end of the dirt wharf. A shower pipe sticks up in the middle of nowhere. You can make a loop by continuing to circle left around the peninsula, passing a smaller harbor, a longhouse with viewing decks set among palms, and coming to the viewing area for Pu'ukohola Heiau that is described above. If you pass the entrance to the port and continue on Highway 270, you reach the smallest jetty in the harbor, where the Kawaihae Canoe Club puts in. There's usually a lot going on in Kawaihae, an underrated place.

South Kohala

GREEN SEA TURTLE, WAINANALI'I LAGOON AT KIHILO BAY

At first blush, the 25-mile South Kohala coast would seem most appealing as viewed from a speeding car in the dead of a moonless night. String-straight Highway 11 passes through vast fields of a'a lava, like piles of broken glass and razor blades, that have poured from several eruptions over the last 200 years, coming from both Mauna Loa and Hualalai. But look again. Every mile or two is an oasis and beach, the best on the Big Island. Some beaches are wild and reachable by hikes, and others are on the grounds of posh resorts. Beach seekers will be as happy as seals in sand.

Farthest north, Kaunaoa Bay is home to the Mauna Kea Resort, a jewel that normally heads the list among word travelers desirous of tropical comfort. Surfing and snorkeling are excellent, and so is the coastal walk to Hapuna Beach State Park, the most-popular beach on the island. The perpetual sunshine, surfing waves, and snorkeling waters of Hapuna draw locals from the rainy climes to the north and east. A hike-to snorkeling beach and turtle tidepools of Puako extend for several miles south of Hapuna.

Just south of Puako, the Mauna Lani Resort boasts a triple-play that may keep you there all day—historic sites, snorkeling and surfing beaches, and coastal walks. An aspect of Hawaii few know about is revealed at the Puako Petroglyphs near Holoholokai Beach Park, and at the fishponds and village near the Eva Parker Woods Cottage Museum.

These ancient sites are melded with surrounding gardens of the resorts. Beach Club Beach and Pauoa Bay, are right off the cover of travel magazines, blue crescents fringed by white sand and coconut palms. The walk from the Mauna Lani to the Fairmont Orchid is from the lap of luxury to the bosom of opulence.

After a day at Mauna Lani, do it all over again at Anaeho'omalu. The beach park at big A-Bay is a winner for surfing and wind sports, and the beach trees of two large ponds that front the bay provide tranquil shade. Going south from Anaeho'omalu is a coast walk to untouched Kapalaoa Beach, a sunbather's haunt. Going north is a coastal hike by anchialine ponds that were vital to surrounding villages. And past this rugged coral coast looms the theme park that is the Hilton, with its monorail, boat rides, museum-quality artworks, and man-made lagoon where you can look dolphins in the eye.

ANAEHO'OMALU

Resorts take a holiday south of A-Bay, where miles of rugged coast and several beaches will swallow up day-trippers. The more obscure is Keawaiki Bay, a half-mile from the highway, a ghost-town retreat that was party-central for the celebrities of the 1920s. A salt-and-pepper beach entices snorkelers, while the rugged hammerhead of Weliweli Point dares anyone to get near the water. Just south of Keawaiki is better-known Kihilo Bay, with a frock of coco palms and turquoise lagoon—swimmers, start drooling. The remains of Kamehameha's huge fishpond contribute to an intriguing backshore at Kihilo and west Hawaii's best black sand beach is to be found at the southern end of the two-mile bay.

After Kihilo, you have an opportunity to take a bird's eye view on the coast at Pu'u Wa'a Wa'a, the rippled butte that lies inland below Hualalai. Aside from its panorama, the old volcanic vent is a rich bird

PAUOA BAY, KIHOLO BAY

KUKIO BAY, PU'U KUILI

habitat, in one of the state's few remaining native dry forests. Then, ho hum, it's back to the coast for more beach hopping between two world-class resorts, the Four Seasons Hualalai and the Kona Village, the high-end little grass shacks that are a Big Island institution. Expect a variety pack at this site of the former Kaupulehu Village. A boardwalk winds through a large petroglyph field at the Kona Village, and sitting below the tasteful lobby of the Four Seasons is the Kaupulehu Cultural Center, quietly one of the best museums in the islands. You can walk a few miles of groomed coastal trail, beside both smashing surf and white-sand beaches. At the north of the coast is Kahuwai Bay, a snorkeler's delight fronting the Kona Village. The south end of the coast features pretty Kikaua Park on Kukio Bay.

South of the resorts at Hualalai are miles of (mostly) open coast, where white-sand beaches await surfers and snorkelers who like to walk, but not *too* far. Kua Bay, known for its clear waters and white sand cove, is a short walk in from the highway. Pu'u Kuili is the landmark south of the bay, a destination view hike. South of the pu'u is Kekaha Kai State Park with its hike-to beaches, Mahaiula Bay and Makalawena. Bring water, pack a lunch, and set out on a snorkeling safari.

AT HILTON RESORT

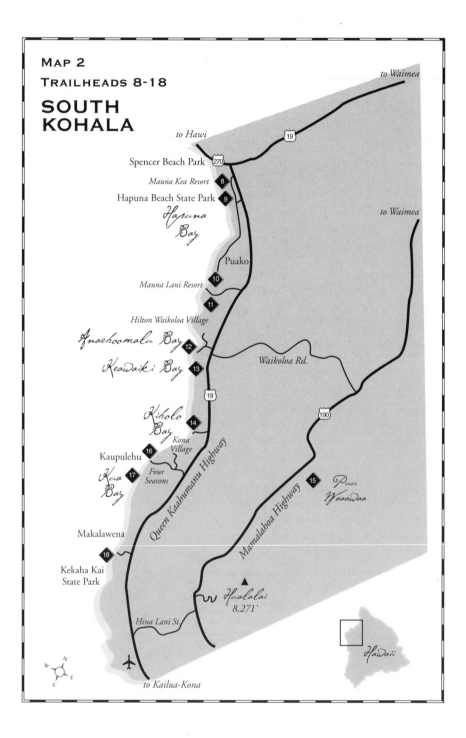

Map 2

Trailheads 8-18

SOUTH KOHALA

to Waimea

to Hawi

19

Spencer Beach Park 270

Mauna Kea Resort 8

Hapuna Beach State Park 9

Hapuna Bay

to Waimea

Puako

Mauna Lani Resort 10

11

Hilton Waikoloa Village

Anaehoomalu Bay 12

Keawaiki Bay 13

Waikoloa Rd.

19

190

Kiholo Bay 14

Kona Village

Kaupulehu 16

Four Seasons

Kua Bay 17

15

Puu Waawaa

Queen Kaahumanu Highway

Mamalahoa Highway

Makalawena

18

Kekaha Kai State Park

▲ *Hualalai 8,271'*

Hina Lani St.

Hawaii

N
W E
S

to Kailua-Kona

SOUTH KOHALA

TRAILHEADS

		8-18
TH :	TRAILHEAD	
HIKE :	HIKES AND STROLLS	
SNORKEL :	SNORKELING, SWIMMING	
SURF :	BOARD, BODYBOARD, BODYSURF	
MM :	MILE MARKER; CORRESPONDS TO HIGHWAY SIGNS	
MAKAI :	TOWARD THE OCEAN	
MAUKA :	INLAND, TOWARD THE MOUNTAINS	

ALL HIKING DISTANCES IN PARENTHESES ARE ROUND TRIP.
ELEVATION GAINS OF 100 FEET OR MORE ARE NOTED. SEE
RESOURCE LINKS FOR CONTACTS AND TELEPHONE NUMBERS.

8.   KAUNAOA BAY   HIKE, SNORKEL, SURF

WHAT'S BEST: The Mauna Kea Beach Hotel is world-renowned for its white crescent beach and spacious grounds. Snorkel, surf, or just kick back.

PARKING: Take Hwy. 19 north from Kailua-Kona. Pass the Hapuna Beach turnoff. Turn left before mm68 toward the Mauna Kea Resort. Stop at entrance station, where you have three options: The first choice is to ask for public beach access; the road swings left in front of the resort to beach parking. A short paved path winds down to the beach. Second, if no beach passes remain, ask to visit the resort. In this case, park in the lot to the right of the resort and walk through the lobby and pool area to the beach. Third, if resort permits are not available, ask for a permit for the Mau'umae Beach trailhead. See *Hike-More Stuff* below for directions to this trailhead.

HIKE: Mauna Kea Beach Hotel (.75-mi.)

Prompted by Hawaii's post-war effort to bring tourism to the Big Island, Laurance Rockefeller and a big bag of money arrived at Kaunaoa Bay in 1960. He leased land from the Parker Ranch and opened the Mauna Kea Beach Hotel in 1965. Westin Hotels took over in 1978, followed by other corporate interests. Although no large village existed here, Kaunaoa Bay was a fishing haven for locals, who would ride horses down the beach to favorite spots. Some of these locals sued the resort in 1973 to attain public access, which was granted seven years later. The Mauna Kea Beach Hotel is commonly rated by luxury travelers as one of the world's best beach resorts.

For the **Mauna Kea Beach Hotel,** from the beach access, make your way up the beach, or wander inland through the spacious lawn area with its towering trees. Stairs lead up from the lawn to the pool area. From there, go left out through the luau terrace to Kaʻaha Point, which forms the north end of Kaunaoa Bay and offers a pleasing view. From the point, continue north around the lava-reef seascape. You'll reach a golf cart path, and, immediately left, a path leads to an elevated tee where Palmer, Nicklaus, and Player opened the course in 1964. If no golfers are around, the tee makes a restful spot to view the coast. *More Stuff:* A nature trail leads from the south end of Kaunaoa Beach to Hapuna Beach State Park. This hike is described from the other direction in TH9, but there's no reason you can't start here.

Additionally, you can access Mauʻumae Beach from the Mauna Kea, as is mentioned in the parking directions above—although the trail from Spencer Beach Park, TH7, is more convenient and scenic. To reach this access, as you drive away from hotel parking, turn left on a private road across from Kamahoe Place that takes you past a maintenance yard. Continue straight, cross over a wooden bridge, and park at a second wooden bridge. A trail leads down through scorched kiawe trees.

SNORKEL: With a gradual sand entry and plenty of fish **Kaunaoa Beach** is among the best spots on this part of the island. Posh facilities and an idyllic setting don't hurt. **Kaunaoa Point**, on the south end of the beach, has slightly better coral, but the northern end toward **Kaʻaha Point** is also first-rate. Check out the surf conditions, since the calmer of the two spots will change from day to day. *Be Aware:* High surf indicates rip currents. Normally, current goes out from the center of the beach to the southern point. Agitated sand will also lessen water quality on higher surf days.

SURF: Kaunaoa Beach attracts bodyboarders as well as board surfers. Bodysurfing novices can ride the foam closest to the beach. Board surfers like the right-break at Kaʻaha Point, at the north mouth of the bay. When conditions are right, you can watch these dudes, and dudettes, do their thing from the luau terrace at the hotel. *Be Aware:* Hotel beach attendants post warnings when surf conditions are adverse, but don't count on it. Impact injuries are common. Look for sand being drawn from the base of waves breaking near shore, which indicates a shallow-water hazard.

9.   HAPUNA BEACH STATE PARK   HIKE, SNORKEL, SURF

WHAT'S BEST: Always-sunny Hapuna Beach, the biggest deposit of white sand around, draws beach lovers from all over the Big Island. You'll find several snorkeling and surfing spots, as well as a coastal trail leading to the cover-girl beach at the Mauna Kea Resort.

PARKING: Take Highway 19 north from Kailua-Kona. Pass Puako Beach Dr. and mm70. Turn makai toward Hapuna Beach State Park on Kaunaoa Dr., continue .25-mi., and turn right into a very large parking area. Drive in and park as close as possible to rest rooms and snack bar. Do not leave valuables in your car.

HAPUNA BEACH

HIKE: Hapuna Beach to Kaunaoa Beach (2.5 mi., 150 ft.)

The huge parking lot at Hapuna Beach is a clue. Only 10 inches of rain falls here yearly, compared to 100 inches or more on the Hamakua Coast and Hilo, only a hour's drive away. On prime weekends, the place is jumpin'. A half-mile of white sand gets scorched by sun and soothed by an almost continual shore break. A lawn and treed hillside rises from the shore, with three trails leading down from the parking area. Shaded picnic pavilions provide respite for the hungry and sun-weary.

To hike from **Hapuna Beach to Kaunaoa Beach**, site of the posh Mauna Kea Beach Hotel, take any of the paths from the parking area and head to your right on the sand. On calm-sea days, wear your swimsuit and haul snorkeling gear. A few hundred yards from the lifeguard stations, a low bluff protrudes into the sand—which the ancients called Ihumoku, or Prow of the Ship. At low tide, you can go around at water's edge. At high tide, skirt inland, not far, and take a footpath to the left that goes under the sprawling branches of a large tree. In a minute or two you'll be at north Hapuna Beach, which sits below the Hapuna Beach Prince Hotel. Continue up the beach and jog inland toward the beach activities kiosk at the edge of the hotel's

lawn. At the far end you'll see a sign for the nature trail. Before rounding the point on the trail, you'll see Hapuna Prince Stairs beach, where a flight of stone steps leads down to a protected patch of sand. The trail then continues around the Bluffs at Mauna Kea, the site of trophy homes. You then round Kaunaoa Point, at the edge of a golf course, where you can take a path down to the south end of the resort beach.

SNORKEL: Though known mainly for surfing, **Hapuna Beach** is also fairly good for snorkeling. If you go beyond **Ihumoku**, the bluff that protrudes to the north, you'll be out of sight of the lifeguards. Snorkeling off this point is good. At the south end, rocky Kanekanaka Point is also where the fishes live. The best snorkeling in the immediate area may be **Hapuna Prince Stairs**, reachable at the far north of Hapuna, as described above in the hiking section. Even on wavy days you can at least take a dunk. When the water's calm, the snorkeling at the rocky point is very good. *Be Aware*: During the winter especially, high surf can create dangerous currents.

A more isolated and very good snorkeling spot is nearby **Waialea Bay**, a.k.a. **Beach 69**. And no, the beach is not named for the sexual proclivities of the free-lovers who camped here in the hippie days, but rather for telephone pole number 69, which used to mark the entrance. To get there these days, pass the entrance to Hapuna Beach, driving south and away from the highway. Continue through over a small bluff on bumpy Old Puako Road. In the bottom of a gully, look makai for telephone pole #71, and turn in on a gouged road that leads several hundred feet to a parking area. Make your way through a fence, passing a new rest room that was built and then abandoned by state parks. The best snorkeling is in the middle of Beach 69, around a little "island" near shore that can be high and dry during low tides. The coral shelves at the far south of the beach are also excellent. This beach can be a bust due to high wind and surf, but on the right day Waialea Bay will be a dream.

SURF: You'll see bodyboarders almost all the time in the middle of **Hapuna Beach**. These guys race down from Waimea and up from Kona to get here. Hapuna can be a great beach for novice wave riders, but you're best off seeking the advice from one of the world's best lifeguards. *Be Aware*: For board surfing, check out **Beach 69**, described in *Snorkel*. You can watch them ride the right-break from the point to the north.

10.   HOLOHOLOKAI BEACH PARK   HIKE, SNORKEL, SURF

WHAT'S BEST: A large petroglyph field entices hikers. But the scenic beach park is also the trailhead for two short coast walks, one to the swank beach at the Fairmont Orchid, the other to the turtle coast of folksy Puako.

PARKING: Take Hwy. 19 north from Kailua-Kona. About .5-mi past mm74, turn makai on Mauna Lani Dr. Pass the entrance station, continue to the round-about, and go right on North Kaniku Dr. toward the Fairmont Orchid and

Holoholokai Beach Park. Just before the hotel entrance, turn right toward the beach park. Park in an improved lot at the end of the road.

HIKE: Malama Trail to Puako Petroglyphs (1.25 mi., 100 ft.); Holoholokai to: Fairmont Orchid (.5-mi.) or Ala Kahakai Trail to South Puako (.5-mi.)

At Holoholokai Beach Park are leafy beach trees, palms, and picnic tables set beside a foaming turquoise seascape, all combining to make a pleasing respite for lunch or relaxation. The **Malama Trail to Puako Petroglyphs** begins on the right at the beginning of the paved lot. The rock carvings displayed at the beginning of the trail are re-creations for people to make rubbings. The paved trail quickly ends, and you'll find yourself weaving under a canopy of kiawes on a surface of dirt and smooth lava, with root and rock tripping places liberally added. After about .5-mile, the trail crosses a gravel road, over a rise from which is the several-acre field of pahoehoe lava. Some 3,000 carvings, dating from 1000 AD to 1800 AD, are scattered about, mostly inside of an oval enclosed by a wood railing and low rock wall. One etching of thirty warriors is thought to show a succession of generations, ending with Kamehameha's cousin and rival Keoua, who was killed at Pu'ukohola Heiau and is buried nearby. *Be Aware:* Not all the petroglyphs are within the oval. Tread lightly.

You can also walk from **Holoholokai to the Fairmont Orchid**, with its artful interiors and cute aquamarine cove. Go to the left as you face the ocean at the park. A rocky footpath leads out of the palm grove and soon reaches a concrete path on the lawn of the resort. Continue on the path to the pool area set back from little Pauoa Bay. You'll want to weave inland to admire the elegant décor of the Orchid. *More Stuff:* The path continues south about .5-mile to the Mauna Lani, which is TH11.

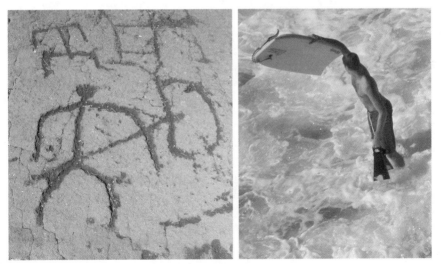

PUAKO PETROGLYPH, PAUOA BODYBOARDER

Going to the right from Holoholokai Beach Park, on the **Ala Kahakai Trail to South Puako Beach**, takes you away from resort world to a miles-long, near-shore reef that is bordered by 1950s beach houses and frequented by surfers, fishermen, and tide-pooling turtles. You'll see the palm grove that marks the coral- and lava-rock embayment soon after setting out on the trail. The "beach" is the last of several Shoreline Public Access turnouts off Puako Beach Drive.

More Stuff: To explore all of the beach community of Puako, get back in the car and go north of the Mauna Lani on Highway 19. Pass mm71 and, .5-mile later, turn left on Puako Beach Drive. Some half-dozen Shoreline Public Access spots are along a 3-mile stretch of sleepy road. About .4-mile in you'll pass Old Puako Road on the right, the back way to Beach 69 and Hapuna State Park. Then, .75-mile from the highway is a right turn to a large parking lot at Puako Bay, a small-craft harbor. At 1.25 miles is Hokuloa Church, dedicated in 1859—the first of 14 churches built by Reverend Lorenzo Lyons, who wrote the now-classic unofficial state anthem, "Hawaii Aloha." On the right, less than .25-mile past the church at a curve in the road, is a 10-foot-wide fenced corridor leading to a rough-sand beach that is shaded by kiawes and palm trees. Look for telephone pole #101. Then, over the next mile, you'll pass several access signs that pop out to shallow tide pools. The best of these is at telephone pole #115. Turtles, no strangers to Big Island beaches, love to feed in shallow waters inside the reef. You can tiptoe through the turtles, but don't touch. South Puako "Beach" is a little more than 3 miles in, at telephone pole #143, before Puako Beach Drive ends at a cul-de-sac.

SNORKEL: Man-enhanced **Pauoa Bay** at the Fairmont Orchid is an ideal pool of warm water to loll about in like a monk seal. It has a sandy entry, with palms gracing the shore. Freshwater intrusion and algae detract from water clarity in the inside pool. For the coral and fish, swim out the lava opening of the pool, and explore the reef to the right. For parking, head toward the beach park, but veer left toward the Fairmont. The public parking lot is to the left of the resort.

Easy entry and safe swimming is to be found at **Puako Bay**, where you enter near the pier and swim out to the north point; but water visibility is not great. The best spot is **South Puako "Beach"** where a rare limestone reef angles to near the shore. You can swim out a channel and go right up the outside of the reef. *Be Aware:* If you're here on a day when the waves are big enough for surfers, then even advanced swimmers should stay clear.

SURF: **South Puako Beach** is known locally as **Ruddles**, because that's the name of a nearby real estate office. Surfers don't waste time thinking up names when they can be out risking their necks on an offshore reef break. Advanced boarders only here. A tamer ride for bodyboarders, as well as the board boys, is the right-break on the north point of **Pauoa Bay** at the Fairmont. You get a good view from shore.

11. MAUNA LANI

WHAT'S BEST: Guests of this fabulous resort must have a hard time leaving. Blue scoops along a white-sand beach are just right for swimming. Palm-lined coastal paths invite strollers. Inland are lake-sized ponds, fringed by an arboretum of tropical trees and a history park.

PARKING: Take Hwy. 19 north from Kailua-Kona. About .5-mi past mm74, turn makai on Mauna Lani Dr. You come to a roundabout, which is past the entrance station. Stay on Mauna Lani Dr., the middle of three options, going toward the resort and historic park. Continue to the resort and park in the large lot to the left of the hotel.

HIKE: Mauna Lani Fishponds and beaches (up to 3.5 mi.); Kalahuipuaʻa Village-Mauna Lani Historic Park (.75-mi.);Coast trail to Fairmont Orchid (1 mi.)

Mauna Lani Resort's mile-long seacoast with white-sand coves, a unique 30-acre history park, and tranquil fishponds make it one of the best places to spend a day at the beach. For the hike to the **Mauna Lani Fishponds and beaches**, head from the parking lot toward the security building that is to the left of the hotel. An asphalt path takes you past the business end of the hotel and onto a lawn area with small Waipuhi Iki Pond on your left. You reach the beach at the Nanuku Inlet, a large protected swimming area. Go left at the shoreline. You'll pass a canoe shed and reach a green carpet of lawn that leads to Eva Parker Woods Cottage Museum. Inside the charming bungalow are artifacts from local sites, such as bone fishhooks, wooden calabashes, and stone tools. On full moon evenings, the cottage is the site for a Talk Story—a medley of dance, chant, music, and crafts. Put a red "X" on your calendar and attend this free event when the timing is right. Just behind the cottage is the largest of the six fishponds; Kalahuipuaʻa, which covers five acres and is nearly 20-feet deep. The path continues past the cottage on a low wall that contains a still-active fish sluice. Here a narrow footbridge and stone wall protrude a 100 feet into the pond, reaching a little hut that is one of the most serene spots on the planet earth.

Next on the path is a small sailboat harbor, and then Beach Club Beach, that is a cove at the southern end of Makaiwa Bay. Hook inland around the shore of Kalahuipuaʻa Pond. An assortment of large native and Polynesian trees line the path, and benches beckon from quiet banks. Breadfruit, kukui, and palms create habitat, and birders will want to sit a spell. You'll come around to the back shore of Kalahuipuaʻa, and pass two other good-sized fishponds on your right, the first called Manoku and the second and larger called Hopeaia. Sturgeon, milkfish, shrimp and mullet—the "pig of the sea"—live in these waters. In ancient times they were raised to delight only the pallets of the aliʻi. Runners would wrap fat fish in seaweed and, like hardcore pizza delivery guys, would run for miles, praying that the fish would still be quivering upon delivery. After passing Hopeaia Pond, the trail reaches a T-intersection. To the left takes you back to the beach. To the right crosses a road and enters the lower part of Kalahuipuaʻa History Park. You can enter the park's trail here, or drive to the upper trailhead on the way to the highway. The trailhead is midway between the Mauna Lani and the roundabout. Look for a sign at Pauao Road.

First-time visitors may not "get" **Kalahuipuaʻa Village-Mauna Lani Historic Park**, especially if the hike is attempted in the noonday sun. A short trail, replete with interpretive markers, undulates through a pahoehoe lava field that was home to hundreds of people for centuries, beginning around 1200 AD. Caves made from collapsed lava tubes are former homes, now missing the crucial layers of woven matting and thatched structures. Many artifacts, such as canoe paddles, fishhooks, and stone tools were recovered in this preserved site after Frances Iʻi Brown sold the property to the Mauna Lani Resort in 1972. One of the best single petroglyphs on the island—a helmeted warrior with upraised spear—is located 15 feet off the paved path to the right (facing toward the ocean), just before you reach the road. And, once crossing the road, where the path enters the fishponds, go right to see the Kulia Petroglyphs.

With all there is to do at the Mauna Lani, you may miss the **Coast trail to Fairmont Orchid** and Pauoa Bay. Grab your snorkeling gear and take the coral- and black-rock path that weaves through coco palms and an occasional heliotrope. Inland are new luxury homes, but they are buffered by a greenbelt of small ponds where you can also find a petroglyph or two. Pauoa Bay, as noted in TH10, is a pleasant place to take a dip.

More Stuff: A trail continues south on the coast from Beach Club Beach for 1.25 miles to 49 Black Sand Beach at Honokaope Bay. From the beach club, go up the paved, railed path alongside condos. The path eventually becomes unpaved, passing between the ridiculously jagged lava cliffs of Waʻawaʻa Point and serene golf fairways. Looking inland from this path you can see all of the Big Island's volcanoes except for Kilauea.

SNORKEL: Beach Club Beach at the south end Makaiwa Bay is at the top of the list among Kohala Coast snorkeling venues. A nice sand beach with easy entry leads to luscious coral heads that are not far offshore. Wave action outside the mouth of the bay can stimulate a southerly current, but conditions are relatively safe inside the bay. Showers, fine sand, and a shaded lawn add to the charm. It's a short hike from the Mauna Lani, as described above. Right in front of the Mauna Lani, the **Nanuku Inlet** is a nice big swimming pool, less than chest deep. Water quality is not excellent and fish are not abundant, but swimming is superb. Large milo trees shade the shore. Snorkeling improves outside the inlet, but heads up since a local sailing canoe replica enters the narrow inlet and makes a daily landing at this beach.

Honokaope Bay, site of **49 Black Sand Beach**, has fairly good snorkeling from its sloping, gritty shores. Tennis courts and a pool for the private homes sit above the little beach. Showers and restrooms are ultra. To drive to 49 Black Sand Beach, loop around the roundabout on Mauna Lani Drive to the far side and go right on South Kaniku

Eva Parker Woods Cottage Museum, Daniel Kaniela Akaka, Jr., Talk Story Dancer, Fishponds at Mauna Lani

Drive. Ask for public access parking at the entrance station. After about a mile you'll reach the 20-space parking lot.

12.   ANAEHO'OMALU HIKE, SNORKEL, SURF

WHAT'S BEST: Where else can you quietly observe centuries-old rock etchings and village ponds, and a few minutes later be reveling in the phantasmagoric opulence of a resort hotel (where you can get face time with dolphins)? Between these extremes are white-sand swimming beaches and a coastal walk to a secluded cove. You can easily spend the day kicking around.

PARKING: Take Hwy. 19 north from Kailua-Kona. Just before reaching mm76, turn makai on Waikoloa Beach Dr. toward Anaeho'omalu. *For the petroglyph preserve:* Drive in .5-mi. and turn right on a cul-de-sac before you get to the Kings Shops. Park off road before the entrance to the Fairway Villas. *For Anaeho'omalu Beach Park:* Drive in .6-mi and turn left on Ku'uali'i Pl. toward Shoreline Public Access—opposite the entrance to the Kings Shops.

For direct access to the anchialine ponds: Continue around Waikoloa Beach Dr., past the Kings Shops, and take the left-hand turn lane toward Shoreline Public Access. This parking area is close to the outer area of the Hilton's guest parking lot. *For direct Access to the Hilton:* Circle around Waikoloa Beach Dr., past the above access, and turn left at an entrance station to the Hilton.

HIKE: Waikoloa Petroglyph Preserve (.5-mi.); Anaeho'omalu Beach Park to: Kapalaoa Beach (1 mi.), or Anchialine Pond Preservation Area (1 mi.) and Hilton Resort (1.75 mi.); Hilton Resort stroll (up to .75-mi.)

For 13 centuries local village people recorded major events and the passage of time on the smooth pahoehoe lava that is the **Waikoloa Petroglyph Preserve**, now enveloped by a golf course and beach villas. Head up the Kings Trail through sparse kiawes. The trail undulates over the near horizon, but the preserve is to the right within the first .25-mile. The earliest carvings are from around 700 AD, while the most recent, like cowboy on horseback, date from the mid-1800s. The circles with dots in the center are thought to mark the birth of boys, and the semi-circles are for girls.

Anaeho'omalu Beach Park is a privately owned recreation area with rest rooms and showers. It was part of Parker Ranch until the 31,000 acres were sold for resort development in the late 1970s. Historical sites, ponds, and hiking trails have been preserved by the resort. Above large Anaeho'omalu Bay now sits the Marriott Outrigger, and the grandiose Hilton is just northward, on the narrow inlet of Waiulua Bay. Locals unwilling to put together seven syllables call this place A-Bay.

To hike to secluded **Kapalaoa Beach**, head to the left as you face the water at Anaeho'omalu Beach Park. You immediately pass the park's most scenic spots, missed by most beach goers who head for open sand. After a few minutes the coastal trail will seem to peter out where surf washes into a mangrove thicket, but press on and you will find a passageway cut through the sprawling trees. Sand dunes await on the other side of the tree-tunnel. Continue up the beach to the far dune and you will find Kapalaoa Beach set in a little white-sand cove fringed by palms, kiawe, and other beach trees.

Going north from the beach park, or to the right as you face the water, a coastal path leads around the sandy bay to its headlands and the **Anchialine Pond Preservation Area**. It then continues around to the **Hilton Resort**. The ponds are about midway; where a spur trail connects from the coast to the anchialine pond parking area. You can use the pond parking to skip the beach walk and enter the Hilton the back way. Starting from the beach park, either walk the sand of the bay or, if Waikoloa's winds are sandblasting, cut behind the beach dune and walk the shores of two large fishponds. Paths encircle these lakelets, the first and larger is called Ku'uali'i, and is connected by a channel to the second, called Kahapapa, which in turn is connected by a sluice gate

ANAEHO'OMALU, THE HILTON

to the sea. *Anae* means "mullet," and *hoʻomalu* means "protected." Hence seagoing royalty would pull canoes in here for fresh fish.

Stick close to shore after rounding the bay. The rock-lined trail continues through leafy kamani trees and passes mounds of bleached white coral that buffet the shore. The pond preservation area will be to your right. Anchialine ponds are brackish pools near the coast where groundwater and seawater percolate to the surface. High tide brings more salt content, while heavy rainfall inland charges the groundwater and brings more fresh water to the mix. The ancients used the ponds for agriculture, drinking, and raising fish and shrimp. Head inland on the paved trail to see the ponds, and then backtrack to continue along the coast to the Hilton. You'll pass some new beachside bungalows. Climb stairs that take you to the resort's pool area, with its swinging bridge and artificial falls. Stay on the paved seaside path to reach the dolphin pool. From there make your way inland to the foyer, shops, and galleries.

The **Hilton Resort stroll** is where a luxury hotel meets theme park. A voluminous entranceway leads to the hotel's free monorail and boat rides. On both you wind through building canyons and gardens, and break out to open to sea views. Beyond these plat-forms, is the Grand Staircase, an expansive portico with 100-foot columns leading right into the water. Or go left at the stairs behind a waterfall to the dolphin lagoon … but don't miss the life-sized bronze of a horse-drawn ancient Japanese carriage. You have to be there to appreciate the scale. The Hilton's Palace Tower has 20-foot high vases and art galore. A man-made lagoon and beach is separated by a grassy spit from the lava shores of Waiulua Bay. For most visitors, the showstopper at the Hilton is the resort's Dolphin Learning Center. At the inner reaches of the man-made lagoon are two pools that are home to a dozen of our brothers and sisters of the sea. Grassy slopes provide a spot to sit down and go eyeball-to-eyeball with these creatures. But the real treat, usually in the afternoon, is when the exceedingly well-trained staff of the Dol-phin Quest introduces small teams of lucky kids. It's a five-ring circus as kids, trainers, and dolphins charge about the lagoon timing out a splash-filled interplay.

SNORKEL: Although surf and sand create murky waters near shore, **Anaehoʻomalu Bay** has some very good snorkeling. You need to swim a long way out, which may deter beginners, and should deter everyone when the big surf is rolling in. Snorkeling tour boats moor offshore in the middle of the bay. Beginners may prefer the south end of the bay, by the beach park. Swim out to depths of 10 feet, with rocks and coral to your left. Water quality improves farther out. Shallow water and algae make the close-in waters at secluded **Kapalaoa Beach** less than ideal. But if you angle out the little cove, keeping close to shore, clarity increases. While not the prime spot for snorkeling, this is a great swimming pool, generally safe. *Be Aware:* Rip current may pick up out-side the cove during periods of high surf.

You can also discretely haul your gear into the **Hilton** and swim in the resort's man-made lagoon, which is open to, but sheltered from, the frothy waters of **Waiulua Bay**.

Once in the lagoon, you can swim up to the Grand Staircase and waterfall, or flipper the other way to the open waters. When surf conditions permit, the bay is an under-rated snorkeling spot, rich with marine life.

SURF: A-Bay is the top windsurfing and kite-boarding spot on the Big Island. Wind riders put in at the canoe hale that is to the left as you enter **Anaehoʻomalu Beach Park**. Board surfers like the area north of the bay, **Kaʻauau Point**, that is between the park and the Hilton. Long-board surfers, who are coming back into favor, can be spied offshore when the surf is up. Due to shallow lava reefs, this is not a learner's locale.

13. KEAWAIKI BAY HIKE, SNORKEL

WHAT'S BEST: In the early 1900s, celebrities and Hawaii's gentry used to gather at this now forlorn estate. You'll feel delightfully in the middle of no-where on this rugged coast—that has excellent snorkeling pools.

PARKING: Take Hwy. 19 north from Kailua-Kona. Pass mm79 and, .5-mi. later, pull off to the ocean side of the highway. You'll see a lava turnout and three palms growing close together.

HIKE: Keawaiki Bay (1.5 mi.) and Weliweli Point (3.25 mi.)

Francis Iʻi Brown, the Great Gatsby of the Big Island, was the grandson of the distin-guished John Papa Iʻi, who spent his long life as a counsel to Hawaii's first three kings and in his later years educated himself and recorded his experiences in seminal history books. His grandson, Francis, owned what later became the Mauna Lani Resort. He also purchased this 15-acre retreat at Keawaiki Bay in 1920 and over the next several decades partied with the likes of Babe Ruth, Mae West, and Bob Hope. Recently the retreat is where author Paul Theroux kayak-camped and wrote about it in *The Happy Isles of Oceania*. In 1956, Francis Brown sold the estate to his grandson and subsequent generations have installed a 10-strand barbed-wire fence around the modest grounds.

To get from the parking area to **Keawaiki Bay**, step over a lava-rock berm, veer left, and go straight toward the ocean on a crushed aʻa lava road. Keep the coco palm grove in your sights. In less than .5-mile, you reach the over-strung fence, where a well-tramped trail leads to the right over fearsome aʻa lava and follows the fence line to the beach. At the coast, go left along the fence line. A palm grove and other beach trees accent the retreat's squat stone cottages with metal roofs. At the far end of this stretch, the stones are worn down to salt-and-pepper pebbles and coarse sand, backed by kiawes and a few palms. This is where you want to do beach time at Keawaiki (pronounce the W as a V) Bay. *More Stuff:* A trail continues south from the beach, around the pahoehoe lava reef to Kawai Point, a highly scenic and recommended side trip that will add up to 1.75 miles round trip to your hike. You pass lava tide pools and reach a coral-sand

KEAWAIKI BAY

camping beach. The trail continues near the coast into rougher lava, but you'll find Kawai Point by veering about 200 feet seaward over the smooth lava reef.

To dramatic **Weliweli Point**, backtrack up the beach past the Brown retreat. You cross a low lava point and reach small Pueo Bay, where in 1859 the molten stampede of jagged lava that is just inland met its match in the relentless Pacific. Stay high on the black-pebble dune as it curls around toward a lone coconut palm, unless some misfortune has since befallen our noble botanical friend. Pause here to gaze inland at Mauna Kea, Hualalai Volcano, and the long slope of Mauna Loa. The lava you see at arm's length crawled 35 miles from Mauna Loa. On the north side of Pueo Bay, footing gets more difficult as you cross chunks of coral and lava, but persevere and you'll soon reach the mound of stone that prior travelers have erected to mark Weliweli Point. You're not in Kansas anymore, Todo. You're on a hammerhead of coral that is being smashed to sand by waves on the Big Island of Hawaii. *More Stuff:* If you double back to the fence corner at the Brown retreat, you can take a lava road that passes a vegetated gulch that is dotted with attractive pools. The rough road hooks back out to the highway, just north of mm78.

SNORKEL: The south cove at **Keawaiki Bay** is protected by a reef that angles north from Kaiwi Point. Snorkeling can be excellent here, provided wave action is not extreme. Beach aesthetics get high marks. Marginally better snorkeling is farther up the shore toward the main house at the Brown retreat. You'll see a lava wall segment at water's edge. Entry is easy here.

Snorkeling is also good at **Pueo Bay**, although the water is normally rougher and you'll find no shelter from the sun. Of underwater interest at Pueo is the freshwater intrusion that can be seen as ripples during periods of calmer surf. You're seeing anchialine ponds in action, as this water is flowing from the ponds just inland, noted above. *Be Aware:* Although snorkeling can be excellent in this locale, wave action creates tricky currents. Observe the seas carefully, and test the current upon entry by floating face down to see if you stay in one spot.

14.   KIHILO BAY

HIKE, SNORKEL

WHAT'S BEST: An enticing view from a scenic point lures visitors to this not-so-secret bay and turquoise lagoon. The place delivers with a black sand beach, hidden swimming ponds, and a rugged coastline thick with tropical greenery.

PARKING: Take Hwy. 19 north from Kailua-Kona. Pass mm83 and, .5-mi. later, turn makai on an unpaved road. Hours for this road are 9 a.m. to 7 p.m., as noted by a Department of Land and Natural Resources sign at a gate just in from the highway. *Note:* Traffic makes this turn dangerous when driving north. You may wish to spot the road on the way by and continue .25-mi. north to a scenic view parking lot and hang a U-turn.

WAINANALI'I LAGOON

For the Wainanali'i Lagoon hike: Continue .75-mi. down the unpaved road and park at a gated road on the right. *For Kihilo Black Sand Beach and Luahinewai Pond:* Continue another .1-mi, to where the road makes a right-angle left (and a rougher road continues straight toward the ocean). Go left a short distance to a Shoreline Public Access turnout on the right, near an octagonal house on poles. *Note:* North of the scenic view parking lot on the highway is another trail down to the bay. Park .1-mi. south of mm81, where the highway cuts through a low hill. Though popular, this option is slightly longer than the access described above, and requires 200 feet of elevation change. You also stand a better chance of getting lost.

HIKE: Wainanali'i Lagoon (2.25 mi.); Kihilo Black Sand Beach and Luahinewai Pond (.75-mi.)

At the north end of 2-mile-wide Kihilo Bay, **Wainanali'i Lagoon** is a luminescent streak of turquoise that is difficult to resist. To walk there, step under the gate from the parking area. After about .25-mile you'll pass a trailhead sign near a gate that leads to beach access. As a side-trip, you can wander this direction and visit a freshwater pool formed by a collapsed pahoehoe lava tube. It's located a stone's throw from the ocean, just south of a large yellow (unless they've painted it) house. About .5-mile from the gate you'll pass another signpost near a third gate. Nearby is the driveway to the architecturally elaborate home of cosmetic magnate Paul Mitchell, who had the place shipped in pieces from Indonesia. Just past that drive, at last, is a Shoreline Public Access sign that leads a short distance through thicket to the beach. At the beach, circle around to the right to a coco-palm lined embayment, inshore of which is a tranquil fishpond. Staying close to the shore, walk the embayment, cross two plank bridges over narrow channels, and continue over a pahoehoe section of trail that leads to the open end of Wainanali'i Lagoon. The lagoon was actually part of a massive fishpond built by Kamehameha the Great in 1810, which was considered an engineering marvel by early Western visitors. Walls 8-feet high and 20-feet wide in places formed a deep-sea fishpond that was nearly two miles around. An 1859 Mauna Loa eruption, which created Lae Hou Point that you can see to the north, destroyed much of the pond. A narrow, .25-mile-long spit that looks like an island lies across the lagoon. This place is turtle city, as noted in *Snorkel*, below.

Kihilo Black Sand Beach and **Luahinewai Pond** are at the south end of Kihilo Bay. From the parking at the octagonal house, head to your left on black sand. Look inland immediately to see the spring-fed pond set below a lava wall and bordered by palms and other beach trees. In ancient times, and well into the 1900s, coastal canoeists would stop in here for fresh water and to maintain the good hygiene for which the Hawaiians were noted. Black sand at southern Kihilo ranges from fairly fine to basketball-sized. You'll find three separate beaches over the southern shore, nuances in a rugged shoreline. From here you could walk the 2 miles to the north end along this beachcomber's beach, although high surf may bully you inland at times. In the 1890s, this end of the bay was where cattle from Pu'u Wa'a Wa'a Ranch (see TH15) were shuttled to their demise via ships offshore.

SNORKEL: **Kihilo Black Sand Beach** is the snorkeling spot on this bay, if you value water clarity, easy entry, and pleasant beach trees. The water gets deep fast, but the average depth of the bay is only about 15 feet. *Be Aware*: Wave action creates strong currents, especially during winter months. At these times, head to the lagoon.

A few months after visiting the Big Island you may find yourself staring through a wall and thinking about the time you snorkeled in **Wainanali'i Lagoon**. You can enter where the trail meets the lagoon, or wade across to the spit, a more private setting. Green sea turtles feed and sleep in the lagoon. Encrusted salt turns their bodies white after they haul out into the sun at the far end of the 5-acre inlet. *Be Aware*: Federal law and common decency require giving the turtles a wide berth. Although startlingly blue, the water is milky in the lagoon. On calm days before a lot of people arrive, you can see a fresh water sheet floating on or near the surface of the 10-foot-deep water. You will also notice a little chill, as the water temps are a few degrees cooler.

15.   PU'U WA'A WA'A   HIKE

WHAT'S BEST: Surrounding this rippled butte above the South Kohala coast is one of the state's few remaining examples of native leeward habitat. The pu'u is visible from everywhere; see what everywhere looks like from there.

PARKING: From Hwy. 19 in Kailua-Kona, take Hwy. 190, or Palani Rd., up the mountain. North of mm22, look for the Pu'u Wa'a Wa'a Ranch gate on the mauka side, at a dirt turnout. The gate is unlocked weekdays from 6 a.m. to 6 p.m. Drive in and veer left immediately. Continue for 2 miles as the road becomes gravel but passable. Park near a small cinder block building.

HIKE: Pu'u Wa'a Wa'a loop (2.75 mi., 525 ft.)

Birders and botanists will particularly enjoy taking a look at an example of native lowland dry forest, which used to be common on the leeward slopes of all the Hawaiian Islands. The Polynesians cleared some of the forest for agriculture, and Westerners did in most of the remaining with irrigation projects and range cattle. For the **Pu'u Wa'a Wa'a loop**, head up through the hunter's gate and road that will be to the left as you face uphill. Although this hike will go uphill and loop around to the right, most of the forest reserve is to the left, so trailblazers can answer their whims and pursue other roads. The route to the top is unmarked and novice hikers may find it a challenge.

The rocky path climbs gradually at the edge of the forest, while across the way the green shoulders and gully of Pu'u Wa'a Wa'a. In the forest, the gray-barked ohia is the dominant tree, with its red bottlebrush flowers and burnt-coffee scent. The squiggly limbed wiliwili, its bark often orange with lichen, will lose its leaves during dry summers. Wiliwili flowers are a peachy-orange, and its berries are coral pink. A common shrub, with little yellow football-shaped fruits, is the ala'a. Among the exotic trees that grow here are the lavender-flowered jacaranda, and the pepper tree, with poisonous red berries. Birdsong is a constant backdrop to these visual delights.

After almost a mile of gradual climbing you reach a saddle where a road arcs left to the forest reserve, and another goes right toward Pu'u Wa'a Wa'a. From here you'll note that mauka face of the old volcanic vent is not steep and rippled like its seaward side, but a more gradual slope. Hook around behind the rise, keeping the scraggly fences and lava walls of the ranch to your right. The last part of the climb is steep. Keep to the right of the crater on the goat trail that leads to the top. Pu'u Wa'a Wa'a is nearly 4,000 feet in elevation, less than half the height of green Hualalai Volcano at 8,271, which rises a few miles southward. Looking north you get a full-frontal of Mauna Kea.

16. KAUPULEHU   HIKE, SNORKEL

WHAT'S BEST: Miles of coastal paths lead to snorkeling coves and pass the tranquil grounds of the Four Seasons and Kona Village. Petroglyphs and interpretive markers impart a sense of history along this striking seascape.

PARKING: Take Hwy. 19 north from Kailua. Pass mm87 and, .6-mi. later, turn makai toward Kaupulehu and Hualalai Resorts. Keep left and stop at the entrance station for the Four Seasons Resort. *For Kukio Bay hikes:* Ask for public access permit for Kukio Bay, which is the south parking area. You turn left from the entrance station and wind down about 1.25 miles to a 25-space parking lot. *For Four Seasons and petroglyphs hikes:* Ask for public access permit for the resort, which is the north parking area. You continue straight from the entrance station and park in spots to the right of the resort.

Notes: If the lot you request is full, ask to visit the Kaupulehu Cultural Center—your ace in the hole. In addition, you can also reach the beach very near the Four Season's north parking area by entering through the Kona Village. To do this, veer right after turning in from the highway. The "greeter" will tell you to try the Four Seasons, and that the Kona Village parking is too far from the beach. True, it is nearly a .5-mile walk, but it is also a large lot. *Last note:* To directly access pretty Kikaua Park at the south end of Kukio Bay, see *Snorkel* below.

HIKE: Kukio Bay parking to: Kikaua Park (1.5 mi.) or Kumukehu Trail to Four Seasons (1.5 mi.); Four Seasons north parking to: Kahuwai Bay (Kona Village) and Kaupulehu Petroglyphs (1.25 mi.); Kaupulehu Cultural Center (.25-mi.)

For both Kukio Bay parking hikes, you begin down the paved path and boardwalk, passing Halau o Kaupulehu. This canoe shed houses a traditional Polynesian sailing canoe and is where school children are told of the craftsmanship, sailing skills, and astronomy that were needed by the ancients to make their trans-Pacific voyages. For the hike to **Kikaua Park**, which is a beauty at the far end of Kukio Bay, depart the path and go left on the beach. At the end of the beach, a trail crosses a short section of lava before reaching the park, which is part of the high-end private development at Kukio.

KINGS POND, KONA VILLAGE

Palms, ironwoods, and the leafy kamani trees are nicely spaced. On the way back from the park, you can make this a pleasant loop hike by veering slightly inland to check out the paths and boardwalk along a grouping of anchialine ponds.

The **Kumukehu Trail to the Four Seasons**—to the right from the Kukio parking lot—is a paved path that skirts a golf course and the jagged seascape left by 1801 a'a lava flow that tumbled down from Hualalai Volcano. Interpretive signs mark the way. Whale watchers will want to pause midway during winter months at Kumukehu Point, before continuing to the Four Seasons.

To hike from the **Four Seasons to Kahuwai Bay and Kaupulehu Petroglyphs at the Kona Village**, you can continue on the Kumukehu Trail. You can also move to the north parking area noted above and wind your way through the gardens of the low slung resort to the coast path. This path comes out near the Kings Pond, a man-enhanced snorkeling pool. Shortly after leaving the Four Seasons, you pass the entranceway for the Kona Village's public parking; look for the chain-link fence. Continue along the beach, passing thatched-roofed swank cottages.

At the crook in the shoreline of Kahuwai Bay are the pool and patio areas. To get to the petroglyph field, cut in between the patios and take a path that runs along a large interior pond. Swans float under spreading trees. At the far end of pond, go right over a little bridge. Keep right and you'll pop out on a perimeter road just opposite the field. A railed boardwalk was built in 1998 to preserve the 400-plus Kaupulehu rock carvings—called ki'i pohaku in Hawaiian. The earliest petroglyphs date from about 1,000 years ago, the most recent from the early 1800s. The origin of some of the etchings is a mystery. Some of the pictures in rock, like the "surfing fisherman" and the ornately drawn sails, are unique. *Note:* This is not a public place. Kona Village offers tours daily at 11 a.m. It further recommends that the best view times, due to the light, are before 10 a.m. or after 2:30 p.m.

The **Kaupulehu Cultural Center** is under the main lobby of the Four Seasons, on the ocean side. Inside are some of the island's experts on Hawaiian culture and crafts, as well as artifacts and replicas that give a hands-on appreciation of what life was like in the 25,000-acre ahupua'a of Kaupulehu. Of particular interest are 11 original paintings that depict village life by Herb Kawinui Kane (KAH-nay). A former Chicago advertising executive, Kane returned to his Big Island home to perpetuate the knowledge of the Hawaiians through his painting and writing. The center is open daily.

SNORKEL: The best snorkeling at Kaupulehu is at **Kahuwai Bay**, offshore **Kona Village**. Use the Kona Village public access, or the north access at the Four Seasons. You'll find coral heads and lots of fish as you swim out toward the point. You can also swim closer to the Four Seasons, where the smooth lava bench gives way to sand. *Be Aware:* Keep an eye out for boat traffic in the bay. A popular scuba diving reef, called Ledges, is outside the bay.

FOUR SEASONS

While its shallow water may put off reef divers, most snorkelers will greatly enjoy **Kikaua Park**, at the south end of Kukio Bay. Either take the first hike described above or drive to the park's lot, which is just south of the Hualalai Resorts' entrance. On Highway 19, look for a makai turn lane that is .75-mile north of mm88. Ask for a public access permit. A 25-space parking lot is less than a mile away, where a paved trail leads to the beach park.

Directly off the point is a dreamy pool with statuesque lava spires just offshore. A formation with a two-legged base is what's left of a lava stack that in Hawaiian mythology represents the local chiefess frozen forever after a love-triangle went bad. A sandy entrance leads to the pool, an excellent place to flipper around.

For deeper water, from this park, take the trail across the lava to the sands of **South Kukio Bay**—a stone's throw away. Entry can be tricky, but you should spot a little channel used by kayakers. Wave action and currents can be a problem here. Likewise, you need to look carefully for entrance points at **North Kukio Bay**, which is accessible from the first lot describing in *Parking* above.

At the **Four Seasons,** just to the left of where the public access trail adjoins the beach is a large **keiki pond** that is ideal for taking a swim, but not great for snorkeling.

WHAT'S BEST: Pick the right day and you'll be happily marooned on your own tropical island, beside shimmering aquamarine waters. When the surf is flat and on weekdays, your only beach mates may be wild goats.

PARKING: Take Hwy 19 north of the airport from Kailua-Kona. Heads up after the road to Hawaii Veterans Cemetery. About .1-mi. after mm88, turn makai where unpaved road meets the highway. A stop sign marks the road.

HIKE: Pu'u Kuili (2 mi., 325 ft.); Kua Bay (1.25 mi., 200 ft.); Both hikes together (3.25 mi., 425 ft.)

For both hikes, start down a road that you will be tempted to drive and soon be glad you didn't. Pu'u Kuili is a clear landmark to your left, rising above a plane of a'a lava. Right away you pass the gate of a lava road, and you will reach another one 10 minutes into the hike. For the easy climb to **Pu'u Kuili,** turn left at the second gate, heading broadside toward the grassy hill. (Roads are part of the Kukio development that is marching southward; see *More Stuff* below.) The road to the pu'u becomes a cul-de-sac. Stay to the left, dropping into a pahoehoe lava gully that supports a grove of stickery kiawes. A rock-lined trail traverses upward to the right, or seaward, on a gentle slope toward the makai side of the pu'u. Once you reach the ocean side of the Pu'u Kuili, it's an easy scamper to the top. An upright pipe marks the spot.

To get to **Kua Bay,** continue down the road that now becomes seriously rutted and you will reach a gate and sign for Maniniowali, the original name for the bay. Go to the right. Once down to the beach, don't take a left-veer to the water, but go straight ahead through another gate. This route soon hooks left, taking you to the sandy beach at the bay. The north side of the little bay is formed by low-lying Papiha Point, a good place to take in the views. *More Stuff:* As the bulldozers move inexorably south from Kukio, so too will recreational developments. Rest rooms, showers, and a picnic area will be built by the developer. A new access road is planned between mm89 and mm88. The access road will fork: The right fork will go to Kua Bay, and a new loop trail to Pu'u Kuili. A left fork will go to primitive camping facilities at Awake'e Bay.

SNORKEL: Kua Bay is known for its turquoise waters and snorkeling can be superb. Get in at the beach and swim out among the rocks that are just off of Papiha Point to the north. *Be Aware:* High surf can roll in here, making for treacherous swimming conditions. The winter surf at times blows away the sand at water's edge, leaving only boulders. Bring along a beach umbrella for shade.

SURF: The shore break at **Kua Bay** draws bodyboarding buffs, and can also be good for body surfing. During higher surf, experienced boarders ride the wild right-break off Papiha Point, a sight to behold.

18. KEKAHA KAI STATE PARK   HIKE, SNORKEL, SURF

WHAT'S BEST: Long sandy beaches with snorkeling coves are set along three miles of undeveloped parklands. Beach hikers will want to spend the day.

PARKING: Take Hwy. 19 north of the airport. About .5-mi. north of mm91, turn makai toward Kekaha Kai State Park. A gate is open from 9 a.m. to 7 p.m., but is locked on Wednesdays. Follow a hellishly bumpy, unpaved road. *For Mahaiula and Makalawena beaches:* Park at a gate your right that is 1.5 miles from the highway. *For Kekaha Kai Beach Park,* continue to road's end at 1.75 mi.

MAHAIULA BAY

HIKE: Kekaha Kai Beach (.25-mi.); Kekaha Kai Trail to: Mahaiula Bay (.75-mi.), and Makalawena Beaches (1.75 mi. to 2.75 mi.)

Kekaha Kai State Park, formerly called Kona Coast State Park, covers some 1,600 coastal acres. The state has plans to improve the access road and put in showers, rest rooms, wilderness camping, and picnic facilities at Mahaiula Bay. An education center, canoe hale, and botanical gardens are also in the works. For now, the waterless rest rooms and barbecue grills under picture-perfect palms at **Kekaha Kai Beach** are the extent of man's handiwork. This beach was called Second Beach by its former owners, and in ancient times it was known as Kaelehuluhulu, which is fun to say. A semi-circle of sand-and-rubble beach curves outward to form the south mouth of Mahaiula Bay, which you'll see around to the right. An alternate way to get to that bay is to pull on the surf shoes and walk the sloping sands past an inshore grove of ironwoods.

For the hikes to **Mahaiula Bay** and **Makalawena Beaches**, beat tracks across the black cinder road on the other side of the locked gate. Make sure to bring a hat and carry plenty of water. A green buffer of kiawes and coco palms hide the bay. Stay on the road and you'll wind up in the center of the half-mile wide crescent of sand. In the 1930s, this bay was part of the Alfred Magoon estate and the scene of days-long parties. Mahaiula was a fishing village in the older days, and the lava tubes surrounding the grounds were burial grounds.

To **continue to Makalawena**, go right on the sand, cutting in front of an open-air bunkhouse. Skirt the shore and then make sure to cut right at a low wall and palm trees. Now you need your shoes. An 8-foot wide crunchy trail leads straight across a'a for a little more than .25-mile before reaching the fine white sand and shade at the backshore of Makalawena. In recent years, locals fought back a 1,000-room resort that was planed for this shore. Continue on the sand trail and head left up a long sand dune which is carpeted green with pohuehue, or seaside morning glory. From the dune, you'll get a look down the beach, about a half-mile long. Midway in the strand is a lava point. The first part of the beach is technically Pu'u Ali'i Beach, but everyone just uses Makalawena, a reference to the ahupua'a name.

At the far end of the beach are parklike grounds, with a picnic table or two set in a stand of ironwoods. Kamani, heliotrope, and other beach trees also stand around look-ing pretty. If you cut inland at this spot you'll find Opaeula Pond, a 12-acre shorebird sanctuary that is home to the endangered Hawaiian stilt, golden plover, as well as waterfowl and the occasional woodland bird. Many of the birds feed on the pond's red shrimp. If you continue over the next little rise from the parklike ironwood grove, you'll find a five-star keiki pond next to a small sand cove. The trail continues north from here, reaching Kaiwikohola Point and the gate of a 4WD road that comes in from Kua Bay. A proposed wilderness campground is just north, at Awake'e Bay.

MAHAIULA BAY BUNKHOUSE, MAKALAWENA

SNORKEL: At **Kekaha Kai Beach** the snorkeling is just okay, due to an exposed near-shore reef. On calm days, however, go right to the sloping sands and you'll see a pretty good swimming spot. **Mahaiula Bay** is the best snorkeling choice at the state park. It is safe and protected, shaded by lovely palms and a spreading heliotrope. Entry is gradual at either end of the bay, although you do have to pick your way though small rocks on the north side. Decent coral heads await offshore, but fish are not copious and water clarity is not among the Big Island's best. Offshore clarity improves, near a scuba divers' spot called Arches.

The south end of **Makalawena** has rocks at the shore break, but you can snorkel at a small opening, just as you top the dune. Or, better yet, cross the first stretch of beach and try the next section beyond the lava point. *Be Aware:* Stinging sea urchins can be a problem at the first part of the beach and a rip current channel goes out the center of this embayment. Go to the far end of the beach and enter near the rocky point. To be totally safe getting wet, try the **keiki beach** that is beyond the ironwood stand, continuing north.

SURF: Boardheads beat up their car's shock absorbers and then come running to catch the right-break at **Kawili Point**, which is the north side of **Mahaiula Bay**. Big surf breaks across the entire mouth of the bay on certain days. You'll find bodyboarders at the north end of **Makalawena**, catching an offshore right-slide. Body surfers will be tempted at this beach, but be very careful of near-shore rocks, as well as rip current.

KAILUA-KONA

Where's the beach?

Arriving at the airport, especially on days when the vog (volcanic smog) is creeping down the barren lava fields, Kona newcomers may be disappointed with the absence of a glitzy run of white sand that is normally associated with a resort area of such high repute. Don't despair. Remember that the big guy, Kamehameha the Great, could have lived anywhere in the Hawaiian Islands and he chose to spend his remaining decade on the shores of Kailua-Kona. Like much of the Big Island, Kona may not deliver the stereotype, but it offers much more after you've taken the time let the magic work.

Just north of town are three beaches, each with its own personality, that provide a quick getaway. Wawaloli Beach Park is a sandy nook with a chilly dipping pond. From the park is a beachcomber's hike to Pinetrees Beach, a surfer's hangout. Just south of Wawaloli, at Honokohau Bay, is a pleasant snorkeling spot at Alula Beach, where you can also sit on a palm point at the mouth of the harbor to watch the deep sea fishermen return with their bounty. But the treasure at Honokohau is the Kaloko-Honokohau National Historic Park, featuring a picturesque swimming lagoon and a coast walk of nearly two miles, leading to a surfer's beach and royal pond. Anthropological sleuths will have a field day.

Closest to Kona is Old Airport Beach State Park, a place to take a stroll with a morning latte or a sunset cocktail, or vice versa, what the heck. A continuous coral-and-sand strip fronts an onshore lava reef, where you can also find some very good snorkeling. You'll have room to roam and a whole runway to park on, a getaway that is nearly walking distance from the hubbub of Kailua.

KALOKO-HONOKOHAU NATIONAL HISTORIC PARK

KEANE'E CLIFFS, KONA COMMERCE, HULIHE'E PALACE

Kailua, or Kailua-Kona as the post office prefers, definitely has the tropical-seaport charm that you expect in the islands. Cruising sailboats anchor offshore, along with occasional luxury liners and the evening dinner cruise barges. Sure, the place has it's tacky shops, but some are downright kitsch, and the historical layers of Old Hawaii are all here—the Ahuena Heiau of ancient times, the governor's Hulihe'e Palace, and Mokuaikaue Church, the first built by missionaries in the islands. You'll also find excellent snorkeling nooks, right there in the buzz of Kailua Pier, and just down Ali'i Drive, is where bodyboarding was born, at Hale Halawai. Bring your camera and get a front-row seat for this flipped-out sport.

Not far down the drive from Kailua is the ancient surfing site at Holualoa Bay, where today's wave riders carry on. What makes the bay doubly interesting is the Keolonahihi State Historical Park that is hiding in plain sight. Unsigned and overgrown, the place is aching for trailblazers with a true sense of adventure. Most of the action farther yet down Ali'i, where snorkelers, surfers, and beach hogs can choose from three parks. The two northerly parks, White Sands and Pahoehoe, are better choices for the summer, since winter's epic surf washes the sand away. But snorkelers can head to Kahaluʻu Beach Park all year long. A reef-protected shore and copious knobs of coral have created a huge fish-lover's pool. For novices, this is the place to test the gear.

A little farther south is Keauhou Bay, where King Kamehameha III was born. The bay is overlooked by many snorkelers, in spite of several good options. You'll also find coast walks north and south. North goes by hidden Heʻeia Bay, a place to check out if you're staying in the area. To the south is the wave-crashing hike to the Kuamoʻo Battlefield, where in 1819 the old guard was defeated by King Kamehameha II, who had instituted reforms that, among other things, brought women to an equal footing with men in Hawaiian social structure. Keauhou serves up a guaranteed one-two punch for those looking for a swim and history hike.

The grandam of this trailhead section is Kealakekua Bay. Site of a major ancient village and Hikiau Heiau, the bay is known mainly as the place where British Captain James Cook ran out of luck in 1779. The bay, particularly at the Cook Monument, offers

HONOMALINO TRAIL AT MILOLIʻI, KEAUHOU BAY

some of the best snorkeling in the Hawaiian Islands. It also has hidden treats, like exquisite Manini Beach Park and Keʻei Village, where you get vistas of the Kealakekuaʻs famous cliffs and a chance to see some non-tourist coastal hangouts. In the same area is Puʻuhonua o Honaunau National Historic Park, which preserves an ancient place of refuge, where vanquished warriors and social miscreants could be safe. A coast hike south from the park is the bell-ringer here, so be sure to check it out. Both in the park, and at Two Step, which is close by, are excellent snorkeling spots in Honaunau Bay.

The Kona coast gets cliffy as you head south from Honaunau through coffee-and-macadamia country, but you can find two roads winding down to out-of-the-way

TWO-STEP, PUʻUHONUA O HONAUNAU

coves. Ho'okena Beach Park is a camper's beach, where both snorkeling and bodysurfing can be good. Trails wind along a wild coast. Farther south, the fishing village of Miloli'i is one of the few that has survived from ancient times, although dugouts have given way to aluminum boats, and thatched huts have been replaced by wood-frames. Still, the village will be high on the list for seekers of true Hawaii, and the short hike south from Miloli'i to Honomalino Beach is a fantasy experience, where coconut palms line a sandy crescent, and dolphins swirl offshore.

South of Miloli'i, the temperate zone continues as you encounter large macadamia groves and native ohia forests. About midway between Kona and Volcano is Manuka State Park, perfectly situated for a picnic or extended hike into native forests. Birders take note. You can choose from a nature trail or longer trek into the forest reserve that surrounds the park. Just south of Manuka, the terrain changes dramatically, becoming a desert buried in a'a lava.

HONOMALINO BEACH, HOLUALOHA BAY, SUPER GIRLS AT SUPER J'S

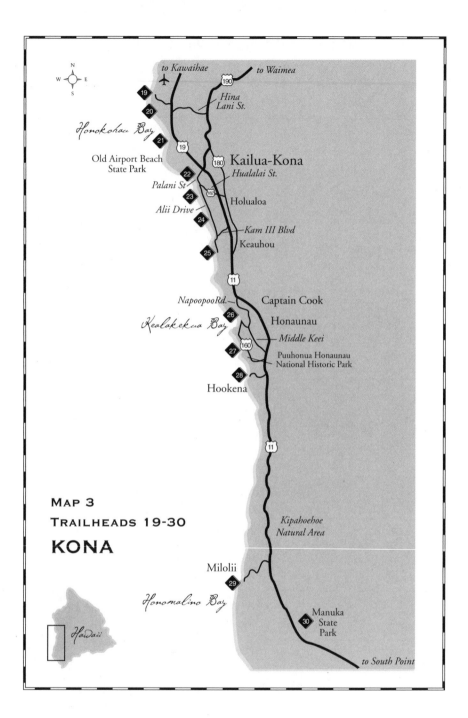

to Kawaihae

to Waimea

190

19

20

Hina Lani St.

Honokohau Bay

21

19

Old Airport Beach
State Park

22

180

Kailua-Kona

Hualalai St.

Palani St

182

23

Holualoa

Alii Drive

24

Kam III Blvd

Keauhou

25

11

Napoopoo Rd.

Captain Cook

26

Honaunau

Kealakekua Bay

Middle Keei

160

27

Puuhonua Honaunau
National Historic Park

28

Hookena

11

Kipahoehoe
Natural Area

MAP 3

TRAILHEADS 19-30

KONA

Milolii

29

Honomalino Bay

Manuka
State
Park

30

to South Point

Hawaii

TRAILHEADS

19-30

TH :	TRAILHEAD
HIKE :	HIKES AND STROLLS
SNORKEL :	SNORKELING, SWIMMING
SURF :	BOARD, BODYBOARD, BODYSURF
MM :	MILE MARKER; CORRESPONDS TO HIGHWAY SIGNS
MAKAI :	TOWARD THE OCEAN
MAUKA :	INLAND, TOWARD THE MOUNTAINS

ALL HIKING DISTANCES IN PARENTHESES ARE **ROUND TRIP.**
ELEVATION GAINS OF 100 FEET OR MORE ARE NOTED. SEE
RESOURCE LINKS FOR CONTACTS AND TELEPHONE NUMBERS.

19. WAWAIOLI BEACH PARK   HIKE, SURF

WHAT'S BEST: Beachcombers and shell-seekers will like this coastal path to a surfer's beach—an out-of-the-way spot that is close to the airport.

PARKING: Go north from Kailua-Kona on Hwy. 19, and continue .5-mi. north of mm95. Turn makai toward the Natural Energy Laboratory of Hawaii on OTEC Rd. Continue .4-mi. to where the road makes a right-angle and park or continue to the improved parking lot to the right.

HIKE: Wawaioli Beach Park to Pinetrees Beach (2.25 mi.)

The facilities at **Wawaioli Beach Park** are courtesy of the nearby energy lab, where scientists study how to use the temperature differential between warm surface water and cold deep water to create a current flow that generates electricity. The Big Island's most westerly land, Keahole Point, is just to the north; winds and currents there are so fierce that even the Hawaiian canoeists of yore would come ashore and paddle a 3-mile fishpond rather than brave the point. All these factors combine for rough water at Wawaioli, where storm surf can wash over the road. But it is nonetheless a pleasant curve of sand, and a chilly keiki pool that is located on the lava shelf between the beach and the rest rooms attracts moms and people with folding chairs.

For the walk to **Pinetrees Beach**, take the unpaved road that is to the left where the paved road turns right. You could shorten the round-trip hike by about .6-mile by driving to just before a gate, where the road becomes a for-real four-wheel journey. An unmarked heiau ruins and Hawaiian checkerboard is just mauka of this parking spot. After the gate, about .5-mile from the paved road, the trail reaches a coarse coral-sand rocky beach that will appeal to tide-poolers and beachcombers looking for seashells. It also appeals to flop campers, who you may see squirreled away amid the kamani trees. Aesthetics increase as the trail reaches the coral-mound monument at the Kohanaiki Shoreline Area. Just through the beach trees from here is the massive mangrove that marks Pinetrees Beach. Hand-painted signs and a newly planted row of coconut palms decorate the shoreline. You will find no pine trees. The story is that a bonged-up surfer thought the mangrove looked like a pine grove from a distance. Whatever, the large clump of greenery is a landmark easily spotted from Highway 19.

More Stuff: A sand trail goes north from the park to Keahole Point. The geographical significance may attract hikers, but the nearby Kona Airport is hard to ignore. Hoʻona Historical Preserve, an ancient gravesite, is near the point. At the airport itself (use the main road in) is the Onizuka Space Center. Named for Hawaii's favorite son, Astronaut Ellison Onizuka, the center features a gravity well, moon rock, theater, model of the Space Shuttle, and a lot of other stuff that will keep families entertained.

SURF: The main break at **Pinetrees** is about 200 yards directly offshore. Shallow water and a rocky bottom make this a spot novices should avoid. Observe the local boys before taking a ride on these waves.

20.   HONOKOHAU BAY   HIKE, SNORKEL, SURF

WHAT'S BEST: A national historic park, locals beach, and sports-fishing harbor combine for a variety show at this close-to-Kailua getaway.

PARKING: Take Hwy. 19 north from Kailua-Kona. After passing mm98, turn makai toward Honokohau Harbor on Kealakehe Pwy. Continue until the road forks. *For the Alula Beach and harbor stroll:* Veer left at the fork and continue to the unimproved parking at the south mouth of the bay. *For Kaloko-Honokohau National Historic Park:* Turn right at the fork and continue along the harbor until the road right-angles left; a gate for the park is on your right. Park in the unpaved lot across from the gate.

Alternate Access: Kaloko Pond, at the north end of the historic park, is reachable via a .75-mile-long unpaved road off Hwy. 19. A gate is open from 8 a.m. to 3:30 p.m. The access is .6-mile north of mm97, where the highway's double-yellow line broadens to a yellow-striped island. In traffic, this can be a dangerous left.

HIKE: Alula Beach and Honokohau Harbor (up to .75-mi.); Kaloko-Honokohau National Historic Park to: Honokohau Beach and Kaloko Pond (3.5 mi.) *Note:* If you have a driver, use the *Alternate Access* to make this a car-shuttle hike.

You'll see **Alula Beach** to the left from the rocky bench at the parking area. It's a decent-sized crescent of white sand and greenery, the ubiquitous kiawe trees mostly,

AIOPIO FISHTRAP AT HONOKOHAU BAY

protected by the lava finger that is Noio Point. Pick a tricky route over the humpback of lava at the shore, or cut left a little and come down the other side of it. At the beach, a tiny walk takes you across the sand to the point. For an added bonus, jog inland to see the ruins of Makaopio Heiau, with its two upright stones, and Hale o Lono.

Honokohau Harbor wasn't developed into a sportsfishing port until 1970. It's sublime spot is the miniature park to the right from the parking area. From this patch of lawn and coco palms you can watch fishing boats return in the afternoon. Black marlin and other large game fish are hung and weighed at the dock of the marina store; these magnificent creatures photographed in the netherworld between being masters of deep blue sea and becoming 1,000 grilled filets with lemon wedges on the side. The marina store is about .25-mile inland from the mouth of the harbor.

Kaloko-Honokohau National Historic Park was made a landmark in 1962 and upgraded to a park in 1978. The development of the 1,170 acres continues, with a new underground visitors center and more interpretive signs in the works. Honokohau Village ruins date from 1,200 years ago. In the early 1800s, the village gardens were a horn o' plenty for Kamehameha, who spent the remaining years of his life just south in Kailua. To walk the length of the park from **Honokohau Beach to Kaloko Pond**, follow the cable along a short trail segment that leads to a canoe hale sitting beside a little cove that will be to your left. The pretty cove is actually a man-made Aiopio Fishtrap. A heiau and anchialine ponds are on its southern shore, if you care to walk that direction. For the hike, head to your right on a tree-shaded road and keep left at a fork near some rest rooms. You'll skirt the sandy shores of Honokohau Bay and pass Aimakapa Pond, a natural 20-acre lake that is home to Hawaiian stilts, coots, and also migrating shorebirds who don't seem to mind that you can see Costco, a mile away.

After passing the pond and fragmented sand strip of the bay, about .5-mile into the walk, you'll veer inland on a lava-rock road under a low canopy of beach trees. In the rocky rubble all along this hike are some 200 archeological sites, ranging from the larger house platforms of the ali'i, to smaller salt pans and stone planters. All of the gardens and thatch-work of these structures are gone—like viewing a former neighborhood that has nothing but foundations remaining. You'll cross a sandy gully, where a Queens Pond lies inland. Near here is thought to be King Kamehameha's burial site, though no physical evidence has been found. Keep following the coast, as footing varies among lava, sand, and dirt, through kiawe and the leafy kamani trees. You'll come upon a palm grove and, extending from it, a 750-foot-long seawall that is the seaside shore of Kaloko Pond. The wall has been restored, and a sprawling mangrove that choked its banks has been cleared to reveal several former homesites. This man-made 11-acre lake was the fish store of ancient times.

More Stuff: The ahupua'a of Honokohau included the green uplands that rise toward Hualalai Volcano. The lands of the volcano are privately owned by the Bishop Estate. You can get a look at its native ohia and koa rain forest. Drive north from Honokohau Harbor and turn inland on Hina Lani Street. At the top, jog left on Highway 190 and then turn right shortly thereafter on Kaloko Drive. Kaloko switchbacks up for about 6 miles. Just before the top, go left at a water tank on Huehue, which ends after less than a mile. A gated road leads left from here to Hinaka Crater. To the right are Kaupulehu Crater and far above it at 8,721 feet the overgrown crater of Hualalai. *Be Aware:* Permission to access these trails may be required. Hiking off trail around here can be dangerous, due to hidden lava tubes and earth cracks.

SNORKEL: Locals do beach time at **Alula Beach**, finding shade in the large kiawes and swimming in a near-shore pool that is protected by a reef. The snorkeling is good. On the other side of the harbor at the historical park, **Aiopio Fishtrap** is a harsh name for an attractive swimming area—a circle of sand with plenty of palms. Just the thing to take a dip and for beginners to try out their gear. But the water can be shallow and clarity is not the best, due to sand and natural algae. You're very likely to see turtles. Turtle Pinnacle, a popular dive spot, is offshore. Snorkeling is also good at **Honokohau Beach**, a few minutes up the trail. Set up on the dune that separates the beach from the pond. Pick your way through salt-and-pepper sand to the large oval swimming area in the middle of the wide bay. An offshore reef protects the shore.

SURF: The waves **offshore Kaloko Pond** beckon the board surfers from Kailua-Kona. Use the north access to reach this spot directly. A shallow reef break and long paddle make this spot dangerous for beginners. You can watch from near the base of the seawall, or head down the trail to the left and pick your way out to the reef.

21. OLD AIRPORT BEACH STATE PARK   Hike, Snorkel, surf

What's Best: You won't want to spend your entire vacation here, but this long sand-and-tide-pool coast is a stone's throw from Kailua and an ideal place for a sunset or sunrise stroll. There's room to roam.

Parking: From Hwy. 19 near Kailua, turn makai on either Kawai St. or Palani Rd. Then turn right, or north, on Kuakini Rd. Follow Kuakini past the aquatic center and playing fields of Kailua Park, where the road jogs left and then right. Pass through a state park gate and park at the end of half-mile-long former runaway. Man, you won't have trouble finding a parking spot.

Hike: Old Airport Beach to: Kukailimoku Point (2 mi.) or Keahuolu Point (1.25 mi.)

Old Airport State Beach owes its inception to big jets. Post-World War II builders did not anticipate the needs of bigger jets and, since there's not enough flat space for adequate extension, the airport was closed in 1970. **Kukailimoku Point**, lies to the south, or left as you face the water. Sand is not scarce, but a storm-washed reef runs along near shore. Rocks encroach farther south, as does the private development inland, now called Kona Bay Estates. In the 1980s, locals who were booted from this historic camping beach set up a tent city in protest. Although camping was never reinstated, a Shoreline Public Access was established, and new surveys showed that 10 acres needed to be snagged from the developer and added to the 110-acre park. Kukailimoku, the site of this conflict, is named after Kamehameha's war god.

Keahuolu Point lies north from the parking area; you'll see pahoehoe lava hills curving seaward. A trail leads from the end of the runway, and very soon leaves the state lands and enters those of the Liliuokalani Trust. Veer left and watch your step, as you follow the rolling lava along the shoreline between gnarly kiawes and the occasional heliotrope. There is a trail, but you will most likely end up wandering. Queen Liliuokalani was Hawaii's last monarch, in office until 1893. From Keahuolu Point you look over the waters of Papawai Bay. You can continue on this rough route farther north to Kaiwi Point, where dive boats commonly anchor.

Snorkel: Papawai Bay has excellent snorkeling, but even experienced flipper fiends need to pick the right day for safe swimming. Access the bay using the Keahuolu hike described above. Though coral is scarce, plenty of fish swim in near-shore currents, which are part of a marine conservation district. Entry is over smooth lava near shore, not easy but not bad. Advanced snorkelers will want to swim out a narrow channel near the point and head north toward **Kaiwi Point**, the dive spot. *Be Aware:* There is usually current in the bay, stronger near the point. Wave action increases this hazard.

When the water is rough at **Old Airport**, locals head to its south end to a **keiki beach**. A small inlet just north of Kukailimoku Point has a protected, shallow swimming pond. Park nearer the entrance gate at the state park to lessen the walk to this beach. You can also take a path from Kailua Park, on Kuakini Street. Walk across the playing field near the swim center, angling left down a short staircase at a chain-link fence. You cross private Kona Bay Drive. From there a Shoreline Public Access sign points to a 50-foot path leading to the keiki beach.

SURF: The reef break offshore of the middle of the park is called **Old Airport** by local surfers. Conditions have to be right for this break to attract much of a crowd. Reef rash and worse await the novice in these shallow and rocky waters. Bodyboarders like the north end of Old Airport, where they brave submerged rocks.

22. KAILUA   HIKE, SNORKEL, SURF

WHAT'S BEST: Kamehameha the Great, who could have lived anywhere he wanted, chose to live his final years at this little bay. Yes, Kailua has its cheesy accents, but you'll also find the romantic charm of a tropical Pacific port.

PARKING: From Hwy. 19, turn seaward on Palani Rd. Continue past a big shopping center and turn left on Kuakini Hwy. Pass the Kona Surf and turn right on Likana Lane; a free public lot will be on your left. *If the Likana lot is full,* go back out to Kuakini, turn right, and continue to Hualalai Rd., where you turn right again. A free public lot will be on the left past the library. *If the Hualalai lot is full,* try the hourly-pay lot that is adjacent to it. Or, continue down to Ali'i Dr. Across the street is Hale Halawai County Park, which has a free parking lot.

HIKE: Kailua Town Stroll (1.75 mi.)

Begin the **Kailua Town Stroll** by walking down Likana and going right on Ali'i Drive. At the corner is the once-proud King Kamehameha Hotel, built in the '70s. Walk through the hotel to check out the museum-quality paintings and ancient memorabilia, like a full feather cape and headdress. Then duck out the back to see Ahuena Heiau sitting on the placid waters of Kamakahonu Beach. This is a recreation of Kamehameha's post-conquest place of worship, where he retired the war god and re-dedicated the temple to Lono, the god of peace and fertility. The island's second monarch, Kamehameha II, or Liholiho, was educated here, which was the capital of the Hawaiian Islands, from 1812 to 1819.

Jog left from the heiau grounds to Kailua Pier, the marlin capital of the world, where the swim portion of the Ironman Triathlon draws a huge crowd every October. Continue down the seawall to the far end of the bay to Hulihe'e Palace, built in 1838 as a home for the Big Island's second governor, John Adams Kuakini. Try the garden path along the seaside wall to get a look at the attractive coral-and-lava rock structure, which is smaller than today's trophy homes. Banyans and other large trees provide atmo-

sphere. Native hardwoods gleam in the interior, which is chockablock with the personal effects of post-missionary royal families. Across the street from the palace is Mokuaikaue Church, built a year earlier than the governor's house. The stone edifice, with a 112-foot steeple, is an upgrade of the thatched-roof model built in 1820 by the first missionaries to arrive in the Hawaiian Islands. King Kamehameha had died less than a year before, and son Liholiho granted the New England preachers a one-year probationary settlement, which was never officially renewed. Go inside to feel the sea-breeze air conditioning of the large building, an innovation of Reverend Asa Thurston.

Continuing along the ocean side of Ali'i, you can jog into the boardwalks of the Kona Inn Shopping Village, where budget-priced tourist stuff is piled in a series of cozy storefronts. In back of the Kona Inn Restaurant, which dates from 1928, is a spacious lawn and seawall where you can contemplate the bay and finish off an ice cream or beverage. Just down the street from the shopping village is Hale Halawai County Park. Behind the drab community center is a palm-lined path that is the grandstand to watch some of the world's best bodyboarders. Go left along the path, in front of the Waterhouse Row restaurants and shops, and watch them peel into Oneo Bay.

MOKUAIKAUE CHURCH, KAILUA WATERFRONT, HULIHE'E PALACE DANCERS

SNORKEL: Parade through Kailua in your swimsuit to try three, good-to-very good snorkeling spots. The best is **Kamakahonu Beach**, behind the King Kam Hotel. A sandy beach with gradual entry leads to the protected inlet between the pier and the Ahuena Heiau. During calmer periods, experienced snorkelers can flipper beyond the pier and angle right toward the deeper water and coral off Kukailimoku Point.

Locals like **Kailua Pier Beach**, a little nook to the left at the base of the pier. Stash your towel and slippers in the wooden shelving on the busy sidewalk made for this purpose, and walk down a short set of stairs. Coral heads are near shore in a large area roped from the bay's boat traffic. At the opposite side of the bay from the pier—the far end of the seawall—is tiny **Kanuha Beach**. This little nook has more privacy than its cousin across the bay. A few rocks provide additional interest for snorkelers. *Be Aware*: Though swimming is normally safe, high surf can make for rough conditions along the seawall.

Surf: As mentioned in the Kailua stroll, **Hale Halawai** is perhaps the island's premier bodyboarding spot. In fact, many claim this surfing-bodysurfing hybrid was invented here. Locals call the beach **Spinners**. A reef just offshore creates a right-break that rolls into little Oneo Bay, which is just south. In the afternoons, the sun backlights the translucent barrels. These guys get some loooong rides. Due to the reef and submerged rocks, Spinners is not for learners.

23. HOLUALOA BAY   Hike, Snorkel, Surf

What's Best: Kings and dudes have been surfing here for centuries. And hiding in plain view next to the bay is an overgrown state historical park.

Parking: From Kailua, go south on Ali'i Dr., past Royal Poinciana Dr. and mm3. Park on the shoulder where the road skirts the bay shore. *Notes:* Other roads lead from Hwy. 11 to Ali'i Dr. You can go south from Kailua and take Kamehameha III Dr. down to Ali'i to approach this trailhead from the traffic-free south end. Activities take place along a mile-long stretch of this road.

Hike: Keolonahihi State Historical Park (up to .5-mi.)

The 12-acre **Keolonahihi State Historical Park** is overgrown and unsigned. As yet, no trails exist among the two-dozen sites that have been identified in the thicket of brush and trees of Kamoa Point. The state purchased the property in 1990, and originally named it Kamoa Point Historical Park. The best way to see it—and to get a cover-shot of the surfers riding into the bay—is to walk the road's shoulder to the south end of the bay. From there walk a seawall to reach a trail that curves toward the point. The going gets tougher when you pass the rocky inlet where the boarders put in. Inland, trailblazers can find heiaus, house platforms, and a shrine that commemorates surfing. *Note:* An easy Shoreline Public Access path is at the south end of the park. Continue south on Ali'i Dr., passing a long chain-link fence, and look for upright pipes and the access sign. You can peer into a lost world as you walk the short path.

SNORKEL: Don't bring your fins to **Riviera Pool**, but do bring the mask and kids, if you have either with you. A .25-mile gravel path ends at a large man-made infinity pool, roughly shaped like the Big Island. Look for a Shoreline Public Access sign about .25-mile south of mm2 on Ali'i Drive. Turn makai into a six-space public parking lot in front of the Kona by the Sea condo complex.

SURF: Holualoa Bay's south point break is a long left slide, usually curling in two or three tiers, known locally as **Lyman's.** Hawaiians have been surfing this spot since waves were invented. The north side of Holualoa Bay, which people call **Banyans,** also sees a lot of action. You'll see cars across from Banyan Mart, which is .25-mile north of mm3. Board surfers also scope the reef break from

HALE HALEWAI AT SPINNERS

Riviera Pool, at a place called **Rivies**, which is just offshore of the Kona Riviera Villas. Shallow reef makes this less popular than the other two places.

24. KONA BEACH PARKS HIKE, SNORKEL, SURF

WHAT'S BEST: Three beach parks await at the south end of Ali'i Drive, one of them the Big Island's most popular snorkeling spot. Don't worry, there's plenty of room in the reef-protected coral pool.

PARKING: Take Hwy. 11 south from Kailua. After mm118, turn makai on Kamehameha III Rd. Continue to the bottom of the hill. Turn right on Ali'i Dr. *Kahalu'u Beach Park* is at mm4.5. Turn left into a large parking lot. *White Sands Beach Park* is just north of mm4. *Pahoehoe Beach Park* is just north of White Sands, near mm3.5. *Note:* Parking lots tend to fill up early on peak days.

HIKE: Kahalu'u Bay stroll (.75-mi.)

Warm up between snorkeling dunks on a **Kahalu'u Bay stroll**, where points of interest lie both north and south. To the north, or right as you face the water, walk the sand and lava wall until you have to hop up to the road. Sitting on the tip of lava is the dollhouse St. Peters Catholic Church. As a statement of virtue, the church was built atop the sacred site of the "pagan" Kuemanu Heiau, where the ancients prayed for good surfing. Righteous, dude. Part of the heiau ruins remain, as does the brackish pool of Waikui, where the fabled board riders would cleanse themselves.

Heading south from the beach park takes you into the lovely gardens of the Keauhou Beach Hotel, where sacred Po'o Pool is a quiet break from the sunny beach scene. Then walk the hotel grounds along the water side and you'll come to the tidal lagoon of Kealiaia, a place to see marine life without getting in the water. Offshore the lagoon is the 4,000-foot semicircle of boulders known as the Menehune Breakwater. Created by fishpond builders that predated the Polynesian voyagers, this man-made feature has been greatly altered by the pounding of millions of waves.

More Stuff: Just south of Kahalu'u Bay, at Makolea Beach, was an ancient settlement where some two-dozen heiaus have been discovered. Most of these are unmarked, and some were destroyed when the hotels were built. Drive south, beyond the now-defunct Kona Lagoon Hotel. You'll see wooden gates at the road, before mm5.5. Walk down through the former resort to reach the rough coral-and-lava beach. Makolea was the major heiau—look for a wooden-pole platform—named for the Big Island's most beautiful maiden; some young girls still journey here to pray for fertility. Although the future for this area is uncertain, plans for a Hawaiian cultural center are in the mix.

SNORKEL: It's best to show up early, by 9:30 a.m. at **Kahalu'u Beach Park**, both to find a parking spot and for the best snorkeling conditions. But, hey, there's always

SPINNERS, KAHALU'U RESIDENTS

room for one more. The half-mile wide bay has been attracting snorkelers since it became a park in 1953. You'll find sandy entrance channels, often made cozy by the legs of fellow fish-seekers, near the lifeguard station. The bay is shallow, protected by a long reef, and filled with just about every colorful fish in Hawaii. Turtles usually join in the fun. *Be Aware:* A rip current empties the bay to the right, heading out in front of the little church. Don't be shy about getting tips from one of the lifeguards. Also, those mushroom rocks offshore are living coral, which have been dying off because of people. Don't step on the coral. One last thing: It's against state law to feed fish in the bay. ReefTeach, a nonprofit group, often sets up at the park pavilion to encourage responsible snorkeling at this heavily used beach.

The snorkeling at **White Sands Beach Park** is not as good, due to a rocky entry and onshore surf. During epic winter surf, the fine sand at this beach leaves overnight, like the gal in a country song. The sand, scrubbed white and clean, gradually returns—hence this park is also known as Disappearing Sands or Magic Sands. Another alias is La'aloa Beach Park. Regardless, during low surf, the best snorkeling is at a rocky inlet south of the park. **Pahoehoe Beach Park**, with a lawn shaded by large trees, is more of a place to sit a spell. During calm conditions, snorkelers seeking solitude swim at a coral-rubble channel that is to the right as you face the water.

SURF: In the shadow of the surfing heiau, experienced surfers ride the offshore reef break at the north side of **Kahalu'u Bay**. The strong rip current and jagged rocks should deter beginners. The heiau is a good place to be a spectator. When the sand is back in the summer, **White Sand Beach Park** is a training ground for bodysurfers who can try a mellow shore break. When surf's up, the point break attracts big-time bodysurfers and lots of spectators. Championship competitions have taken place here.

KAHALU'U BEACH PARK

25. KEAUHOU BAY

WHAT'S BEST: King Kamehameha III was born at this deep inlet, today the starting point for snorkeling, canoeing, and a coastal hike. Nearby is another rugged coast walk, where the last battle among Big Island royalty took place.

PARKING: *For all activities:* Take Hwy. 11 south from Kailua-Kona to Kamehameha III Rd., which is south of mm118. Turn makai and continue to the bottom of the hill. *For Keauhou Bay and Kuamo'o Battlefield* go left on Ali'i Dr. *For Keauhou Bay,* pass mm6.5 and turn right on Kaleiopapa Rd., follow to the end and park near the docks. *For the Kuamo'o Battlefield hike,* pass the turn-off to the bay, and continue on Ali'i through a new development. Park at a signed trailhead on the left, where the road makes a sweeping right.

For He'eia Bay: At the bottom of the hill on Kam III Rd., go straight across Ali'i Dr. Turn right on Manukai and look for a Shoreline Public Access sign on your left, just past He'eia Way. *Note:* If you continue on Kamehameha III Rd. you reach a cul-de-sac on north side of Keauhou Bay a stone's throw from the parking described above.

HIKE: Keauhou Bay (up to .5-mi.); He'eia Bay (1.25 mi.); Kuamo'o Battlefield (1.5 mi.)

Begin the **Keauhou Bay** stroll on a lush path along the cliff near the modest dockside buildings. In 1814, Kalani Kauikeaouli, or Kamehameha III, was still-born in the shade of this cliff, and massaged to life by a kahuna on the very rock that now has a plaque that commemorates his birth. By age 11, both the boy's father, Kamehameha the Great, and elder brother, Liholiho, or Kamehameha II, had died. Although Kauikeaouli was now king, the monarchy was ruled at first by matriarchal prime ministers—his mother Keopuolani, and Kam I's favorite wife, Queen Ka'ahumanu. Rebelling against the womens' abolishment of the old kapu system, the young king spent his youth gambling, boozing, surfing, and chasing girls. Some things never change. But after his beloved sister died in 1836, Kamehameha III embraced his responsibility and became Hawaii's longest ruling monarch—for 29 years until his death in 1854.

Okay, from the end of the short path, walk across the dock area, passing the Fair Wind snorkel tour company to the seawall that protects Keauhou Park. Up a grassy hillside is the storage shed for the local canoe club. Picnic tables and large trees make this a good sitting spot. A mile-long holua sled track, the longest in the islands, used to come down to the bay from what is now Kamehameha III Road. It was covered with grasses and weavings to cushion the rocky, high-speed ride. Competitions were boisterous.

From the parking off Manukai Street, a short path leads less than .25-mile down to tiny and wild **He'eia Bay**. At the bottom veer right, past the chirps of a bird study station, to a lava-and-coral path near the water. Go right, toward the low point with a lone kiawe tree, and pick up a cinder path that runs alongside the seawall of Kanaloa Resort. Although the trail continues all the way to Makolea Beach at the old Kona Lagoon Resort, you'll probably want to turn around a bit past the Kanaloa's pool.

KEAUHOU SUNDECK

From the Aliʻi Drive trailhead, a wide gravel path leads toward the **Kuamoʻo Battlefield**. In November of 1819, six months after the death of his father, young King Kamehameha II used muskets to defeat the forces of Chief Kekuaokalina. The conflict was over reforms brought on by the new king, at the behest of his mother, Keopuolani, and Kam I's favorite wife, Queen Kaʻahumanu. The royal women simply ate beside the king at a formal feast, thus flaunting the age-old system of kapus that, among other prohibitions, limited the rights of women. All the kapus were thus questioned, and the battle was on. One of jewels on the hike is near the beginning, where the path makes a 90-degree left turn. When the big surf arrives, locals take a short trail to the right to Kualanui Point, where the big ones roll by and explode against the lava shore. The main path continues alongside the frothy waters of Maihi Bay. As the trail climbs, you reach a cattle gate. Head up

KUALANUI POINT

off-trail to Kuamoʻo point for a great view and a look at a 20-foot square lava shrine with a kiawe growing in the center.

The main trail continues over cobbles. You'll see walls and other ruins, and pass a recently staked area near the shore, where improvements are planned to commemorate this site. Beyond this point, the road becomes a trail and the trees get larger. You'll come to a wooden gate, where crude livestock pens tell of a former ranching venture. Vowel fans will want know that this scallop on the coast is called Paʻaoao Bay.

SNORKEL: Keauhou Bay has excellent swimming and good snorkeling. Entry is easy from rock steps that lead down from the seawall. Water clarity improves as you swim out, though the bay is not known for visibility. Stay to your right, fairly near the shore, and you'll soon be swimming over a goodly number of coral heads. Although not a significant risk, you need to keep an eye peeled for boat traffic in the bay. The **Keauhou Sundeck**, is a familiar name for teensy-weensy **Mukukanekaula Island**, which sits a few feet offshore at the south mouth of Keauhou Bay. As you drive down Kaleiopapa Road toward the bay, turn left on Ehukai Street, at Shoreline Public Access sign. Continue for less than .25-mile, and look for a path on the right, just before the entrance to the refurbished hotel. A 100-foot garden path curves between houses to a smooth lava reef, with the sundeck offshore—a rock platform sticking about eight feet above the water. Snorkeling is excellent around it and the onshore rocks. Offshore of this area is Manta Ray Village, a nighttime dive spot where the hotel's searchlight attracted the billowing creatures. *Be Aware*: Big surf and tidal surge can make entry iffy, or downright dangerous. Watch the water for at least 10 minutes before entering.

KAYAK TAKEOUT NEAR COOK MONUMENT, KEALAKEKUA BAY

SURF: Board surfers try the offshore break at **Heʻeia Bay**, a.k.a., **Walker Bay**, after Reverend Shannon Walker who ran a youth camp here in the old days. The main hazard is the point-blank slam of the waves into a bouldered shore. Bodyboarders also try their luck at this little bay, usually on the south point.

WHAT'S BEST: The cliffs rising above Kealakekua Bay are the Big Island's signature seascape. This is where Captain James Cook took his last breath, and where you'll find some of the best snorkeling in the islands.

PARKING: Take Hwy. 11 south from Kailua-Kona. Veer right toward Kealakekua Bay, on Napo'opo'o Rd., which is at mm111. *For Captain Cook Monument:* Park immediately on the left after veering from the highway. You'll see a turnout big enough for several cars. *For all other activities:* Continue on Napo'opo'o Rd. for about 5 mi. At the bottom, you'll come to stop sign and a T-intersection, directly across from which is Napo'opo'o Wharf.

HIKE: Captain Cook Monument (4.25 mi., 1,325 ft.); Manini Beach Park (up to .5-mi.); Ke'ei Village to: Palemano Point (1.5 mi.) and Mokuohai Bay (3 mi.)

The hike and snorkel to **Captain Cook Monument** is a two-punch knockout, not to be missed by Big Island adventure seekers. From the parking spot, cross the road, walk down a couple hundred feet, and take a wide path that is right at telephone pole #4—not the driveway with a stop sign and chain at pole #5 that is next to it. You'll know you're on the right path when you pass a dirt drive that veers to the right a minute or two into the hike. The trail then descends through seed cane, under big mango trees. You pound down on a steady, straight grade for the first mile. The vegetation becomes scarce as you approach the trail's only switchback, an a'a lava perch that overlooks Ka'awaloa Point. Hang the left here and take another long ramp to the bottom.

CAPTAIN COOK MONUMENT

At the bottom, the wall-lined path heads under the shade of big kiawes straight to the water, where kayaks often land. Although the monument is a short distance to the left, you may wish to go straight to see the plaque that marks the spot of Cook's last stand, on February 14, 1779. During low tide you'll see it on a rock, under the curling horizontal branches of a large tree. Monumental ironies surround Captain James Cook's death, not the least of which was that this man, among the greatest of all seafaring navigators, could not swim to the safety of a rowboat that rescued other members of his party from these slippery rocks.

Walk over to the monument itself. The 28-foot white spire was erected by some of Cook's countrymen in 1874 and is actually British sovereign soil. Not many people explore the backshore of this northern mouth of the bay. If you do, you'll find numerous remains of Ka'awaloa Village, including several heiaus. Puhina O Lono Heiau, where the bones of the English faux Lono were interred, is off the trail on the way down, just north of the switchback. (Cook arrived during the Makahiki festival and the Hawaiians first thought him to be an incarnation of their god of peace and fertility, Lono.) *Be Aware:* Conditioned hikers will have no trouble with this walk, but bring plenty of water and sun protection. A good strategy is to leave very early and do your snorkeling before the tour guys and kayakers arrive, around 10 o'clock.

Manini Beach Park is one of the most dramatically scenic spots on the island. It's easy to miss. Go left at the Napo'opo'o Wharf, continue about .25-mile and turn right on narrow Manini Beach Road. Park where the beach road curves left, by a house that sits on the water. You'll see a short beach access trail leading to the little beach park, with its row of palms and view across the bay to the cliffs of Kealakekua. You can continue out the seaward end of the park to see the storm-washed point. If you keep hooking left, for less than .25-mile, you reach locals' coral cove, tiny Kahauloa Bay.

Ke'ei Village, with its lava walls surrounding weathered cottages, blue-tarp awnings, and eclectic outdoor furniture, is a quiet corner tucked away from touristville. On nice surfing weekends the place will be jumpin'. At noon on Wednesdays you might not scare up a cat. To get there, turn left at Napo'opo'o Wharf and continue less than .5-mile to open lava fields. Turn right on unsigned, unpaved Keawaiki Road, which is the last right on the way out of Kealakekua Bay. (The one-lane paved road continues 3 miles to TH27, Pu'uhonua o Honaunau.) Another bumpy dirt road joins from the right after .25-mile, and you may wish to park here. To do so will add about a half-mile to the round-trip hiking distances. Or continue driving until the rocky road turns left and reaches the first buildings. Park on the right across from the first house, making sure not to block the driveways. One of Ke'ei's attractions is the grotto on the smooth lava bluff at the water's edge near this parking place. Groaning waves wash into three, land-locked caverns formed by large collapsed lava tubes.

To get to the awesome bay view at **Palemano Point** and continue around to the man-made pool at **Mokuohai Bay**, start down the village road. Lava walls and tropical trees

KEʻEI VILLAGE SEAWALL

line the route, and the detail of village life will be too much to take in on one pass. You then walk along a mortared seawall that takes you to the run of sand and coral rubble that is Keʻei Beach. Palemano Point is beyond the beach, on the low, pahoehoe lava fields. You'll see a 4-foot-high upright pipe that marks the spot—the south mouth of Kealakekua Bay. Across a mile of water is the Cook Monument, and the white Kaʻawaloa Lighthouse sits seaward of the monument, looking like its twin. You gotta be there to appreciate this oil-painting view of the bay. Jog inland, but stay on the smooth lava, to continue to Mokuohai Bay. You can spot the place by looking for the large pavilion of Maluhia Camp, fringed by coco palms and a lawn. The cool (literally) thing here is a swimming pool set in the lava reef a few hundred feet offshore of the pavilion. Look for lava wall sections. On the walk back you cut inland behind the pavilion and take a shaded road that leads back to the village.

The inland area is where the Battle of Mokuohai took place in 1782. Hawaiian Chief Kalaniopuʻu had just died, leaving lands to his son, Kiwalao, while the war god Ku was entrusted to Kamehameha, then a strapping 24-year-old. A power vacuum created a struggle for land. The Kamehameha's forces were greatly outnumbered by those of Kiwalao and other island chiefs, but the Lonely One was joined by his older mentor, the famed warrior Kekuhaupio, who was born in Keʻei. They were able to use the treacherous aʻa fields to outmaneuver the enemy, and the victory established Kamehameha's reputation.

SNORKEL: Take the plunge off the concrete jetty at the **Captain Cook Monument** to find snorkeling unsurpassed in the state. By late morning, tour boats normally lay anchor and drop dozens of flipper fiends, who are joined by a fleet of plastic rental kayaks that put in a mile away at Napo'opo'o Wharf. Only a few people hike down each day. A multi-species coral reef extends hundreds of feet to the left and right of the monument, boiling downward to blue water 50-feet-deep offshore. If you swim out into the bay you may see some of the 100 or more spinner dolphin who make their home in this 315-acre state underwater park. Oodles of fish swim the reef, so bring your marine ID card.

Snorkeling is also good-to-excellent at the **Kealakekua Bay State Historical Park**, though a winter shore break can make entry difficult. To reach the park, turn right at the Napo'opo'o Wharf and drive a short distance to road's end. If you sense crowds, park at the wharf. Walk to the right of the seawall in front of the heiau to the cove—and if you don't like the boulders on the beach, blame Hurricane Dot, which dropped them on top of the sand in 1969. Swim out to the rocks to the left, and keep circling that way to find the best coral and fish. *Be Aware*: Shore break can knock you down and create unwelcome current, so be mindful. Watch out for body boarders, too.

In spite of new rest rooms and other improvements, the historical park isn't where you want to spend the whole day, but you'll want to see Hikiau Heiau. Once adorned with thatched platforms and an array of akua ki (wooden carvings of gods), this 18-foot high fortress was the first thing the crew of the Cook's *Endeavor* saw when they sailed into Kealakekua in January of 1779. Also atop the 2,500-square-foot platform were the crossed poles with tapa cloth hanging from them, symbols of the god Lono and the Makahiki peace-and-harvest festival that took place over the winter months. These symbols of Lono mirrored the white sails of the ship's mast. Thousands of Hawaiians took to their canoes and Cook was welcomed as an incarnation of Lono. Everything was hunky-dory when the British sailors left, but a broken spar forced their return. Makahiki was over. When one of the ship's dories was stolen for its iron nails, the local chief Kalaniopu'u was taken hostage. The crisis ended with Cook's killing and the death of several Hawaiians on the shores of the bay where the monument now stands.

Though wave action commonly makes snorkeling **Napo'opo'o Wharf** a ridiculous notion, during calm periods this is a better spot than the beach park. Go toward the left of the wharf and look for steps that are near the end of the wharf's concrete bulkhead.

You can also snorkel at **Manini Beach Park**, although better choices nearby make this a less-popular destination. Look for a narrow sand channel through the reef, to the right just as you enter the park grounds. Shallow and rough water hampers entry. Snorkel to the right, inland.

SURF: Bodyboarding is a big draw at **Kealakekua Historical Park**, and on normal days this is a decent learner's beach. The action is usually at the section closest to the seawall, which is also a good spot for watching. Board surfers like the triple-tiered left-

break at **Manini Beach Park**.
They paddle out via the sand
channel to the right as you enter the park. For a great viewing
spot, walk to the coral-and-
rubble lava on the point. From
here, imagine the 25-foot-high
waves of Hurricane Iniki in
1980, breaking in a wall across
the entire mouth of the bay.
Ke'ei Beach is a status surfing
spot with a rich tradition—and
a big offshore break onto a shallow reef. Broken boards and
bones are not uncommon. Long rides are the lure. When visiting by canoe in the
1840s, Mark Twain told of a surfer who "would fling his board upon a foamy crest and
come whizzing by like a bombshell." Those guys are still doing it. Bring binoculars to
get a look.

27.   PU'UHONUA O HONAUNAU   HIKE, SNORKEL

WHAT'S BEST: This well-designed place of refuge, a national historic park,
attracts scads of visitors. But the coastal trail and excellent snorkeling nearby
keeps them coming back.

PU'UHONUA O HONAUNAU, MANINI BEACH PARK

PARKING: Take Hwy. 11 south from Captain Cook. Just south of mm104, turn makai at Hwy. 160, a.k.a., Keala O Keawe Rd. Continue downhill for about 4 mi. and turn left into the Puʻuhonua o Honaunau National Historic Park. *Notes:* And admission is charged to enter the park. The visitors center is open daily from 8 a.m. to 5:30 p.m. The beach park is open to 11 p.m. on weekends and holidays. Finally, you can also get to the park by taking a 3-mile, one-lane paved road along the shore from Kealakekua Bay.

HIKE: Puʻuhonua o Honaunau National Historic Park (.25-mi.); Puʻuhonua Beach Park to Kiʻilae Village coastal trail (3 mi., more or less)

Tourist tongues had it easier when **Puʻuhonua o Honaunau** was called by its anglicized misnomer, City of Refuge. Like other such spots in the islands, it was where defeated warriors, outcasts, and violators of the kapu system could go voluntarily to escape punishment. When justice was a swift club, people didn't break out of jail, they ran for it. A specialized kahuna would decide when people had served their time, which for minor kapu violations was overnight. An appropriate stay at the refuge appeased the gods, who would otherwise punish everyone with earthquakes, tidal waves, volcanic eruptions, or other calamities. The park's premier attraction is the Great Wall—10-feet high, 7-feet thick, 1,000-feet long—that was built without mortar in 1550 to separate the royal residences of Honaunau from the grounds of the puʻuhonua, or place of refuge. Coco palms sway over the park's re-created structures and interpretive center, all set beside little Keoneʻele Beach, a canoe landing that is an inlet of Honaunau Bay. Thatched-roofed Hale o Keawe, where the bones of 23 chiefs were interred, is prominent on the grounds, as is Alealea Heiau, a platform for sports and games. On most days, you'll see antiquity in progress as canoe carvers, weavers, and other Hawaiian artisans ply their trade. In 1920, the grounds became a county park, which halted a deterioration that had begun with the reforms of Kamehameha II in 1819. City of Refuge National Historic Park, all 180 acres of it, came to be in 1961. Since it never was a city, and for other reasons, the name was changed in 1978.

Puʻuhonua Beach Park is a pretty strip of sand, shaded by false kamani and coconut palms. A broad pahoehoe reef buffers the coast, and whales pass by outside the surf line in the winter. Many visitors, but few locals, overlook this park. To get there, go to the left as you drive to the far end of the parking lot, and take an unpaved road. You'll cross a narrow lava section, and one access to the village trail on the left, before the road curves left on its quarter-mile journey to the park's beachside tables. The gate for the **Kiʻilae Village coastal trail** is at the far end of the picnic area. After a few minutes of walking, walls and enclosures of the village will appear to the left as the route veers toward the greenery-topped Keaneʻe Cliffs that curl inland around it. The sand and coral beach to the right, Alahaka Bay, offers wading opportunities. After hiking over wide-open lava, you reach a junction for the trail that begins at the unpaved road near the visitors center parking lot. You could loop back that way, to the left, though kiawe trees and village ruins.

KEIKI POND AT PUʻUHONUA BEACH PARK

TWO AT TWO STEP

The more scenic choice is to continue down the coast. About a half-mile into the walk, the road meets the cliffs, by climbing up 20 feet or so on a cobblestone section. At the top of this rise, look to the left for a cave, which turns out to be a 150-foot-long lava tube that you can duck-walk through to an opening in the cliffs over little Ki'ilae Bay. For generations, locals have jumped from here, as well as from the cliffs to the right of the cave opening, but park personnel have been cracking down on this frivolity. The trail continues south. The route is actually an 1871 road that goes for several miles to Ho'okena, TH28. From the cliffs, you walk beside big kiawe trees, heading due south and away from the ocean. Loa Point sprawls to the west. Footing is not the greatest, but the path is wide and pleasant. A little more than a mile from the trailhead you come to the south boundary of the national park. Right after that the kiawes thicken to be an annoyance, but open up again after a short distance on some pristine sections of the old road. You can turnaround whenever, or tough it out for another 45 minutes of power striding to get a look toward Ho'okena.

SNORKEL: Those in the know head for **Two Step** at **Honaunau Bay** for the best drive-up snorkeling on the Big Island of Hawaii. To get there, turn right on a one-way lane just before the entrance station for the national park, and continue a short distance to the boat ramp area where the road makes a 90-degree right turn. Parking is usually jammed. There's a convenient, reasonably priced private lot across the street run by local guys. The two steps, which are actually three or four, are opposite the entrance to this parking lot. Walk across the smooth lava reef. You come to a ledge that has another ledge beneath it that gets washed by waves, and beneath that is a third, submerged ledge. Sit on the top ledge, gear up, then drop the fanny to the step below and use the submerged step to slide into water that is at least six feet deep. Off you go.

Very clear water and lots of fish and coral await in the big oval that is Honaunau Bay. You can hug the shore or swim over toward the reefs at Pu'uhonua o Honaunau. Waters near shore will be around 30-feet deep, but the coral gets closer to the surface farther out. Angle to the right about 200 feet, and you'll see an "ALOHA" written in cinder blocks on a sandy bottom. On rough water days, some people and kids enter at the Kapuwai boat ramp nearby, although a shallow reef makes it iffy to swim out to the deeper water. *Be Aware*: Swell surge can raise the water several feet at the Two Step entry. Relax and let the swells lift you up. If waves are crashing on the upper reef, however, only advanced snorkelers will want to get in.

Keoneʻele Beach, the little beach that is a canoe landing at **Puʻuhonua o Honaunau**, is also an excellent snorkeling spot. Turtles often loll about in the cove. Entry is easy over sand, and you can swim out over the reef, to the right, and be in the same waters that are offshore Two Step. The catch is that park rules prohibit leaving anything on the beach at this sacred spot. So, swallow your dignity, don the swimsuit only, and walk to the beach with only your gear. To avoid burning feet on asphalt, figure out a way to fasten your slippers to your person, and take them for a swim. Although not a snorkel spot, the **keiki pond** at Puʻuhonua Beach Park is a scenic place for picnicking families to take a dunk. About midway in the park, walk out to the reef a hundred feet or more. You'll see an amorphous shaped pool.

28.   HOʻOKENA BEACH PARK   HIKE, SNORKEL, SURF

WHAT'S BEST: While not on everyone's "A" list, this popular fine-sand cove offers a remote hiking coast and, on the right day, good snorkeling.

PARKING: Take Hwy. 11 south from Captain Cook and the Hwy. 160 jct. South of mm102 and the school, turn makai on signed Hoʻokena Beach Rd. Continue down for about 2.25 mi. and veer left along a low lava wall to an unpaved parking lot at the beach park.

HIKE: Hoʻokena Beach Park to: Kealia Beach (.75-mi. or more), or Kalahiki Beach (1 mi.)

Now popular among campers, **Hoʻokena Beach Park** in the late 1800s was a bustling trading village, where island beef and other commodities would go by steamer to Honolulu. Author Robert Louis Stevenson got his trousers wet at Kupa Landing. The ruins of the landing are in front of the parking area on the north end of the beach. Cliffs and a shock of tropical trees lie behind a gray crescent beach that receives the shore break of Kauhako Bay. By 1930, automobiles ran the steamers out of business and the trading town was no more.

To walk to **Kealia Beach**, begin at the beach park along the coast in front of a picnic pavilion. You'll immediately come to where an unpaved lane joins the coast; you can drive to this point by turning right across from the entrance road to the beach park. After a few minutes the road passes the crumbling walls of the old Catholic church that was abandoned after storm damage in the late 1800s and relocated to become the

Painted Church above Kealakekua Bay. Across the way is the coarse white sand of Kealia Beach. As you continue along the coast, coral chunks and lava rocks abound on the low onshore reef that extends for about 2 miles to Loa Point. After less than .5-mile on this coastal road, you reach houses and need to veer onto the lava.

Kalahiki Beach lies south of the beach park, along the low-lying lava of Limukoko Point. Walk the sand and skirt the cliffs—a route that may be impassible during high surf or high tide. A strand of coral sand and rock wraps around the point. Leafy kamani trees and beach kou join coco palms. Inland, trailblazers willing to endure overgrown vegetation can explore Kalahiki Village, site of a number of heiau ruins.

SNORKEL: Most people snorkel **Kauhako Bay** at **Hoʻokena Beach Park** on the south end, taking advantage of an easy shore access. But you'll see more coral and fish in the deeper waters of the landing ruins, located by the parking area. Entry at the landing is more difficult, over rocks and some concrete, but you can't have it all at Hoʻokena. *Be Aware*: Surf can make water visibility poor. More experienced snorkelers can try their luck at **Kealia Beach**, or at other entry points north of the beach park. Snorkeling can be very good, but surf and current can cause problems.

SURF: Bodyboarders like the left-slide into **Hoʻokena Beach**. The rollers are best in the summer, but winter storms also draw the short boarders.

29. MILOLIʻI   HIKE, SNORKEL, SURF

WHAT'S BEST: This authentic fishing village doesn't woo tourists and its links to ancient times may not be apparent to the untrained eye, but seekers of Old Hawaii will want to pay a visit. The hike-to beach nearby is one of the island's eye-popping goodies.

PARKING: Take Hwy. 11 south of Captain Cook and Hoʻokena. Pass mm89 and turn makai on signed Miloliʻi Rd. Follow down for 5 mi., to the end of the road. Park by the basketball court and picnic pavilion.

HIKE: Miloliʻi Beach Park to Honomalino Beach (1.5 mi.)

Outboards may have replaced canoe paddles, but the fishermen still net opelu, or mackerel, on the shallow waters, making Miloliʻi one of the few fishing villages that has survived to modern times. The rocky inlet just north of **Miloliʻi Beach Park** is where a cultural center is being developed to teach and preserve the old ways. This effort was furthered in 2003 with the launch and blessing of a traditional canoe, the first such ceremony in 85 years. A cultural event of a different nature took place at the shack that sits above the inlet, when Elvis filmed his 1962 bomb, *Girls, Girls, Girls!* And more recently, Hawaii's singing legend, the late Israel (Iz) Kamakawiwoʻole staged one of his last concerts in this hamlet. Near the picnic pavilion is yellow Hauoli Kamanao, the little church with big mana that hosts cultural events. In the 1980s, locals were able to convince backers of a resort complex to stay away from quiet Miloli'i.

For the five-star walk to **Honomalino Beach**, take the road between the church and basketball court, threading your way on a wall-lined path that displays a boggling array of 'keep out' signs meant to scare tourists away from this well-used, public trail. Lagoonlike Ako Pond will come up on your right. You'll need to cross a heap of black rocks that front homes, on the other side of

HONOMALINO BEACH

which is the pond's sandy beach. Then jog inland 50 feet, where a hand-drawn sign marks the trail—which continues to the right over rocks and kou branches. You drop into a gully, and climb up a bit, passing a tree-shaded cemetery on the left and a sacred fishing shrine on the right. Shortly after the sacred site, the path pops out to an exposed section of a'a lava and follows a utility line toward a good-sized palm grove. After this straight stretch, you'll come upon Honomalino and probably want to skip madly across the curving black-sand dune dotted with coconut palms. The snapshot view of the beach is from palm-covered Kapulau Point, the little tab that frames the north side

CANOE BLESSING AT MILOLI'I

of the bay. *More Stuff:* Trailblazers with happy feet can continue on a coastal trail south from Honomalino for 4 miles to Niuou Point and Okoe Bay, site of the Ahole Heiau and Holua, a slide. Additionally, if you want to see how vegetation fights its way through a'a lava flows, pull off Highway 11 before Miloli'i at mm90.5. A sign for Kipahoehoe Natural Area Reserve will be on the left, and on the right a crunchy road drops seaward. Ohia trees and ferns punch through the flows, dating from 1919.

SNORKEL: There can be no doubt of your genius if you have the good sense to be sitting in palm shade watching spinner dolphins circle the blue waters off **Honomalino Beach**, joined from time to time by a breaching whale farther out. You can snorkel on either end of the beach, nearer the rocky points, but the north side by Kapulau Point may yield more marine life. This beach has eroded some 75 feet in modern times and may not be here a century from now. Like all black sand beaches, the land giveth and the sea taketh away. *Be aware:* The water gets deep, right at the shorebreak.

Off the trail to Honomalino is a nice snorkeling nook, in tiny **Omaka'a Bay**. When you cross the gully below the cemetery, head 100 feet seaward and you will see a coarse-coral patch. You won't do much swimming in this small pool, but a fair few fish will be present near shore. Turbulence and rocks make swimming out from here not a good idea. At **Miloli'i Beach Park**, snorkeling can be good from the lava fingers that protrude from ironwood grove at the shore. *Be Aware:* The water gets deep fast, right at the shore break.

SURF: **Miloli'i Beach Park** is a locals beach, since a shallow reef break and a long paddle out can get newcomers in trouble. The local guys gather south of the beach park, way offshore near Moku o Kahailani rock.

30.   MANUKA STATE PARK   HIKE

> **WHAT'S BEST:** Birders, botanists, and tree-huggers will make a special point to visit this native and exotic forest. Everyone else can appreciate the serene and expansive picnic spot, a refuge midway between Kona and Kilauea Volcano.

> **PARKING:** Take Hwy. 11 south of Miloli'i. At mm83 enter the Manuka Natural Area Reserve. Before mm81, turn mauka at Manuka State Park.

HIKE: Manuka Nature Loop (2.5 mi., 400 ft.)

Enveloped in a 26,000-acre natural area reserve, **Manuka State Park** has towering trees that surround a lawn and picnic area, plus comfort facilities. The 13-acre park section, established in 1952, sits just above the highway, an easy pull-off to take a break and short stroll amid the chirps of many birds. The **Manuka Nature Loop** starts at the back of the parking lot. (It's advertised as 2 miles, but is actually longer, with difficult footing in sections over a'a.) Interpretive signs along the way label many of the 50 indigenous and

130 introduced trees and shrubs. Keep your eyes peeled for Hawaii's state flower, the mao hauhele, a yellow hibiscus bush, as well as its cousin, the red-flowering hibiscus known as hau heleula—this trail is one of their few homes in the state.

The trail steps up a steady grade. A limb-and-leaf dome is high overhead, shading a healthy understory that includes lush ki and ferns. In about a mile you'll reach the Pit Crater. This overgrown, volcanic maw is an example of why you want to stay on trail. From the crater, the path hooks left. More ruins mark the highest elevation of the loop, near trailside marker #13. From here the trail makes a downward chute through vines, before reaching the last, too-long, homeward run through aʻa lava and ohia.

More Stuff: A popular 4WD trip is Road to the Sea, a 7-mile, swath of bumpy cinder. The road begins just north of mm79; look for the Shady Grove Farms fruit stand. The road travels through a 1908 Mauna Loa flow and reaches Humuhumu Point, a cone that is being eroded by the sea to form a green sand beach. About .25-mile before reaching the coast, a road veers right from Road to the Sea and goes to Awili Point, which is the green-and-black sand beach north of Humuhumu. Finally, big-league wilderness hikers who really want to wander native forest can attempt the Kaheawai Trail, an ancient route that drops 1,900 feet over 6 miles, and reaches the coast, about 3.5 miles south of Manuka Bay. The trailhead is hard to spot: Go south of the state park and continue .25-mile south of the reserve boundary sign. The trailhead is on top of a 15-foot high bank on the makai side of the road. If you continue a short distance to the turn at Aloha Boulevard (boulevard?) and hang a U-turn, you can more easily see the trailhead sign. Only experienced hikers should try this trail. Most hikers make it a car-shuttle by going south at the coast to get a ride up on the Road to the Sea.

MANUKA STATE PARK

Mauna Loa

KILAUEA IKI CRATER

Mauna Loa is not spectacular at first sight, looking from a distance like an oval soup dish turned upside down, albeit a large dish, 30 miles by 60 miles. As seen on the horizon, the shape looks like the profile of a shield, hence the term "shield volcano." Then you learn that the "Long Mountain," when measured from its base on the seafloor, is nearly twice as high as Everest and is easily the planet's most massive mountain, containing 100 times the earth of mainland volcanoes, like St. Helens and Rainier. All this size has come from lava squirting up from the Pacific's Hot Spot, piling up and spreading out like cake batter.

And the fat lady hasn't sung yet. The big mountain has begun to inflate, and in 2002, the neighboring volcano of Kilauea sent forth a renewed river of lava toward the sea. Both cones are part of the huge Hawaii Volcanoes National Park, but the recent event has caused scientists to believe that they may also be geophysically related, so that swelling of Mauna Loa means more lava at Kilauea. Or perhaps a new eruption is brewing at Mauna Loa, which in 1984 sent a stream of lava to within 4 miles of Hilo.

Nobody knows for sure what's in store, but all visitors to the world's most active volcanic zone will appreciate that geology is not the study of rocks, but rather of rocks in *motion*. This appreciation will be underscored if their visit coincides with the next stage of Mauna Loa, the Giant Landslide Stage, when scientists speculate that the entire 4,000-foot-high mass of Kilauea may break loose and slide into the sea.

One of the best views of Mauna Loa is from South Point, where the southwest rift zone tapers gently into the sea. Yes, this is the most-southerly land in the United States, but

MAUNA LOA

to the Polynesian trans-Pacific voyagers this land was the far north, the end of a 2,000-plus-mile journey in open sailing canoes. A heiau commemorates this feat, first accomplished around 100 AD.

As you round South Point and proceed through Na'alehu, you have two opportunities to visit the shore before the highway heads up the volcano. Whittington Beach Park has serene ponds where shorebirds are happy, along with dock ruins from when cane was king—a pleasing rest stop or picnic place. Punalu'u Beach Park is a lovely black sand crescent on the tour-bus circuit; you can take in a large heiau here and enjoy an unusual lava trail over imbedded smooth rocks.

Inland from these beach parks is the volcano that doesn't get any respect, Ninole, lying in the heart of the Kau Forest Reserve. Old volcanic vents have eroded into buttes and filled in with rain-forest greenery. You can get up close in Wood Valley, or at several other trailheads into the forest reserve. Just up the mountain from the Kau Forest is the Ainapo Trail, the backdoor to the summit of the long mountain. Although few will attempt the grueling crusade to the summit, the lower reaches of the trail are a birdland forest, home to the Hawaiian goose, the nene.

Kilauea Crater is the centerpiece for Hawaii Volcanoes National Park, delivering scenic delights unsurpassed by any of America's mainland wonders. An 11-mile drive around the crater, the former lake of lava, can be done as a day trip. At Volcano House you're in a fern forest with a view over the expanse of lava. On the other side of the crater, you're in a steaming moonscape, site of the Halemaumau Crater, which spewed red-hot as recently as 1974. In between are excellent short hikes, like one to the floor of the Kilauea Iki Crater and the tourist-trot through the dripping cave that is the Thurston Lava Tube. Circling the caldera are the park's visitors center, Volcano House Hotel, Jaggar Museum, and Volcano Art Center, all top-notch attractions.

Stealing the thunder from Kilauea Crater—at least during the last two decades it has been roiling lava—is Pu'u O'o, which is off Chain of Craters Road. The 20-mile road drops to the coast, passing a dozen inactive craters before reaching sea level. Where the lava meets the sea is a towering plume of sulfuric steam. Depending on the day's conditions, and that's a big 'depending,' you can walk to view the steam or to see the actual lava creeping inexorably over land. From Pu'u Huluhulu, which is a short hike from upper Chain of Craters Road, is a long view of the fuming volcano. Pu'u Loa Petroglyphs, one of the islands better sites, is also down this road.

Hilina Pali is a 2,000-foot cliff reachable by a fork off Chain of Craters Road. Give it top marks as a view drive, with the potential to add on hikes of varying lengths. The stone hut at road's end is dramatic, set above the pali with a commanding view of the seacoast to South Point. The coastline below the pali has several shelters with water that combine to make for an excellent backpacker's circuit. Day hikers who want an all-day sucker can strap on the pack and go.

THURSTON LAVA TUBE, HALEMAUMAU CRATER, PU'U LOA PETROGLYPHS

The upper slopes of big mountain are also part of the national park. A 10-mile drive takes you to the Mauna Loa Lookout, at almost 7,000 feet, where the summit trail begins. The lookout is a prime viewpoint for Kilauea Caldera, and a place to start up the mountain and gain an appreciation for its massive, domelike shape. On the way to the lookout is a fun family hike through a native forest that was spared lava flows, and is one of the better native-bird-viewing trails.

The windward side of Mauna Loa is lush and green, and includes the Ola'a Rain Forest that is also part of the national park. You can catch a glimpse of these botanical marvels on a memorable hike through a

PART OF MAUNA LOA OBSERVATORY

tree fern forest (these things are as high as giraffes) in the Maka'ala Forest, which shares a border with the rain forest. Just down the mountain from this fanciful trail, is the Big Island's best rain forest hike, a challenging jaunt into the dank and ferny recesses of the Kahaualea Natural Area. The kicker for this hike is a view of the active volcano, Pu'u O'o, about a mile away.

MAKA'ALU TREE FERNS

To see the north side of Mauna Loa, you need to head up to the middle of Saddle Road—from either Kona or Hilo, take your pick. The Pu'u O'o Horse Trail is part of the old paniolo route, when the cattle from Parker Ranch were driven through the saddle and down to ships in Hilo Bay. The trail takes you across pahoehoe lava fields at 6,000 feet, fringed by ohia and koa forests, with the two big mountains rising like twin Kilamanjaros, north and south.

If you really want to hike to the summit, the Mauna Loa Observatory Road is a best-kept secret. Beginning near the road to Mauna Kea, this paved tract is a way for passenger cars to get to the weather observatory at 11,000 feet. North Pit is still a bit of a stroll— about 8 miles round-trip and 2,000 feet —but it's definitely doable. Regardless, the view of Mauna Kea, Maui, and Hualalai are fabulous from the observatory. If you want to thank someone for teaching the human race about global warming and harmful particulates in the atmosphere, this is the place to do it. These under-funded scientists are watching out for Mother Earth— and keeping an eye on Madam Pele, who occasionally sends streams of lava their way from lofty heights.

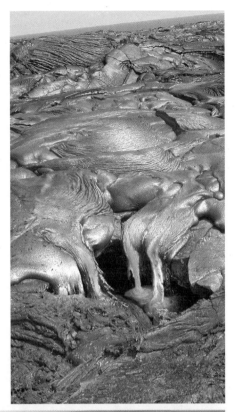

FRESH LAVA AND THE ACTIVE PUʻU Oʻo

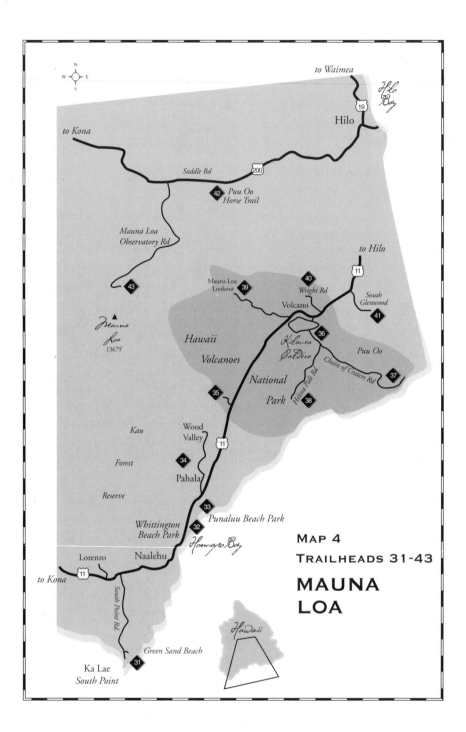

N
W · E
S

to Waimea

Hilo Bay

19

Hilo

to Kona

Saddle Rd

200

42 Puu Oo
Horse Trail

Mauna Loa
Observatory Rd

to Hilo

11

43

Mauna Loa
Lookout

40

39

Wright Rd

South
Glenwood

Volcano

41

Mauna
Loa
13679'

Hawaii

36

Kilauea
Caldera

Puu Oo

Volcanoes

National

Chain of Craters Rd

37

35

Park

Hilina Pali Rd

38

Kau

Wood
Valley

11

Forest

34

Pahala

Reserve

33

Punaluu Beach Park

Whittington
Beach Park

32

Honuapo Bay

Lorenzo

Naalehu

MAP 4

to Kona

11

TRAILHEADS 31-43

South Point Rd

MAUNA
LOA

Hawaii

Green Sand Beach

Ka Lae
South Point

31

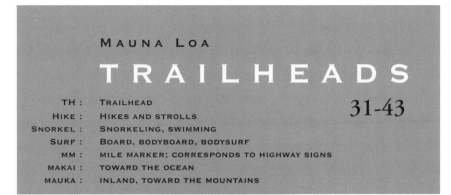

MAUNA LOA

TRAILHEADS

TH :	TRAILHEAD	**31-43**
HIKE :	HIKES AND STROLLS	
SNORKEL :	SNORKELING, SWIMMING	
SURF :	BOARD, BODYBOARD, BODYSURF	
MM :	MILE MARKER; CORRESPONDS TO HIGHWAY SIGNS	
MAKAI :	TOWARD THE OCEAN	
MAUKA :	INLAND, TOWARD THE MOUNTAINS	

ALL HIKING DISTANCES IN PARENTHESES ARE ROUND TRIP.
ELEVATION GAINS OF 100 FEET OR MORE ARE NOTED. SEE
RESOURCE LINKS FOR CONTACTS AND TELEPHONE NUMBERS.

31. SOUTH POINT   HIKE, SNORKEL

WHAT'S BEST: Stand at the most-southerly point in the Hawaiian Archipelago, with nothing between you and Antarctica but the deep blue sea.

PARKING: Take Hwy. 11 south of Miloliʻi. Pass mm70 and, .5-mi. later, turn makai on signed South Point Rd. Continue on the one-lane paved road, past the wind farm generators, and veer right 10 mi. from the highway at a fork. Go another mile and park at an unpaved lot on the right.

HIKE: Canoe Ladders, Kalalea Heiau, and South Point (up to 1.5 mi., 150 ft.); Green Sand Beach (4.75 mi., 250 ft.)

Ka Lae, "The Point," is where the first Polynesian voyagers are thought to have made landfall, and the entire southern tip of the Big Island is a national historic landmark. As a mini-side-trip after entering the landmark—where the road forks—look on your right after .1-mile for a spur road that gives you a good look at the cliffs. But keep your foot over the brake. Broken Road leads to a cliff, where the county project to provide fishermen with boat access was taken out by storms less than a year after its construction in 1955. Fishermen still must rely on the **canoe launch ladders** that descend a 30-foot cliff at the parking area. The deep seas are sometimes safe enough for swimming, but even the ancients were wary of the turbulent Halaea Current, named for a chief whose canoe was swamped and swept away.

To get to the **Kalalea Heiau** and the actual **South Point**, walk down the grassy road that parallels an old wall leading away from the canoe ladders. Within a quarter-mile you'll see the heiau (or the 40-foot-square low walls that remain), which is dedicated both to fishing gods and to the success of the long oceanic voyages. The two rocks nearby the heiau are symbols of Kuʻula, the fishing god, and his son, Aiai. Continue down the gradual slope to South Point, where the land gently tapers into the sea, on this the southwest rift zone of Mauna Loa. This taper continues down another 43,000 feet under the ocean's surface. Vegetation is scarce along this windswept shore, where currents from both sides of the island join.

SOUTH POINT CANOE LADDERS

Since all the major Hawaiian Islands are well south of Florida, the more significant geographic fact is that South Point is the tip of the 1,600-mile Hawaiian Archipelago.

For the popular hike to **Green Sand Beach**, veer left at the fork in the road that is 10 miles from the highway. After about .5-mile you'll pass a small house, billing itself as a Kalae Information Center and offering paid parking. Parking fees are not required; the paid lot constitutes private enterprise in action. Continue .2-mile and park where the road makes a circle. You'll see the boat launch area at Kaulana Bay down the rutted slope from the parking area. Walk that direction. *Be Aware:* Leave your car free of valuables. Bring water and prepare for wind and sun.

Following a road, hang a left at the bay, passing through a pipe gate. Over the next mile or so the road undulates along low bluffs. At times, two or three routes interweave along the coast; it doesn't matter which you select. After about 1.5 miles you reach a grassy plain, from where Puʻu Mahana is visible. This cone sits above Mahana Bay, where the beach is located. After crossing the grassy plain, you come upon the 80-foot cliff that forms the south shore of the bay and the olive green beach. The trail down is over the lip of this cliff. Once you hop down, it's easy. A rock ledge and path traverses downward and inland, making a little switchback just above the beach. You can also get down by skiing down the sand that slopes up from the inside of the bay's crescent. The beach owes its color to olivine, a gemstone that is eroded by wave action from the base of the puʻu. Intact stones are rare in the sand. The sluicing action of the waves separates olivine from other minerals in the lava, and the green stuff settles on top.

More Stuff: A short drive from Green Sand Beach, the Puʻu Ki Petroglyphs will attract gung-ho Indiana-Jones types. The hike is almost 5 miles round-trip, exposed to harsh weather on a lava road. To drive to the trailhead, on the way to South Point, pass mm78 in Ocean View and turn makai toward the post office—on Prince Kuhio Boulevard. Then make your first left on Maile Drive, continue a mile past four roads, and turn makai on the fifth street, which is Kohala. Go down to the end of Kohala and park. Walk about 2 miles toward the ocean, and veer left before reaching the coast at Pohue Bay. The large field of rock carvings lies near the puʻu on the mauka side.

SNORKEL: Don't make the drive to snorkel **Kaulana Bay**, but on a calm day this is the best spot around South Point, also the *only* spot. A boat landing provides easy entry, and the harbor offers protections from the swells. **Green Sand Beach** is better for wave play than snorkeling, but it's hardly worth the effort of dragging your gear along on the hike. Plenty of people swim at the beach, so, if the conditions are calm, you may have a memorable experience—swim toward the puʻu and the rocks on the north side of Mahana Bay.

HONUAPO PONDS

32. WHITTINGTON BEACH PARK   HIKE, SNORKEL, SURF

WHAT'S BEST: This by-passed park is the most serene coastal scene between South Point and the Kilauea Caldera.

PARKING: Take Hwy. 11 south, past South Point Rd. and Naʻalehu. Descend a long grade, pass mm61, and, .5-mi. later, turn makai into Whittington Beach Park. Continue .25-mi. to an improved parking lot near rest rooms.

HIKE: Whittington Park and Honuapo Ponds (up to .75-mi.)

You won't find hiking trails at **Whittington Beach Park**, but you will find an interesting stroll along the shore of Honuapo Bay, which has twice been turned from thriving community to ghost town by raging tsunamis. The fishing village was wiped out in 1868. The sugar cane port, took the knockout in the big wave of 1946, although by then truck transport had limited its use. You can see the pilings and other ruins off the lawn area of the park. Large mangos and a smattering of coco palms add to the scene.

To see the placid **Honuapo Ponds**, take the unpaved lane that veers to the left as you enter the park. You come to decrepit concrete slabs associated with the sugar days, several of them connected by short road segments, Continue left to reach the ponds. Even after the destructive wave of 1868, these ponds were essential for feeding fresh mullet and other fish to the burgeoning population of sugar cane workers. Shorebirds now enjoy the waters, including the white-tailed tropic birds that nest in nearby cliffs.

SNORKEL: Under freakishly calm conditions, the base of the wharf ruins at **Whittington Beach Park** is an excellent place to snorkel. Fish like decaying pylons. But you are more likely to encounter rough seas unsuitable for dipping a big toe.

SURF: If there are waves, then there will be surfers. This maxim is proven at the south point of **Honuapo Bay**, off Whittington Beach Park, where the wave slicers ride a he-man left-break. Summer months are the best.

33. PUNALU'U BEACH PARK   HIKE, SNORKEL, SURF

WHAT'S BEST: Pick a time when tour buses aren't lined up and you'll see why this is Hawaii's most popular black sand beach. At any time you can find solitude on an intriguing coastal hike.

PARKING: Take Hwy. 11 south from Kona, past Na'alehu and Whittington Beach Park. About .25-mi. after passing mm57, turn makai on Alanui Rd. Continue nearly 1 mi. as the road loops left and park in improved lot on right, next to a picnic pavilion.

HIKE: Punalu'u Beach Park to: Kane'ele'ele Heiau (.5-mi.), and smooth rock trail to Nahuluhulu Point (2.5 mi.)

Punalu'u Beach Park, known also as Black Sand Beach, has attracted tourists since the late 1800s, when it was a stopover for volcano-bound visitors. Its place name, "diving springs," derives from the sweet fresh water that issues from the middle of the bay. Villagers would dive with gourds to get to it. The Pahala sugar industry created a need for a port on rough Kuhua Bay, and a railway ran up the mountain to the fields. All these historical threads, including the most recent, defunct resort that sits near the ponds at the backshore of the beach, have been frayed by 50-foot tsunamis. From the parking area, which is the county campground, take the short walk to the curve of black sand that is backed by coco palms. (Before you do, you may wish to check out

PUNALU'U (BLACK SAND) BEACH

the tide pools to see if any turtles are around.) **For both hikes,** continue around the sand to the old concrete slabs at the far end of the beach. The slabs are all that's left from a World War II military installation, there to prevent the Japanese from coming ashore. At the mauka side of the slabs, take an unmarked trail up about 15 feet to the a'a lava bench. Go seaward at the top of the bench, toward Kahiolo Point, and you can't miss **Kane'ele'ele Heiau,** since it is more than 500-feet square. You should see a platform raised by poles, called a lele, where Hawaiians leave offerings to this day.

For the **smooth rock trail to Nahuluhulu Point,** cross over the crunchy a'a lava along the inland wall and walk toward the ocean along the north wall until you see the trail to your left. Flat, smooth stones embedded into the sharp a'a continue intermittently for at least .25-mile—all that remains of this unusual ancient trail. Go through a green gully and come up where a Jeep trail enters from the left. Continue right around the black rock and coral rubble of Keone'ele'ele, a storm beach. You then hit more of a dirt trail through dwarf kiawe, and there may be cows on the trail as you continue to the rounded Nahuluhulu Point. A good walking trail continues another 1.5 miles to a beach below Kamehame Hill.

SNORKEL: Kuhua Bay at **Punalu'u Beach Park** is known more for its mean rip current than snorkeling, but on the right day intrepid snorkelers can give it a try. A lava reef fronts much of the beach, so you want to go left as you face the water and enter at a small boat ramp, near the ruins of the old sugar pier. The bay offers lots of turtles and decent water clarity. *Be Aware*: Unfortunately, the best entry point is also the mainline for the rip-current express. Use caution at all times and stay out when the surf is up.

The better chance for snorkeling is nearby **Ninole Cove**. Use the above parking directions, except turn toward the Seamountain Resort instead of continuing to Punaluʻu, and park at the golf course lot. A path leads to the small cove. A sand channel or two will provide decent entry points, and lava pools at the shoreline are good keiki pools. Stay within the cove and exercise caution. On the aʻa lava bench above the cove are the remains of Kaieie Heiau, associated with the ponds that were the best swimming holes around until flash floods of the early 1980s brought tons on boulders upon them. Geology happens in real time on the Big Island of Hawaii. Speaking of which, if you stare at the ocean horizon due east from Ninole Cove for 10,000 years, you will see the emergence of Hawaii's next island, Loihi, now a 15,000-foot-high seamount that is boiling lava into water 3,000-feet deep above its summit.

SURF: Submerged rocks and swift current at **Punaluʻu Beach Park** limit surfers, who usually don't pay attention to such details. When conditions are right, you'll find board riders attempting the right-break at the south end of the beach, which is **Puʻumoa Point**. The rocks off the point that are obstacles for surfers also serve to slow down the erosion of the black sand beach. But unless Mauna Loa cooperates with a new landslide of hot aʻa, the beach will be a goner after a few more lifetimes.

34. KAU FOREST   HIKE

WHAT'S BEST: Tucked below the dry slopes of Mauna Loa and above the Kau Desert is a lush rain forest. Adventure seekers will be tempted into this exotic habitat, the green hills of which are former volcanic vents.

PARKING: From Kona, take Hwy. 11 south. Access to the forest reserve is at three points, strung along 20 mi., described below beginning with the closest to Kona. Wood Valley, the farthest, is the prime choice if you can only do one. *For Lorenzo Rd. access:* Pass mm70 and, .25-mi. before reaching South Point Rd., turn mauka on Lorenzo Rd. Continue up for about 1 mi. and park at road's end, near gates to large estates. *For Naʻalehu access:* Continue on Hwy. 11 past mm65 to Naʻalehu. Turn mauka on Kaʻalaiki Rd. and then turn left on Makino Rd. Park at the far end of the cemetery. *For Wood Valley access:* Continue on Hwy. 11 to mm52 and turn mauka toward Pahala. Follow Kamani Rd. a few blocks, turn mauka on Pikake Rd., and continue uphill. Pikake becomes Wood Valley Rd.

HIKE: Wood Valley walkabout (3 mi., 300 ft.); Naʻalehu to Haʻao Springs (7.5 mi., 750 ft.); Lorenzo Road to Puʻu Akiʻi (2.25 mi., 575 ft.)

From the highway, you get the Cinemascope view of the 50,000-acre **Kau Forest Reserve** after passing Whittington Beach Park heading north toward Volcano. Inland are green buttes, including the prominent Pu'u Enuhe, all of which are former cones of the extinct, 100,000-year-old Ninole Volcano. Erosion caused deep valleys around the cones, but subsequent lava flows from Mauna Loa have partially filled them up. The whole zone is a rain forest, carpeted in greenery.

For the **Wood Valley walkabout**, continue up Wood Valley Road, passing Norfolk pines and Macadamia trees, for about 4.5 miles, to where the road makes a 90-degree left turn. The unpaved trailhead road is to the right at this turn, but you should go left for a short distance to see the Wood Valley Temple. The 25-acre Buddhist retreat was dedicated in 1980 by the Dali Lama. Terraced gardens surround the colorful buildings. Continue up the paved lane, now called Wood Valley Loop, to take a couple-mile drive along a country lane that is enveloped in flowering gardens and exotic trees. Keep making lefts and you'll wind up where you started.

To get out and walk, backtrack to the 90-degree turn and head up the unpaved road to the right. Go left at the first fork (the right fork continues to Kapapala Ranch), and park anywhere. Indigenous koa as well as forestry-planted trees buffer the unpaved road, and woodland birdsong is pronounced. After about .5-mile, keep left where another road goes right. Keep left, passing around the Buddhist center. There are many routes in the forest. Wood Valley is about being there, not getting anywhere; how Zen.

The **Na'alehu to Ha'ao Springs** hike is a difficult-to-describe trailblazer's special, since you pass through a crosshatch of former cane field roads. Walk the road from the

WOOD VALLEY TEMPLE

cemetery and stay the course, an undulating contour—resisting the urge to head up the mountain. After 1.25 mile, give in to this urge, and angle up right on a major road. You'll climb amid greenery for several hundred feet, and reach a junction with the Ha'ao Springs Trail that comes in from a different access in Waiohinu. The steep route continues to the lush springs, and then much farther up the slope to Mountain House, a hunter's shelter.

The hike from **Lorenzo Road to Pu'u Aki'i** is a bushwhacker route on a newly established public access. You may be in knee-high grass from the get go, so watch for overgrown rocks. From the cul-de-sac parking spot, step up the hillside and follow the wide easement between fences. You lose the private property and enter unkempt forest. The pu'u will be to the left, hard to distinguish from the contour of the hillside. The return leg of this hike serves up big ocean views. *More Stuff:* If you continue to contour left at the pu'u, you hit the ancient Pali o Kaeo Trail, which goes all the way up Mauna Loa. This trail pierces 115,000 acres of the Kahuku Ranch, which are being purchased by the National Park Service to add some 50 percent more land to Hawaii Volcanoes National Park. Only prepared backcountry hikers should venture here.

35.   AINAPO TRAIL   HIKE

WHAT'S BEST: Day hikers may be reluctant to walk the entire 20-plus miles and 10,700 feet to the top of Mauna Loa. Fair enough, but consider checking out the forested birdlands that lie at the start of the trail, home to the endangered nene, or Hawaiian goose, that is the state bird.

PARKING: Driving north on Hwy. 11 from South Point, pass mm41. About .3-mi. later, turn mauka on Ainapo Rd. and proceed through a gate and sign noting the Kapapala Forest Reserve. Pass a hunter checking station, and park in the open field. *Note:* Ainapo Rd. continues for 8 mi., climbing several thousand feet through Kapapala Ranchlands to the Ainapo Trailhead. The suggested hike is on the lower portion of the recommended four-wheel drive road.

HIKE: Ainapo Trail sampler (4.5 mi., 1,100 ft., more or less)

For the **Ainapo Trail sampler,** cross the meadow and begin the gradual ascent on the ranch road. You may well see nene soon into the hike, as they often waddle and flutter in the lowlands of the sparse native forest. The walk begins at 2,500 feet. Ohia trees, with red bottlebrush flowers are quite large at this elevation, and you'll also see some koa, which have pointed leaves similar to some eucalyptus. The higher you climb, the more sparse and smaller the trees become. The top of Mauna Loa is an alpine desert.

About 1.5 miles into the hike—after ascending 650 feet—stay to the right at a fork in the road. A half-mile and 300-plus feet after the fork, you'll pass the scattered ruins of the ancient village of Ainapo. In the late 1700s, during the Battle of Bitter Rain, an army of Kamehameha's men led by Chief Kaiana retreated to this point until reinforcements from Kona came to bail them out. Another .5-mile and 300 feet above Ainapo village, the road crosses another contouring Jeep trail in Keakapulu Flat. Those who haven't turned around already will probably want to do so here. *More Stuff:* Contact the state Department of Land and Natural Resources and Hawaii Volcanoes National Park if you're entertaining thoughts about doing the full monty to the top of the trail. Water holes and shelters aid in the walk, but it is considered challenging.

36.   KILAUEA CALDERA   HIKE

WHAT'S BEST: This former lava lake—four miles across from rim to rim—is the centerpiece of Hawaii Volcanoes National Park, unsurpassed in scenic beauty by any of America's monuments. Take the drive around the rim and sample a variety of landscapes, from the bizarre to the sublime.

PARKING: From either Hilo or Kona, head to mm28.5 on Hwy. 11 and turn into Hawaii Volcanoes National Park. Stop at the entrance station, pay the admission fee, and pick up a map. *Note:* Hikes are described from the entrance station, going to the right, or counterclockwise, around the 11-mile Crater Rim Drive.

HIKE: Kilauea Visitors Center-Volcano House-Volcano Art Center (.75-mi.); Steaming Bluff (.25-mi.); Kilauea Overlook to Jaggar Museum car-shuttle (.5-mi.); Halemaumau Crater Overlook (.5-mi.); Devastation Trail to Pu'u Puai car-shuttle (.5-mi.); Iki Crater loop (4 mi., 400 ft.); Thurston Lava Tube (.25-mi.)

Notes: These hikes are the headliners on a Kilauea Crater day trip. The best longer-hike suggestions are described in *More Stuff* sections. The visitors center elevation is 4,000 feet. Bring warm clothes and rain gear. **Hawaii Volcanoes National Park** came into being in 1916 with a stroke of the pen by President Woodrow Wilson, but it then included Haleakala Volcano on Maui and did not include all of today's nearly quarter-million acres. The whole park was declared an International Biosphere Reserve in 1980.

The **Kilauea Visitors Center**, on the right .25-mile from the entrance station, has excellent films and displays, but its remarkable feature is an abundance of enthusiastic and informed staff. When the lava is flowing, the center has the energy of a newsroom on deadline. Many visitors miss the **Volcano Art Center**. As you face the visitors center, go left to the ranchstyle building sitting by itself—which is the original Volcano House, built in 1877. Aside from its historical appeal, the nonprofit art center is one of the best places to buy fine art in the state. Prices are surprisingly reasonable, whether you're looking for fine art or a memento. Upon leaving the center, jog right across the trees and lawn to see an authentic hula platform and thatched building.

The **Volcano House Hotel** is across the street from the visitors center. Hawaii's oldest operating resort has gone through many incarnations (moved, rebuilt, burned down) since its beginnings in the mid-1800s. Walk through the hotel to the observation area in the rear for your first look at of Kilauea Caldera, a view that is at once panoramic and detailed. To the right on the walkway you'll find the old concrete pillar that held the first view-scope for the Hawaii Volcanoes Observatory, put there by founder Thomas A. Jaggar in 1912. Before leaving the hotel, check out the lounge to see its oil paintings and fireplace that has burned wood continuously for more than 100 years.

Having viewed this opening triple play, jump back in the car and proceed .75-mile to the **Steaming Bluff**. A short walk out to the rim greatly enhances the experience. The spur trail joins the Crater Rim Trail at the bluffs, an ethereal stroll. Next up on the drive is the Kilauea Military Camp, a mishmash of structures serving as a resort for servicemen. But anyone can go in to avail themselves of cheap gas and cafeteria food. The **Kilauea Overlook** is about 2.25 miles from the entrance station. In 1823, Missionary William Ellis became the first Westerner to see the caldera from this spot, although at the time it was 500-feet deeper. Currently, the magma, or molten rock reservoir, is about 2 miles beneath the caldera floor.

For the **car-shuttle hike to the Jaggar Museum**, go the overlook, which is on the Crater Rim Trail, and head to your right. Fast runners may beat the driver, who must turn in at 2.75 miles to get to the museum parking lot. Vog (volcanic smog) lingers in the viewshed of Halemaumau, the crater within the Kilauea Caldera, a mile from the museum's observation area. Science-heads will enjoy displays and everyone will get a chill from Her Kane's red-hot portrait of Pele. Next door to the museum is the current Hawaiian Volcano Observatory, not open to the public.

More Stuff: At almost 4 miles from the entrance station, the Kau Desert Trail crosses the highway. Masochists in training can take off on a 9-mile, arid trek to a trailhead on Highway 11 that is at mm38.25. About .5-mile after this junction, on Crater Rim Drive, the Southwest Rift will have special appeal. You can stroll over a moonscape created by a 1971 lava flow, small steps for a man, big steps for mankind.

The **Halemaumau Crater Overlook** is 5.5 miles from the entrance station, directly opposite the caldera from the Volcano House Hotel. A short walk through a post-apocalyptic landscape, complete with toxic fumes, leads to an observation platform 250 feet above the crater floor. Halemaumau is the home of Goddess Pele, who traveled from the northern islands of Kauai and Ni'ihau before finding this home. Pele had a duplex at Halemaumau until 1790, when a large explosion turned two craters into one. Since then some 20 eruptions have taken place, including one in 1974 that sent a curtain of fire skyward. For two decades, ending in 1924, the crater was a dazzling lake of lava. On one occasion, the crater floor collapsed 400 feet. The view you get on your visit, therefore, may change at any moment, subject to Pele's whims.

More Stuff: The Halemaumau Overlook is the trailhead for two longer hikes. The most popular is a 3.5-mile jaunt across the caldera floor to Volcano House. Splatter fields and explosive debris will be found on the caldera floor, on top of flows dating mostly from the 1970s. But the last segment of the hike, is a study in native plants, including the creeping fern, uluhe, and the red-berried ohelo bush. You can also try the Byron Ledge Trail, which branches off the Halemaumau Trail after about a half-mile. You follow a vegetated ledge above the caldera floor and come to the Devastation Trailhead, almost 3 miles from Halemaumau. Both these options are better as car-shuttles. Equip your pack and avoid the noonday sun.

The **Devastation Trail to Puʻu Puai Overlook** is actually lush compared to the southwest zone. You'll find the trailhead at 7.5 miles from the park entrance, opposite Chain of Craters Road. Take the right fork at the beginning of the easy-walking path. You'll skirt an ohia fern forest, lousy with birds. The big cinder hill that is Puʻu Puai will be to the left. Keep one eye to the ground and you may find Pele's tears, black droplets of lava, or Pele's hair, glassy black filaments, both a result of molten rock blowing skyward

IKI CRATER

and cooling in the air. Shuttle drivers will find the Puʻu Puai Overlook parking lot on the left, a half-mile down the road from the Devastation Trail.

The trailhead for **both** the **Iki Crater Trail loop** and **Thurston Lava Tube** hikes is 9.3 miles from the entrance station, or only 1.5 miles if you turn left after entering the park. **For the Iki Crater**—perhaps the premier hike at Kilauea—head down the stairs across the street from the lava tube. You switchback through a rain forest before spilling onto the fractured floor of Iki Crater. Iki, more properly called Kilauea Iki, erupted in 1959. Steam rises in cracks all around, as you follow a cinder path straight across the tilted pahoehoe tabletops. Green walls, 400-feet high, rise on three sides. The trail heads toward the open end of the crater. Snake up a jumble of lava and veer to the right. At the green edge of the crater—a little more than 2 miles into the walk—you'll reach a railed stairway section. Up you go, in trees now, keeping right at two trail junctions over the next .5-mile. You then reach the Crater Rim Trail, where you keep right again, over a pleasant ascent of .75-mile to the Kilauea Iki Overlook. Cross this parking area and gobble up the last .5-mile on a splashy view section of rim trail.

Try to avoid the big tour buses at the **Thurston Lava Tube**, a.k.a. Nahuku. And for an exciting add-on to this stroll, bring a flashlight. You begin looping down through an ohia and tree fern forest that is a rich bird habitat. The lava tube, lit by dim lights, has a dripping ceiling about 15-feet high. Lava tubes are formed when the surface of fast-moving pahoehoe lava cools and hardens. The hot lava continues to flow underneath until the source ceases, and the tube drains. After about .25-mile, you emerge from the tunnel and complete the loop walk. Trailblazers with flashlights, however, can take a less traveled section of Nahuku that begins at the tube's exit, behind an unlocked gate. The tube continues for another 1,000 feet into darkness, a safe way to get a thrill.

WHAT'S BEST: Lava, get yer red-hot lava! Until Madam Pele decides otherwise, the flowing lava meets the sea at the bottom of this 20-mile drive from the visitors center. Along the way is a hike with a view of the fuming crater, and another to a petroglyph field that has survived centuries of lava flows.

PARKING: From either Hilo or Kona, head to mm28.5 on Hwy. 11 and turn into Hawaii Volcanoes National Park. Turn left after passing through the entrance station, continue on Crater Rim Dr. for 1.5 mi., then turn left on Chain of Craters Rd.

HIKE: Pu'u Huluhulu (2.75 mi., 300 ft.); Pu'u Loa Petroglyphs (1.25 mi.); Pu'u O'o flows and steam plume (1.25 mi., more or less)

Extending eastward from Kilauea Caldera are a **Chain of Craters**, more than a dozen of them covering the first 12 miles of the east rift zone. Nearer Kilauea, the pu'us are overgrown with greenery. Midway, the lava flows date from the late 1960s and early 1970s, and in the eastern section, the molten rock has been bubbling out of Pu'u O'o since 1983. The road follows the earliest craters and the middle zone, and then drops down the 1,000-foot Holei Pali to where present day flows enter the ocean with a towering plume of toxic steam.

From the top of **Pu'u Huluhulu** you are about 6 miles from the action at Pu'u O'o, close enough to get a good look, but binoculars will heighten the effect. Head down

DEVASTATION TRAIL

Chain of Craters Road, perhaps stopping at several of the jungly craters on the way—small Lua Manu, steaming Puhimau, forested Koʻokoʻolau, and Pauahi with its commanding viewing platform. Look left for Mauna Ulu, and take the spur road to a large parking lot. Walk down the road and hang a left at the trailhead—where pahoehoe lava from 1970s flows covers the road.

The Puʻu Huluhulu Trail, which is a little longer than the trailhead sign indicates, curves through a pahoehoe lava field, marked by rock cairns and yellow reflectors to aid night-time hikers. Vegetation is scarce, mostly dwarf ohia. The indirect route swings left around the lava field and then back right along the base of forested cone. Make sure to go left on the spur trail up the puʻu, rather than continuing on the Napau Trail. You make several switchbacks through trees large enough to cast welcome shade. A viewing area is to the left at the top. In your glee at viewing fuming Puʻu Oʻo, don't forget to look inland at mammoth Mauna Loa and Mauna Kea. Puʻu Oʻo has been gurgling lava since 1983, including 43 fountain bursts reaching as high as 1,500 feet. In 1997 the cone had grown to over 1,000 feet when a catastrophic collapse lowered it to its present 825 feet in less than 24 hours. Who knows what will happen tomorrow?

More Stuff: You'll need a free permit, available at the visitors center, to strike out to Napau Crater, which gets to within about 2 miles of Puʻu Oʻo. The walk is a heatstroke special, over the barren lava of Mauna Ulu and passing the Makaopuhi Crater. Wilderness camping is available at Napau Crater, which is about 7.5 miles from trailhead parking. A day hike is feasible, but leave early and don't skimp on water. The danger warnings about staying away from the crumbling slopes of Puʻu Oʻo are for real.

The **Puʻu Loa Petroglyphs** field is 13 miles down Chain of Craters Road, below the Holei Pali. A marked trailhead will be on the left, before the road makes its big left turn and continues up the coast. A highlight on the way down, near mm9, is Kealakomo, a picnic pavilion set at cliff's edge with a spectacular view. The petroglyph hike takes you across old pahoehoe lava to a wooden-railed walkway from which you can view the most concentrated rock carvings in Hawaii. Many of these kiʻi pohaku, the ones with circles and semicircles with dots, commemorate births. Sailing images are also present at this field, which is near the landing point of Polynesian migrations. Some of the petroglyphs were moved to near the visitors center, saving them from the 1990's eruptions. *More Stuff:* The Puna Coast Trail is across the street from the petroglyph trailhead. The trail leads 6.5 miles to primitive coast campsite at Apua Point.

The **Puʻu Oʻo flows and steam plume** hike can change with Pele's moods. You'll want to check in with park rangers before heading down. If the current pattern holds, you'll drive about 20 miles to the end of Chain of Craters Road, to barricades at off-street parking. After sunset, cars may line the road for a half-mile or more. From the end of the road, rangers normally mark a path with yellow reflectors to a viewing area of the steam plume. Similarly, if fresh flows are in the vicinity, a path may be marked to them, with distances ranging from a few hundred yards to a mile or more. Puʻu Oʻo has

added some 700 acres to the coastline during its current outburst. At times a few acres gets dramatically subtracted, when an overhanging cliff of lava collapses into the sea to become an instant black sand beach. At temperatures of 2,100 degrees, molten lava can melt through anything in its path and goes wherever it wants. Walking across the gleaming, crunchy new lava is not dangerous, but you need to heed precautions and be prepared. An average of one visitor a year has died viewing the volcano during the recent eruptions. Daily, yes daily, it sends 2,000 pounds of sulfur dioxide skyward. *Be Aware:* Burns, explosions, lethal vapors, heat exhaustion, and broken bones are some of the treats awaiting the oblivious hiker.

Pu'u O'o Lava Gas and Toxic Steam

More Stuff: You can watch the Holei Sea Arch fight its losing battle with the surf by taking a short, signed trail toward the ocean about a mile before the end of Chain of Craters Road. On the return leg of this stroll, look mauka to the Holei Pali and notice the a'a lava streaks dripping over the cliffs, frozen in time since the 1970s.

38. HILINA PALI   HIKE

WHAT'S BEST: This 2,000-foot sea cliff is the gateway to the Big Island's most appealing coastal wilderness.

PARKING: From the entrance station at Hawaii Volcanoes National Park, turn left on Crater Rim Drive for 1.5 mi., and then turn left on Chain of Craters Road. After 2 mi., turn right on Hilina Pali Rd. and follow 8.5 mi. to road's end.

HIKE: Hilina Pali Overlook (.75-mi., 150 ft.); Ka'aha Shelter (7.75 mi.; 2,100 ft.)

Aside from being the nexus for excellent, backcountry hiking, the **Hilina Pali Overlook** is one of the sublime view spots on the Big Island of Hawaii. The road down is pot-hole paved and easily navigated by passenger vehicles. About 3.5 miles into the drive, you pass the newly improved Kulanaokuaiki Campground, where the 6.5-mile Mauna Iki Trail connects with the Kau Desert Trail access on Highway 11. The road continues through scrub and grasslands until reaching a comparative oasis at the overlook, where an attractive stone hut is bordered by small koa trees and other greenery. Walk down the face of the cliff on the Hilina Pali Trail to get a huge view of the coast.

To reach the **Ka'aha Shelter**, think like a goat and descend the cliff face, dropping most of the hike's 2,000-plus feet in 2.25 miles. Then you need to veer right, at a junction where the Hilina Pali Trail goes left toward other primitive campsites at Halape and Keauhou. From this trail junction, the downgrade is much more gradual over the next 1.5 miles through lava grasslands. Then, at another junction with a connector trail that comes in from the left, you drop over a 200-foot lip and make the last .25-mile to the shelter. Water should be available at the Ka'aha Shelter, but you'll want to check with park rangers beforehand, and bring a pump or water treatment tablets. *Be Aware*: Although highly unlikely, if you feel the earth shake when you're down here, head up the trail fast. Localized earthquakes can create tsunamis that arrive without time to sound warnings.

More Stuff: This coastal wilderness has an excellent trail system connecting four shelters, all with catchment water supplies. The Pepeiao shelter is a cabin with actual beds, while the Ka'aha, Halape, and Keauhou shelters are three-walled. All are in arid grasslands with big sea vistas. Permits are free, and so is the advice you should get from park rangers before embarking. Wind and sun exposure are the downside.

39.   MAUNA LOA LOOKOUT   HIKE

WHAT'S BEST: A bird park delivers with tweets galore amid a stroll through old growth native trees. Or keep driving higher to get a smash-bang view of Kilauea Caldera and a taste of the long trail up 'Long Mountain.'

PARKING: From the entrance road to Hawaii Volcanoes National Park, head west, or toward Kona, on Hwy. 11. Pass mm30 and Pi'i Mauna Dr. Before mm31, turn mauka on Mauna Loa Rd.

HIKE: Kipuka Puaulu loop (1 mi., 200 ft.); Mauna Loa sampler (3.75 mi., 700 ft.)

For the forested **Kipuka Puaulu loop**, commonly known as Bird Park, continue 1.5 miles on Mauna Loa Road to the turnaround. The trailhead is on the right. Stay to the left on the loop trail and you'll soon be striding by 50-foot koas and smaller ohia trees. This habitat is completely surrounded by the Keamoku lava flow—an island of vegetation that is called a kipuka. At the hike's midway point, a couple of benches invite birders to sit a while. Nearby, a ferny lava tube will attract the curious. Fearless black pheasant will be in plain sight along portions of the trail, more obvious than the native woodland birds. Look for the bright-red apapane, which has black wings and tail and loves to swill sweet nectar from the ohia blossoms. Another red one is the i'iwi, slightly bigger and with a curved bill, and the yellow ones are most likely amakihi, the Hawaiian honeycreeper. Cardinals, the crew-cut red guys, are not native. On the loop's homestretch, vines, ferns, and leafy ti buffer the path, and a bench beneath an enormous koa, about 100 feet off the trail, begs for a sitter.

For the **Mauna Loa Trail sampler**, continue through an open gate up the road, which becomes Mauna Loa Scenic Strip and climbs to an elevation of 6,662 feet over 10 miles of smooth pavement. On the drive up—half the fun for this trailhead— you get glimpses of Mauna Loa, but the big view from the lookout is of the Kilauea Caldera. After a half-mile on the scenic strip, you pass through Kipuka Ki, a mile-long ecological area surrounded by lava. Large trees form a tunnel at the lower portions of the drive, but flora dwarfs after you get above 5,000 feet. The stone kiosk of the Mauna Loa Lookout is in a grove of native trees. Even with the head start from the lookout, you'll need to walk more than 18 miles one-way and climb 6,500 feet to reach the summit. But a shorter hike reveals the mountain's tremendous mass. You start on a contour over red, smooth lava, and then traverse up to your right for a half-mile, reaching the margins of the black a'a of the Keamoku flow. Here you head more directly up the slope, weaving through red rock. The trail becomes less distinct, and you

MAUNA LOA LOOKOUT, NENE, THE HAWAIIAN STATE BIRD

need to follow rock cairns. The temptation is to keep pushing upward hoping to catch a glimpse of the summit. But this is folly. The gently curving slopes of Mauna Loa translate to a horizon that keeps moving away as you climb.

Pick your turnaround spot and enjoy the view on the way down—but keep a sharp eye on the trail that is easy to lose. Measured from base to summit, Mauna Loa is the second highest on the Big Island, and the second highest on the planet earth. The current estimate for its summit height is 56,000 feet from its submerged base. But the amazing statistic is its mass. At some 19,000 cubic miles, you could fit more than 100 mainland volcanoes, like Rainier and St. Helen's, inside of it. *More Stuff:* Known locally as the Trail of Tears, the Mauna Loa Trail is a challenge for any backpacker. All of it is exposed to wind, sun, and harsh temperatures. The Red Hill Cabin provides shelter 7.5 miles from the lookout, at just over 10,000 feet. The next cabin is near the summit, a long 11.5 miles and 3,000 vertical feet away. Obviously, check with park rangers to obtain permits and information on this hike. Also, see TH43, Mauna Loa Observatory, for more on the summit, and the "easiest" route there.

40.   MAKA'ALA TREE FERN FOREST   HIKE

WHAT'S BEST: This enchanted rain forest of giant tree ferns may have you seeing elves. The trail provides easy access to the fringes of the Ola'a Forest Wilderness, part of the national park.

PARKING: Drive toward Hilo on Hwy. 11 from the entrance to Hawaii Volcanoes National Park. Pass mm27 and turn mauka on Wright Rd. After 2.5 mi. the road makes a 90-degree left and, .5-mile farther, turn right on Amaumau Rd. Follow for 1.75 mi. to a cul-de-sac. Drive (or walk) a grassy two-track road from the cul-de-sac for .25-mi. to the trailhead.

HIKE: Maka'ala Tree Fern Forest (2 mi., 150 feet)

Begin the hike through the **Maka'ala Tree-Fern Forest** by heading up the trail opposite the road leading in—not by going left on a utility road. The trail's early portions are typical, as you tread soft dirt and cross through muddy sections with the aid of inlaid steps made of rust-colored tree-fern trunks. You will be enveloped by greenery, as the trail curves and undulates. Close by to the right is the border for the 100,000-plus acres of the Ola'a Wilderness. Although companion ohia trees are present, you are essentially in an intimate tunnel of the fronded trees, called hapu'u in Hawaii. Some are 25-feet high. After a wondrous mile, near some large shaggy ohias, you reach a fence marking the boundary of the 12,000-acre natural area reserve.

More Stuff: Trailblazers can continue by hopping the fence and taking the public trail into the Kulani Forest Reserve. Other access to this reserve is via the Stainback High-

Maka'ala Tree Fern Forest

way, which heads mauka from Highway 11 a few miles south of Hilo. To explore the Ola'a Forest, check with the park service to see if they've added access. If not, hiking will be dangerous and nearly impossible due to thick foliage and, more to the point, earth cracks that can mail you to nowheresville in a heartbeat.

41. KAHAUALEA RAIN FOREST   HIKE

WHAT'S BEST: Get beyond the beyond after only a short distance into a native Hawaiian rain forest. Then, as an added bonus, keep trekking to a view of Kilauea's east rift zone and see Pu'u O'o blowing its stack about a mile away.

PARKING: Take Hwy. 11 toward Hilo from Hawaii Volcanoes National Park, or head toward the park from Hilo. Turn makai on South Glenwood Dr., which is .25-mi. on the Hilo side of mm20. Continue 3.5 mi. as the road becomes Captains Dr. and then Ala Kapena Dr. Park at signed trailhead for Kahaualea Natural Area Reserve. Leave your car free of valuables.

HIKE: Kahaualea Natural Area to Pu'u O'o viewpoint (7.5 mi., 350 ft.)

Pack rain gear, plenty of water, food, a rabbit's foot, and a hiking pole before entering the 17,000-acre **Kahaualea Natural Area**. The trail corkscrews through ferny muck, roots, and mossy upheavals of lava on its way to the **Pu'u O'o viewpoint**. And make sure to follow the trail, which should be marked by plastic ribbon at eye-level branches in critical places. If you encounter heavy rain or fog, turn back. No, it's not *that* bad, but you want to respect this hike. It starts out innocently enough on some grassy straight sections, over the roots of a towering canopy of ohia and koa, and beside an understory of several varieties of fern and shrubs.

About a mile into the rain forest, you'll cross a shallow gully and step over one of several earth cracks in the trail. After this point, the trail becomes a drunken snake, slithering left and right, hiccuping up and down 6 to 12 feet. At 2 miles, you'll reach a clearing of sorts, mostly moss and ferns, and think you're nearly out of the woods. But, no. The trail continues toward daylight in the trees that seems to get close without arriving. Finally, after about 2 hours of diligent marching, and maybe 10 minutes after stepping over the third earth crack, you'll notice the forest trees dwarfing in size and losing their vigor. Then you reach the last of them, those that were blocking your view, and you peer like a pagan at the fuming vent of Pu'u O'o. You won't find a better place to bust out the Tarzan yell. *Be Aware:* Don't be lured closer. Aside from lethal fumes (tons of sulfur dioxide are sent airborne each day) and collapsing lava tubes, you may not be able to find your way back to the Kahaualea Trail. If you don't feel like an odyssey, just walk in from the trailhead and hang around. You may see more by being still than stomping along purposefully. Branches twist ornately, decorated by moss. Birds circulate in all directions.

SADDLE ROAD TRAILS

42. PU'U O'O HORSE TRAIL   HIKE

WHAT'S BEST: A trail on the open plateau between the two most massive mountains on earth imparts a large sense of place—and you'd never guess it was Hawaii. (This is a different Pu'u O'o than the lava-spitting one.)

PARKING: From Kona, take Hwy. 190 toward Waimea and near mm7, turn right on Saddle Rd. Continue past the Mauna Kea Rd. turnoff. Turn off to the right .5-mi. after passing mm23. Parking is at a rough lava turnout. *From Hilo,* take Hwy. 200, Waianuenue Ave. west from town. *Note:* See *Free Advice & Opinion* for tips on driving Saddle Rd.

HIKE: Pu'u O'o Horse Trail (up to 7.5 mi., 200 ft.)

Cattle and paniolos hoofed this trail in the 1800s, contouring around Mauna Kea from Parker Ranch, coming through the saddle on the way to Volcano town, and thence to awaiting ships in Hilo Bay. The Pu'u O'o Ranch and the old cone are on the Mauna Kea side of Saddle Road; see TH65. So get along little doggies, and don't forget to pack rain gear and equip your pack for a wilderness hike. The **Pu'u O'o Horse Trail** weaves through pahoehoe lava and native ohia, roughly on the boundary between the Upper Waiakea Forest Reserve and the Ainahou Nene Sanctuary. About .5-mile into the hike, you'll drop into a large grassy swale fringed by large koa trees and affording a big view of both Mauna Loa and Mauna Kea. You climb gradually from this swale, veering left over pahoehoe lava flows from 1855 that have had time to weather. Both right and left are islands of vegetation, kipukas, with old growth koa as the cornerstone of a rich bird habitat. The trail gets curvy and you have to keep your eyes peeled for worn areas and rock cairns to stay with it. Still angling left, you cross over a more recent flow from 1881 before the horse trail joins Powerline Road. You can return on this straight road, which is easy to follow and joins Saddle Road about .5-mile east, toward Hilo, from the Pu'u O'o trailhead. *Be Aware:* Start early on this hike, since fog and rain are not uncommon later in the day.

More Stuff: Toward Hilo from the Pu'u O'o Horse Trail parking are several more public trails. Recreational appeal is marginal, but trailblazers may be interested. The Powerline Road is at mm21.5, and takes off to the right, or south, over a hellish a'a lava field, and continues all the way to the Ainapo Trail. A couple of miles farther, on the right at mm18.4, is the Kaumana Trail. This promising Na Ala Hele state hiking trail never gets far from the highway and is disappointing. On the right at mm16, you'll see the wide swath of the Tree Planting Road. Mountain bikers will be most interested in this forested pathway 10 miles long, running between Saddle Road and Stainback Highway. Beyond Tree Planting Road, about .25-mile but on the Mauna Kea side of the highway, is an access to the large Hilo Forest Reserve. Desolate slopes support wiliwili trees, a suitable place to wander off and have existential thoughts.

43.   MAUNA LOA OBSERVATORY   HIKE

WHAT'S BEST: Though no cakewalk, this trailhead is by far the easiest way to get up Mauna Loa. You begin at 11,150 feet, where you can take a look around the installation that is keeping an eye on the world's atmosphere.

PARKING: Heading toward Hilo on Saddle Rd., Mauna Loa Observatory Rd. is .25-mi. past mm28, on the right—just past the road to Mauna Kea and the Pu'u Huluhulu trailhead. Passenger cars can make the 17.5-mi., 4,500-foot climb to the trailhead, but use caution. Turn on your lights, avoid potholes, and drive down the center of the white line. *Notes:* See *Free Advice & Opinion* for tips on driving Saddle Rd. Gas up. Start early to avoid the marine cloud layer which generally rises in the afternoon. Bring warm clothing, water and food.

HIKE: Mauna Loa Observatory (up to .5-mi., 100 ft.); North Pit (7.75 mi., 2,000 ft.)

Ascending on the lower end of the observatory road, you'll drive through a Marslike ocean of a'a, deposited by several eruptions in the late 1800s and in 1935. On the left is the Ainahou Nene Sanctuary. To acclimatize to the altitude, stop for 30 minutes or so, about 8.5 miles from the bottom, where the observatory road makes a sweeping right turn at a telecommunications installation. You'll see public parking at the end of the paved road. The **Mauna Loa Observatory** is a short hike up the hill. It's an assemblage of metal buildings and boardwalks looking like an Arctic outpost laid down on lava instead of ice. Although the public is welcomed, no staff are assigned time to deal with visitors. To put it tactlessly, don't be a pest. Now under the auspices of the National Ocean and Atmospheric Administration and other agencies, the MLO has been keeping tabs of the air we breathe for 45 years. Gases, particulates, and aerosols are all measured, including carbon dioxide, which has increased 20 percent during the years of study. Yes, global warming, depletions of the ozone layer—the charts are on the walls of these faraway buildings; read 'em and weep. But don't forget to marvel at the view of Mauna Kea, Maui's Haleakala, the Kohala Mountains, and Hualalai Volcano.

For the hike to **North Pit**, start down the a'a lava road heading east from the parking area. After a little more than .25-mile, the Observatory Trail joins the road, and you want to go left. Thus begins a steady climb over mostly pahoehoe lava on a route marked by precious rock cairns, 2- to 3-feet high. Don't space out and lose these babies, especially coming down when they're harder to spot. The four-wheel drive road continues up the mountain, too, making five switchbacks on the way, crossing the trail three times. Think like a mule on this steady but not-too-steep grind. A slow pace will ward off the effects of thin oxygen. You'll eventually reach the lip of the pit, elevation 13,120 feet, a little inlet off the larger crater of Mokuaweoweo Caldera, spreading out before you in a three-mile oval. It is not deep or precipitous, but the austere caldera is one of the world's most distinctive topographical features, the barren dimple upon the most-massive mountain. *Be Aware:* If it's not obvious already: Only seasoned hikers should attempt this hike and prepare for severe weather.

More Stuff: Several trails intersect where Observatory Trail ends at North Pit. The Mauna Loa Summit Trail comes in from the left—see TH39—and also continues to the right for 2.5 miles and 500 higher feet to Mauna Loa's peak. If you go left from North Pit, the trail rims the other side of the caldera, passing small Lua Poholo Crater on the way to Mauna Loa Cabin, 2 miles away, and up another 150 feet.

MAUNA LOA OBSERVATORY AND SUMMIT TRAIL

FISHERMAN AT MOKU OLU

Hilo's rain is legendary. Proverbs lament the perpetual gloom that mercilessly brings hundreds of inches of rain each year down upon the people. When the King Kalaniopu'u died in the late 1700s, the young warrior Kamehameha earned his stripes by defending the sunny lands of Kona from the covetous grasp of Chief Keawemauhili of Hilo, who, when you peel away the political squabbling, seems simply to have been desirous of some of that dry west-side air.

Today, east-siders have laid down armaments and picked up big umbrellas, to them as much a part of Hawaii as sunglasses and swim fins. And don't knock it until you've tried it, since strolling through a warm downpour in a rain forest garden is among the unique memories to take home from the islands. To be fair, the rain comes in buckets, not drizzles, and it's interspersed with generous displays of tropical sunshine that make Hilo glisten like Eden. Unless you see Hilo and Puna, you will miss the mind-boggling greenery that says, "Hawaii." Most of the world's supply of exotic flowers is flown out daily from the east side.

Once the capital of the islands, Hilo has a sense of place that would otherwise be absent on the Big Island. Show up on a Saturday or Wednesday for the farmers market and crafts fair and you'll be wandering through a romantic bazaar of a faraway land. Roam the dilapidated-and-gentrified city blocks of historic Hilo, and you will be transported to the 1950s. This old section was spared two horrific tsunamis, in 1946 and 1960, which tragically wiped out communities that crowded the bay. Two parks—Bayfront and Waiola River—are expansive greenbelts that compliment the bustling funk of the historic section.

Hilo Bay is below the saddle between Mauna Loa and Mauna Kea. The waters running off these two great peaks join to form the Wailuku River that runs through the old town, spanned by several quaint bridges. A couple of miles up the hill is the Wailuku River State Park, home to Rainbow Falls and Boiling Pots, a series of turbulent pools that lie below Pe'epe'e Falls. Both of these attractions receive the big tour buses, but you need to visit these "destructive waters" to further appreciate Hilo's sense of place.

Then head to nearby Liliuokalani Gardens and Moku Ola, a.k.a. Coconut Island. The gardens are of formal Japanese design. The little island, reachable via footbridge, is protected by the post-tsunami breakwater across part of Hilo Bay. Excellent snorkeling and swimming are available. From the island is a stunning view across the bay to Hilo, with the world's highest mountains lofted above. Put Moku Ola high on the list of places to stand and take in the immense beauty of the Big Island.

The outer portions of Hilo Bay are home to a half-dozen beach parks that are locals playgrounds on weekends. Just north of town is Honoli'i Beach Park, a black-sand beach in a jungle gorge that is Surf City. When the larger waves roll in, spectators line

the cliff above the beach. Heading east of Hilo, for 5 miles outside the breakwater, are several beach parks buffeted by an arboretum of tropical flora. You won't find long runs of white sand, but you will discover several, man-enhanced lagoons, which are excellent for snorkeling. You can pick a favorite, but be sure to see Onekahakaha, Carlsmith, and Richardson Ocean Park. They're not far apart, and each has its own personality, proving once again that the unique is typical on the Big Island.

East and south of Hilo, Puna's Kehena-Pohoiki Scenic Coast drive plays second fiddle to none in the Hawaiian Islands when it comes to tropical scenery. Starting farthest south, Kalapana is a bay that was filled by lava in the 1990s, and now sports the newest black sand beach with a view of fuming Pu'u O'o. Just up the scenic drive is Kehena Black Sand Beach, tucked into a lush shore. A few delicious miles north of Kehena are the bluffs of Mackenzie State Park, set in the largest ironwood grove in the state. Isaac Hale Beach Park, where locals and fishermen hang out, is the next stop north of Mackenzie. Its stout wharf provides an underrated pool for snorkelers. Only a mile or

RICHARDSON OCEAN PARK, ORCHIDS, SHIPMAN HOUSE

so farther up the coast is Ahalanui County Park, which alone makes the trip along the coast worthwhile. A man-made warm pool is set at ocean's edge, dappled with the shade of palms and other beach trees—a free resort spa that is rarely if ever crowded.

The Waiopae Pools, which are not far north of Ahalanui, can be nominated as Hawaii's best snorkeling venue. A dozen or more pools, from waders to Olympic-sized, adorn a broad reef at the south shore of Kapoho Bay. Colorful coral competes with sparkling fish for your attention. You have to walk out a couple hundred yards to this unusual spot. On the north side of Kapoho Bay is Cape Kumukahi, the eastern-most spot in the Hawaiian Archipelago, which boasts the purest air you can breath in the world at sea level. The lighthouse at the point escaped the lava of a 1960 eruption by a few feet. You can take a short hike to the dramatic cape, or a slightly longer one to the warm Kapoho Sea Pool, which lies off the north shore of the bay.

Lava Trees State Monument lies inland from the Puna coast, in papaya-and-orchid country. A fast-moving lava flow in the late 1700s, about 12-feet deep, clung to tree trunks which later burned away, leaving these weirdly formed statues. A canopy of enormous monkeypod trees and a ground layer of ferns and leafy ti complete the scene, which is more like walking through museum grounds than on a park trail. Birds go wild in the native ohia forest that envelops the monument.

APE CLIMBS MONKEYPOD AT LAVA TREES STATE MONUMENT, KEHENA-POHOIKI SCENIC DRIVE

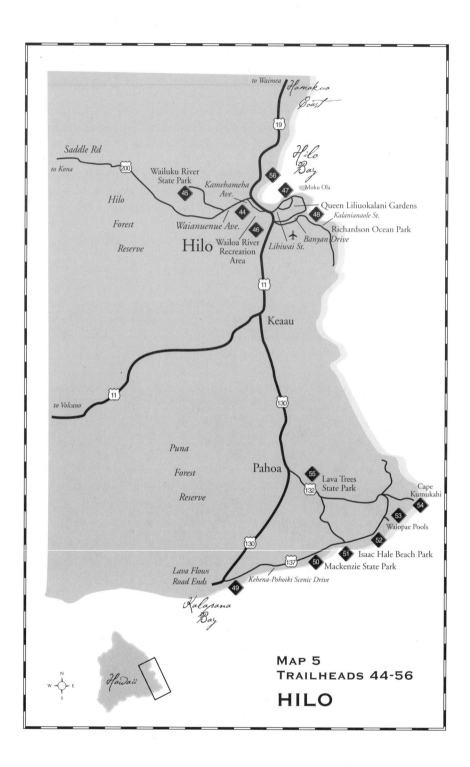

Map 5
Trailheads 44-56
HILO

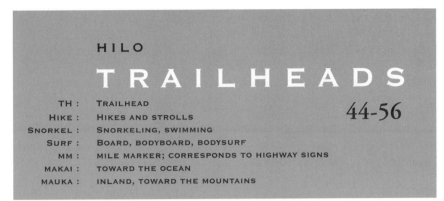

HILO

TRAILHEADS

TH :	TRAILHEAD
HIKE :	HIKES AND STROLLS
SNORKEL :	SNORKELING, SWIMMING
SURF :	BOARD, BODYBOARD, BODYSURF
MM :	MILE MARKER; CORRESPONDS TO HIGHWAY SIGNS
MAKAI :	TOWARD THE OCEAN
MAUKA :	INLAND, TOWARD THE MOUNTAINS

44-56

ALL HIKING DISTANCES IN PARENTHESES ARE ROUND TRIP.
ELEVATION GAINS OF 100 FEET OR MORE ARE NOTED. SEE
RESOURCE LINKS FOR CONTACTS AND TELEPHONE NUMBERS.

44. HILO TOWN
HIKE, SURF

WHAT'S BEST: Yes, it rains in Hilo, and that's why it's so beautiful. Having survived tsunamis, the pre-war old-town section has soul and charm, plus a greenbelt for a coastal stroll.

PARKING: From Kona, take Hwy. 190 to Waimea and continue on Hwy. 19, approaching from the north. (This route is a little shorter than Hwy. 11.) After crossing the river on the steel (singing) bridge, turn right on Waianuenue St., and then immediately turn left on Kamehameha Ave. Pass Kalakaua St. and park in the public lot that extends for several blocks.

HIKE: Hilo Town (1.25 mi.); Bayfront Park (.5-mi., or more)

If at all possible, time your visit to **Hilo Town** for a Saturday or Wednesday morning to take in the Hilo Farmers Market. From the parking lot, follow the old-fashioned storefronts for a block or two to Mamo Street. The market covers the equivalent of two square blocks. One side has just about every fruit and vegetable you've ever seen, plus numerous tropical varieties only Dr. Zeuss could dream up, and overflowing buckets of fresh flowers and herbs. Your nose will be as active as your eyes. Across the street from this organic orgy is a bonanza of hand-crafted potential souvenirs—sarongs, shell jewelry, blown glass, ceramics, wood carvings, instruments, condiments—just go and ye shall find. The market is under awnings, providing welcome shelter, rain or shine.

Historic Hilo hangs as loose as hula hips, so loose some of it appears ready to topple. You can see much of it by making a loop. Start by heading up Mamo Street from the farmers market and going right on Kilauea Avenue. Across to the left, is Hawaiian Force, the place to go to pick up locally designed clothing with a cultural flair. After a block, Kilauea becomes Keawe Street. Dip left on narrow Furneaux Lane to check out the 1925 Ancient Order of Foresters Building. Continue on Keawe and cross Haili Street, featuring the Art Deco Palace Theater, also built in 1925 and still thriving. Farther down Keawe, jog left on Kalakaua to see the Old Police Station, now a cultural center with the hipped roof of an old Hawaiian hale. Next door is the Hawaiian Telephone Company Building, designed by C.W. Dickey, who is credited with creating a 20th century style by fusing Hawaiian with California Mission. Across the street from these buildings is Kalakaua Park, which King David Kalakaua named for himself (a.k.a., the Merrie Monarch, who was known for extravagant expenditures that weakened the monarchy). Some of the park's trees are more than 100 years old.

A block after Kalakaua Street, hang a right on Waianuenue Avenue. Look left before you do to see the Burns and Pacific buildings, vintage wood-frame styles that have become rare in Hawaii. Down the block, where the avenue meets Kamehameha, is Koehnen's Building. Fine gifts in this family-owned store may draw your eye, but take a look at the koa walls and ohia floors. Then turn right on Kamehameha and go one block back to Kalakaua to the Pacific Tsunami Museum. Killer sea waves are as much a part of local cultural and natural history as are volcanoes. Inside are a variety of interactive displays and videos. The main videos take place in a vault, since this is a former bank building, designed in 1930 by Dickey.

Finish up your loop by continuing down Kamehameha. On the way you'll pass the S.H. Kress Building, a 1932 Art Deco. After crossing Furneaux, you'll see the Caribbean-styled Vana building, with tiled roofs and arched windows and then comes the S. Hata Building, built in 1912, another renaissance revival gem. Inside you'll find the Mokupapapa Discovery Center for Hawaii's Remote Coral Reefs, a new museum that explores the two-thirds of the state that few people know about—the 1,200-mile archipelago northwest of Kauai that is the nation's largest conservation area. A 2,500-gallon saltwater aquarium and touch-screen videos help bring the reef to life.

Bayfront Park is directly across the highway from Hilo Town, a greenbelt that stretches for 1.5 miles, from the Wailuku River to the Wailoa River. On this end is a large gazebo, Mo'oheau Park, where community gatherings take place. Wharves and dock buildings used to crowd a bustling shoreline, but, in a cruel stroke of nature's urban planning, 30-foot waves wiped them out—in 1946 and 1960.

More Stuff: To further appreciate Kamehameha the Great, head to the county library, which is a few blocks up Waianuenue Avenue. That big coffin-shaped stone in front is the Pohaku Naha, all 3.5 tons of it that was delivered from Kauai by canoe centuries ago. As a test of royal blood, a young Kamehameha was able to move this stone and later was bestowed custody of the war god, Ku. To see the stately Shipman House (now a B&B), where Jack London sojourned in Hawaii, turn right past the library on Kaiulani Street and continue a short distance after crossing the river. For a more ancient history—and a scenic look at Hilo's bridges and river—take a look at Maui's Canoe (Ka

Waʻa O Maui), which is close by: Go back down Waianuenue and turn left on Kinoʻole. Cross the river on the Wainaku Bridge, built in 1919. Park, and walk back onto the bridge. That gouged-out finger of bedrock downstream is the legendary site where the demigod Maui left his canoe when he rescued his mother at Rainbow Falls.

On rainy days, Lyman Museum gets foot traffic. Its bureaucratic curbside appeal belies a fine collection of artifacts and cultural history that await inside. The Mission House on the grounds dates from 1839. To get there, head mauka from Kamehameha Avenue on Haili Street and continue a few blocks to the corner of Kapiolani.

BRIDGE TO MOKU OLU, PALACE THEATER, LUANA A.B. NEFF STANDING IN THE DOORWAY OF HER STORE

SURF: In the old days, before the breakwater and inshore canal projects made Hilo a safer place to live, the break offshore **Bayfront Park** was one of the best in the islands. Bodyboarders and surfers still ride the tiers, but only during big winter swells.

45. WAILUKU RIVER STATE PARK   HIKE

WHAT'S BEST: Two scenic waterfalls are just a few miles from Hilo, up the river that joins the runoff of Mauna Loa and Mauna Kea. Go early.

PARKING: Coming south into Hilo on Hwy. 19, cross the steel (singing) bridge and turn mauka on Waianuenue Ave. Continue about 1.5 mi., and keep right on Waianuenue where Hwy. 200 veers left. Shortly thereafter, turn right on Rainbow Dr. and continue to the Rainbow Falls parking lot on the right.

HIKE: Rainbow Falls and pools (.5-mi.); Boiling Pots (up to 1 mi., 125 ft.)

Wailuku River State Park spreads its 16 acres along a roiling mile of the river, which comes down the saddle from the island's mammoth twin peaks. You should arrive in the morning to have a chance of seeing the misty spectrum of color for which **Rainbow Falls** is named—and to avoid the big tour buses that hammer the place. The falls' twin white waters join at the top and fall 80 feet. A cave behind the falls is where the demigod Maui rescued his mother, the goddess Hina, from Moʻo Kuna, the giant eel lizard, and she was darned glad he did. The hot tip here is to head for the pools that lie just above the falls. Go up the stairs to the left and continue into a dip beneath a huge banyan. Look right for an opening cut through an 8-foot high rock bank, and you'll find a well-used trail that leads a short distance to the pools. (A sign warning of swimming dangers marks the trail.) You can wander up the river and dip when the water is low, but doing so during swift flows is dangerous, like the sign says.

To get to **Boiling Pots**, continue on Rainbow Drive, which loops back out to Waianuenue. Pass Waiau and turn right on Peʻepeʻe Falls Street. A short paved walk takes you to the overlook of the "boiling pots," a succession of pools connected by both underground and surface flows. Basalt lava columns line the pools, and upstream you can see Peʻepeʻe Falls. A slippery, unsigned trail leads down to the pools, to the right as you stand at the railing. This is a fun wade-around under calm conditions, but when the pots are boiling to venture into them is suicidal. It's not called Wailuku (Destructive Waters) for nothing.

More Stuff: Spelunkers and other people fond of dark, dank holes will want to know that Kaumana Caves County Park is not far away. Head back down Waianuenue and turn right on Highway 200, which is Kaumana Drive heading up the mountain. Pass Akala Road on the right and mm4, and look .25-mile later for the park on the right. Park on the shoulder across the highway, and grab your flashlight. Steep, railed stairs lead into a mossy cavern, created by a collapsed lava tube from an 1881 flow. To the right you can make your way about 200 feet over broken sheets of lava. Then the going gets thick. Trailblazers can take the route less traveled, to the left, where you can squeeze through a less-obvious opening and have relative easy going thereafter.

46. WAILOA RIVER STATE RECREATION AREA Hike

WHAT'S BEST: If you're staying in Hilo, don't overlook this huge pond-side park for a tranquil picnic spot or sunset stroll.

PARKING: Coming into Hilo from the north on Hwy. 19, cross the steel (singing) bridge, continue along the bay shore, and cross the bridge over the river. Turn mauka immediately on Manono, pass the boat launch, and turn right on Pi'ilani. Pi'ilani ends at Park Rd., where you jog right into the large parking lot.

HIKE: Waiakea Fishpond to Kamehameha statue (.75-mi.)

Huge trees—palms, mangoes, monkeypods—are spaciously placed along the 150 acres of lawn, picnic tables and open water at the **Wailoa River State Recreation Area**. Scalloped footbridges invite you to head across Waiakea Fishpond, the largest body of freshwater on the island. Fed by high-volume springs and a stream, the pond was the exclusive grey mullet fish tank for three generations of Kamehamehas, and hence is also known as the Royal Pond. No doubt Impressionist painters would have been inspired by the tropical reflections cast upon its placid waters.

To reach the **Kamehameha statue**, cross the first bridge and veer right at the shoreline, setting your course for a second scalloped footbridge that crosses an arm of the fishpond. Off to the left is the modernistic Tsunami Memorial and Japanese Immigrant

KAMEHAMEHA STATUE, WAIAKEA FISHPOND BRIDGES

Museum, there to honor the souls living in the settlement that was swept away. This recreation area was a thriving community before the big wave of 1960 hit—killing 61 people and demolishing 300 structures. The Kamehameha statue will be to the left after crossing the footbridge. On the return leg, angle toward the ocean side of the pond to where it narrows and behold the Wailoa River. You can then tell your friends you've seen the shortest river in the United States—about one-third mile.

47. LILIUOKALANI GARDENS

HIKE, SNORKEL

WHAT'S BEST: The ancients believed swimming at this tiny island would cure what ails you. Maybe, but for sure you'll get a five-star, romantic view of Hilo and a chance to stroll formal gardens that could be in Kyoto.

PARKING: Coming into Hilo from the north on Hwy. 19, cross the steel (singing) bridge, continue along the bay shore, and cross the wide highway bridge. Turn left immediately on Lihiwai and then go right on Banyan Dr. Continue .25-mile and turn left on Lihiwai, a one-way through Liliuokalani Gardens. Then turn right immediately on Keli'ipio toward Moku Ola.

HIKE: Moku Ola and Liliuokalani Gardens (.75-mi.)

A concrete footbridge spans the narrow channel leading to **Moku Ola**, which is also known as Coconut Island. A tiara of palms surround the island's several acres of lawn. This is the perfect place to take a midday rest, as in ancient times when ill people came to bathe in the island's curative waters; Moku Ola means island of healing. From the bridge you get a view that makes you fall in love with Hilo, and anyone else nearby. The town sits across the waters of Hilo Bay, with the 13,000-foot-plus peaks of Mauna Loa and Mauna Kea rising in the background.

LILIUOKALANI GARDENS

Liliuokalani Gardens, built in honor of the queen who was the nation's last ruling monarch, are across the quiet street from the island's parking lot. Curving footbridges of stone and painted hardwoods connect little islands in Wiahonu Pond. Sloping lawns around the shore are graced by large banyans, mangos, palms, and kukui. The serene land-

MOKU OLA DIVING TOWER

scape was designed by the University of Kyoto's Kinsaku Nakane. In ancient times, a sacrificial heiau stood on the peninsula.   .

More Stuff: If you continue around the peninsula on Banyan Drive you reach Reeds Bay County Park. A pool adjoins the head of the bay, called Ice Pond. On a hot day, dip a toe and find out how the pool got its name. Across the narrow bay is one of those sublime spots, where under the shade of banyans and palms is an evocative view of sailboats anchored in the small harbor. To get there, veer left at Banyan Way as you drive past the park and then go left when you get to Kalanianaole Avenue. Look immediately on the left for a Shoreline Public Access sign at the Reeds Bay Clinic.

A touching attraction, the Waiakea Tsunami Memorial Clock, stands where you turn onto the peninsula on Lihiwai. It is forever stopped at 1:04, as a tribute to all who lost their lives when the tsunami struck in the dead of night, May 23, 1960.

SNORKEL: Cute **Moku Ola** is also one of the east side's better and most convenient places to swim. Protected by the vast breakwater, surf is calm and water clarity is good. As you walk onto the island, head to the right, and you'll find the 15-foot **diving tower**, a two-tiered mortar-rock structure that has survived at least two tsunamis. High school kids do flips from the top. The inlet on the inside of the tower is a sea pool, known as **Pua'akaheka**. If you're feeling a bit sick, take a swim around the rocks that lie opposite the tower in this inlet. Ailing Hawaiians, under the supervision of a kahuna, would do so for its healing properties.

TSUNAMI MEMORIAL CLOCK

HILO FARMERS MARKET, LELEIWI BEACH PARK, RICHARDSON OCEAN PARK

48. HILO BEACH PARKS HIKE, SNORKEL, SURF

WHAT'S BEST: Pick a sunny day and you'll understand why Hawaiians flock to this 5-mile strip of coast that boasts five beach parks with protected sea pools, sand patches, gardenscapes, and sections of wild reef. On the weekends, all the BBQs will be smokin'.

PARKING: Head to the junction of Hwys. 11 and 19 in Hilo, which is across from Banyan Dr. Then go east on Kalanianaole Ave., or Hwy. 137. Further directions are given below, starting from the junction.

HIKE: Onekahakaha Beach Park (1.25 mi.); Carlsmith Beach Park to Pohakea Point pandanus grove (.5-mi.); Leleiwi Beach Park to Richardson Ocean Park (1.5 mi.)

Take a gander as you pass by Keaukaha Park and Puhi Bay. Then veer left on Apapane, go left again off Keokea Loop, and drive to end of this cul-de-sac for parking near a Public Shoreline Access sign. This spot is the hidden entrance to **Onekahakaha Beach Park**. (For the main beach parking lot, you can continue on Apapane, or the highway, and turn makai on Onekahakaha Road.) This park features a small cove, lagoons, a wave-bashed point, and a huge sea pool. A short shaded path leads to Lihikai Beach, a patch of white sand and coral rubble that is a locals hideaway. Circle around this small beach to the blunt Keokea Point, where the boomers roll in. Ironwoods join palms at the shore. Across the base of this small point are the ponds of the beach park. Continue past the ponds and you'll get to the main park grounds, with lawns and picnic pavilions of one of the Big Island's first public parks, dedicated in the 1930s. This is the east side's most popular family beach, owning to its huge, protected sea pool.

James Kealoha Park and **Carlsmith Beach Park** share opposite sides of the same small bay, just down the road at mm4. Kealoha is more of a local kids parking spot; you'll want to park at Carlsmith, which is across the inlet next to the six-story Mauna Loa Shores apartments. A path leads by an attractive pond and trees to the park's reef-protected shore. Tiny Scout Island sits close to shore near the point. Across the street from the park is 30-acre Loko Waka Fishpond, which is a marine marvel in that some 100-million gallons of freshwater a day permeate is porous lava bottom. All that rain from Mauna Loa's lower rain forests has to go somewhere.

For the instant getaway to the **Pohakea Point pandanus grove**, take a forest trail that begins on the other side of the big apartment building. You'll find Shoreline Public Access parking. The path is a tree tunnel through dense flora, including the ape (AH-pay), or elephant ears, and vines. Avoid a path that branches to the right and you'll soon hit the thicket of pandanus trees, called hala in Hawaii, which are used in the weaving of baskets and hats. Watch your step as you navigate the lava-rock shore, with its tide pools that draw fishermen.

CARLSMITH BEACH PARK

Leleiwi Beach Park is less than a mile down the highway from Carlsmith. On busy weekends, you might want to park on the right after Koloa Street. Pick a path along the intricate, tree-lined shore which features tide pools and ponds, heading to your right as you face the water. Beyond Leleiwi's picnic pavilions walk the top of a low lava wall to reach **Richardson Ocean Park**. The structure at the shoreline is the ocean center in front of which is an inlet with a small black sand beach. Continue around the shore in front of the center and walk by the park's larger black sand beach, Waiolena, which sits at the end of the lovely, yes lovely, garden path that is the park's main entrance. Hooking around the beach gets you onto Leleiwi Point, the smooth lava point that protects the east end of the beach. *More Stuff:* Undeveloped Lehia Beach County Park lies just beyond Richardson at road's end, the home of permanent tent campers.

SNORKEL: **Richardson Ocean Park** offers very good snorkeling, under the right conditions, but it is not the best swimming among this coast's beach parks. Try the inlet in front of the ocean center, or the Waiolena black sand beach, the park's easiest place to get in. Lots of rocks make for good fish habitat and interesting swimming, although chest clearance will be a problem in spots. You'll also get a chill from freshwater intrusion in places. *Be Aware*: Rip current can accompany even moderate surf at this park, although it is mostly reef-protected. The rock in the center on the bay is known as "suck rock" because of the powerful current.

Carlsmith Beach Park has an excellent swimming sea pool, complete with stairs leading down from a small dock area. You'll have to compete with leaping kids. The water is stand-up deep. Under lower surf conditions, check out Scout Island and the rocks off Pohakea Point. The bay at **James Kealoha Beach Park** has deep water snorkeling with good visibility, but wave action often makes swimming unsafe.

The big, sandy-bottomed sea pool and **Onekahakaha Beach Park** is a parent's dream, and anyone can have fun swimming around, protected by a boulder reef. Lawns and even some precious white sand await in between dips. At the far end of the beach park, to the left past the ponds, is **Lihikai Beach**, a locals favorite. Sand channels make for adequate entry. *Be Aware:* Be very mindful of rip currents caused by wave action. Ditto for a second natural pool at the beach park, where current sweeps past the breakwater.

For a bracing freshwater swim, go native and try the **Akepa Pools**. Protected by a reef from the sea's direct blasts, several open ponds make for a swimming park frequented by teenagers. They're onto something. The pools are between Carlsmith and Leleiwi beach parks. Look for Akepa Street on the mauka side of the road, across from which is Shoreline Public Access. You'll feel like you've made a minor discovery.

SURF: Board surfers ride the rocky break off **Keokea Point** at Onekahakaha Beach Park—not a good choice for beginners. The point, also known as **3-Miles**, is a good grandstand for watching. More popular is the offshore break at **4-Miles**, which is the bay shared by Kealoha and Carlsmith beach parks. Most popular of all is **Richardson Ocean Park**, where a consistent surf breaks at the reef extending from Leleiwi Point. Rocks and riptide make this a ride for experienced board heads only.

49.   KALAPANA LAVA BAY   HIKE, SNORKEL

WHAT'S BEST: Eruptions of the 1990s filled this bay with lava, but a new black sand beach has formed. A short walk yields a view of the active volcanic cone that has done the damage. Down the road is a hidden black sand beach.

PARKING: From Hilo on Hwy. 11, drive about 6 mi. toward Volcano and turn makai toward Pahoa on Hwy, 130. Bypass Pahoa and keep right on Hwy. 130 to mm21. Veer left on Ahia Rd. for a short distance to reach Hwy. 137. Then go right and park in a cul-de-sac.

HIKE: Kalapana Lava Bay (1.5 mi.); Kehena Black Sand Beach (.25-mi., 100 ft.)

From the parking area, an arrow painted on the asphalt points seaward toward **Kalapana Lava Bay**, your course for a path that leads over pahoehoe lava. Midway to the surf, look back inland to notice the curve of coco palms that once lined a serene black sand beach and Harry K. Brown Beach Park, a bay now filled with lava. Some 200 homes were destroyed, along with a Kaimu Beach Park, perhaps the island's prettiest black sand beach. Also gone is the Wahaula Heiau, one of the oldest, having been built in 1250 AD. As you follow the sketchy path, look inland to your right and you'll see Pele's latest incarnation, Pu'u O'o, adding more land area to Hawaii and destroying anything in its path. At the shore, a new beach has formed, which took place when hot lava met cool water, sending silicates into the air which rained down as black sand.

Don't try to be among the first to swim here, as currents and undertow will make you among the last. All the young coco palms, many of which are from Shipman House in Hilo, have been planted by resilient islanders. To see the steam plume created when Mrs. Lava meets Mr. Sea, head right down pahoehoe mounds along the shore—but exercise caution on this crumbly landscape.

Kehena Black Sand Beach is a few miles from Kalapana. Just before mm19 on Highway 137, pull in makai at a turnout. As you face the ocean, go left on a steep, short trail down a small promontory. It's a hands-on descent, dropping onto a big dollop of black sand that is backed by a cliff dripping with tropical greenery. Pele made this beach in a 1955 eruption, and thoughtfully added a new point of land that has inhibited the sea from reclaiming the beach, the inevitable fate of all true black sand beaches. The beach survived a 1975 earthquake which dropped the shoreline 5 feet in a jiffy flat, an incident that is evidenced by a severed concrete stairway that is on the right side of the promontory as you walk down. The broken stairs point toward another portion of the beach, which is less popular because surf often sweeps to the cliffs. Given nature's fury, you might want to nap with one eye open on Kehena Beach.

SNORKEL: Kehena Black Sand Beach, also known as **19-Mile Beach**, is the sandiest spot to take a dip on the coast for many miles. It's known for swimming, rather than snorkeling. People who want to be naked also gather at this beach. *Be Aware*:

KEHENA BLACK SAND BEACH

Kehena is exposed to the open sea. The sand drops off steeply and undertow can be a problem during high surf.

50. MACKENZIE STATE PARK

HIKE

What's Best: The largest ironwood grove in Hawaii is a pleasant rest stop along a spectacular coastal drive.

Parking: From the junction of Hwys. 130 and 137 in Kalapana, go left, heading north. See the previous trailhead for directions to Kalapana. Pass mm14 and, .25-mi. later, turn makai at sign for Mackenzie Park.

Hike: Mackenzie State Park (.75-mi.)

For a dozen miles north of Kalapana, Highway 137 is known as the Kehena-Pohoiki Scenic Coast, a blacktop penetrating tropical gardens the equal of those on Maui and Kauai. And unlike those awesome coast drives, you don't wind in and out of stream valleys, since rain runoff on young Hawaii seeps into the porous lava, and hasn't yet had time to erode. The scenic drive, a country lane beside sea-washed buffs, is a tree-tunnel of breadfruit, palms, pandanus, and other varieties right out of a tropical tree-finder manual. A number of turnouts invite timeouts on this sleepy road.

The 13 acres of **Mackenzie State Park** are surrounded by hundreds of acres of the Malama Ki Forest Reserve. The huge ironwood forest that shades the coast was planted in the early 1900s by Ranger A.J.W. Mackenzie, a Scotsman who arrived on the Big Island as a teenager in 1890. The well-liked ranger was killed in an auto accident in 1938, as a memorial plaque indicates. Unique lava tables and stools stand near a rock picnic pavilion, an inviting campground in spite of its lack of water. Heading to the right from the picnic pavilion, within .25-mile, you will find a heiau ruin, enhanced by shrines of recent visitors. Near the ruins is a cave, opened by a collapsed lava tube. Appearances notwithstanding, the droppings are not needles and cones and the ironwood is not even related to a pine, according to those zany botanists. The tree is a salt-resistant transplant from the South Pacific. You can also walk the bluffs to the left, or north at Mackenzie; the Mahinaʻakaʻaka Heiau, lies about .75-mile in that direction. *Be Aware:* Earth cracks can be partially hidden, so watch your step. Also, as signs indicate, sleeper waves have swept fishermen from the cliffs at the shoreline.

51. ISAAC HALE BEACH PARK

Snorkel, Surf

What's Best: On weekends this beach park gets more action than its scenic assets seem to warrant. But the non-touristy surfer-and-fisherman scene has its charms, including good snorkeling and a hidden warm pool.

PARKING: Best accessed as part of a trip up Hwy. 137, on the Pohoiki Scenic Coastal Drive. From south of Hilo, follow Hwy. 130 past Pahoa to the coast and go north on Hwy. 137. The beach park is north of mm12, where Pohoiki Rd. joins the coast.

SNORKEL: To the right of the boat trailers and blue-tarp campsites is the **Pohoiki Breakwater** and boat launch. Snorkeling here is fairly good, in protected clear water. Combine that with the safety provided by the breakwater and the easy entry of the ramp, and you've got yourself a decent-plus snorkeling site. The **Pohoiki Warm Spring**, a temperate pool, is a short walk away. Head in front of the cottage around the shore of the small bay, and look for a well-used path heading into the dense vegetation. It's not far out of view. This cozy pool, roughly 10-feet across, is for apres snorkel.

Serviceman Isaac Hale (HAH-lay) was killed in 1951 during the Korean War. His family had received the coastal property as part of a land swap with the Puna Sugar Company in the early 1900s. Prior to that, since this was the only boat launch for miles, the area supported a community built around mills for coffee and timber.

SURF: Bodyboarders, including kids and learners, ride the left-break at the tip of the breakwater into little **Pohoiki Bay**. Walk to the end of the breakwater for the Kodak view. Boys and girls on bigger boards head for the treacherous reef break that is to the left, or north, of the boat parking area. A'a lava and shallow break present hazards at this surf spot, called **Bowls** by some of the locals.

52.   AHALANUI HOT POND   SNORKEL

WHAT'S BEST: How much would you have to pay to luxuriate in a warm pool set beside the blue Pacific in a coco palm grove? Zip. This county park is an awesome freebie.

PARKING: Best accessed as part of a day trip up Hwy. 137, the Pohoiki Scenic Coastal Drive. From south of Hilo, follow Hwy. 130 past Pahoa to the coast and go north on Hwy. 137. Ahalanui County Park is near mm11, just north of Isaac Hale Park and the junction with Pohoiki Rd. A paved parking lot is secured by a chain-link fence.

SNORKEL: Leave the flippers in the car at **Ahalanui County Park**, but the mask will be useful in this man-enhanced seaside pool—an oval about 200 feet by 50 feet heated by geothermal energy to just under body temperature. A underground channel from Kilauea's east rift zone warms the pool, which used to be chilly until the 1960 eruption altered the subterranean waterworks. High tide brings slightly cooler temps, but the thermostat is set to Pele's mood swings and could change at any moment.

AHALANUI COUNTY PARK, ISAAC HALE BEACH PARK

Surrounding the pool is a paved path-slash-sundeck. Entry is made easy by several rock stairs. Swimming with the humans in the chest deep water is a variety of fish and the occasional eel that washes over a dam and spillway where the pool meets the ocean. Previously called Pualaʻa Park and shown on some maps as Secrets Beach, Ahalanui has been a county park since 1994.

A lifeguard is on duty from 9:30 a.m. to 4:45 p.m., but the park is open from 7 a.m. to 7 p.m. *Be Aware:* Signs warn of health hazards in the pool, a result of a legal effort by the wife of a man who died after developing an infection when he entered the water with a skin disease. County officials report no common health problems.

53. WAIOPAE POOLS   SNORKEL

WHAT'S BEST: Some say these coral-rich tubs serve up the best snorkeling on the island. The wildest imagination could not conjure this broad reef of tide pools connected by channels—adventure snorkelers … go!

PARKING: Drive south from Hilo and go makai on Hwy. 130 toward Pahoa. Take the Pahoa bypass and veer left on Hwy. 132, Kapoho-Pahoa Rd. Continue several miles to the stop sign and junction with Hwy. 137. Turn right, or south. After mm9, turn makai on Kapoho Kai Dr., toward Vacationland. After .6-mi., turn right on Hoʻolai and then keep left as the lane becomes Waiopae St. Park at public access, where a cable crosses an open area. *Note:* Leave car free of valuables.

SNORKEL: A broad pahoehoe reef extends several hundred yards at the south end of Kapoho Bay, in which there are a dozen or more swimmable depressions, the **Waiopae Pools**. This spot is also known as Kapoho Tidepools, or, less frequently, as Champagne Cove. Pools richest in coral and other marine life are about 200 yards from the road—curve to the right as you walk out. Flippers aren't necessary. Pull on Tevas, reef booties, or any shoe you can walk in and then get wet. Some of the pools are more for wading, but farther out they are Olympic-sized, up to 10 feet deep and chockablock with multi-colored coral. At high tide you can swim channels that connect pools. Sometimes you need to instantly evolve and walk. Stay well inshore of the breakers, as currents drain the tide pools at the edge of the reef. The fish are not giants, but they are plentiful, and you'll run out of fingers trying to count the different species of coral.

More Stuff: Green Lake, a locals swimming hole, is just up the road from the Waiopae Pools. Look for a gate near mm8, mauka from the highway, across from Kapoho Beach Road. A short walk takes you to the large lake, in a gardenlike setting. Permission to access this lake may be required, though the trail is well used.

54. CAPE KUMUKAHI   HIKE, SNORKEL

WHAT'S BEST: Breath the freshest air in the world while standing on the most-easterly land in the Hawaiian Archipelago. This spot has big mana.

PARKING: Drive south from Hilo on Hwy. 11 and go toward Pahoa on Hwy. 130. Take the Pahoa bypass and then veer left on Hwy. 132, the Pahoa-Kapoho Rd. Continue for nearly 10 mi. to a stop sign at the junction with Hwy. 137. Go straight and continue for 2 mi. to the end of the unpaved road.

HIKE: **Cape Kumukahi loop (1.25 mi.); Kapoho Bay Sea Pool (2.5 mi.)**

Cape Kumukahi, or "First Beginnings," was given new life by an eruption in 1960, just 4 miles inland. Flowing lava extended the coast a half-mile seaward on either side of the cape. The lighthouse was spared by a few feet, a benevolent act by Pele, some say. A beacon has replaced the lighthouse, but you can still see where the fresh lava parted. The 400-foot high Kapoho Crater rose inland from the cape, 30 miles down the Chain of Craters on Kilauea's east rift zone—which extends another 70 miles into the sea.

For the **Cape Kumukahi loop**, head straight for the ocean from the unimproved parking area near the light beacon. A tank road heads over the pahoehoe—not the crunchy a'a road that goes to the right, which is the return route. The path is defined as much by where you can't walk, that is, the jumbled a'a that flanks the route. Never mind, in a few minutes you'll hit the road that loops around from the parking lot. Go left on the packed lava chunks and you'll soon reach the east point, marked by a stack of stones. It's debatable whether the rock pile on the point is one of the Kings Pillars, which are believed to have been erected by Chief Pi'ilani of Maui in the 1500s to help his canoes navigate the treacherous waters. Some archeologists believe Kings Pillars to be just another name for the natural rock formations. On the return leg, stay on the a'a road to loop around to the parking spot, passing the road to Kapoho Bay on the way.

The **Kapoho Bay Sea Pool** is south of the lighthouse. Start out on the four-wheel drive road to the right as you face the water. Near the shore, the black sand beaches have mostly been blasted away by tidal action, but some sand has been tossed up to the cliff to make hanging beaches. The pool is a nook just inside the tip of land on the north side of the bay.

More Stuff: The Kuki'i Heiau is one of the older ruins, and is mostly overgrown. Seeking a place to make astronomical observations in the 1500s, Chief Umi is believed to have erected the edifice, which is roughly 40-feet square. Restoration efforts are planned. Trailblazers can explore this site by taking a road to the right as you drive out from the lighthouse, which is located .25-mile before reaching the highways. Drive in and park at a gate. Then take the road going up the hill to the left, before you get to a little cemetery. The top is about 250 feet and .75-mile away.

SNORKEL: The **Kapoho Bay Sea Pool** is geothermally heated, though not as warm as Ahalanui Park, and frequented mostly by locals, though not as many as the Waiopae Pools. It gets confused with these other two places. To get there, take the hike above. When the tide is right you can dip into the depression beside the bay (kapoho means depression) and be elated at your discovery. No need to take flippers on the hike over, but reef shoes will be nice.

55.   LAVA TREES STATE MONUMENT   HIKE

WHAT'S BEST: Twisted lava statuary line a garden path beneath a towering canopy of leafy trees. Only birdsong interrupts the hush in this park.

PARKING: From Hilo, go south on Hwy. 11 and turn on Hwy. 130 toward Pahoa. Take the Pahoa bypass and veer left on Hwy. 132. The park will be on your left, near mm2.5.

HIKE: Lava Trees loop (.75-mi.)

Begin the **Lava Trees loop** on the groomed path. The park's old growth monkeypod trees tower a hundred or more feet, creating a green, backlit dome. Ape, or elephant ears, creep skyward up the tree trunks and ferns and ti cover the buckled lava ground that opens here and there with mysterious earth cracks. In this setting are the lava trees, created in the late 1700s when a fast-flowing pahoehoe eruption coated the trunks of ohia trees up to a depth of 12 feet. The lava flowed away or down into the earth cracks, leaving the hot earth-goo congealed to the moist trunks, which eventually burned and rotted away leaving the lava molds. Dozens of these weird, Giacometti-esque statuary seemed to have been placed about by a curator. Add a little moonlit fog and you'd have a recipe for the willies. This dramatic effect is complimented by a cacophony of tweety birds which inhabit the ohia forest that surrounds the monument's 17 groomed acres. About 10 minutes into the walk, look for a spur trail that leads up some steps to a shelter with benches—the perfect place to kick back, zip the lip, and listen.

More Stuff: When in this neck of the woods you are close to two attractions that will interest families and rainy-day sightseers. The first is the Panaewa Rainforest Zoo. The 12-acre county park, with free admission, is home to some 75 critters, including the ruler of the roost, Namaste, a white Bengal tiger. (Primates may beg to differ.) The grounds include 100 varieties of palms, and a bamboo-and-rhododendron garden frequented by roving peacocks. To get to the zoo, take Highway 11 south of Hilo to mm4 and turn mauka on Stainback Highway. Continue 1.25 miles and turn right at signs, which also point toward an equestrian center. Hours are from 9 a.m. to 4 p.m., daily.

LAVA TREES STATE MONUMENT

SCOPING SURF AT HONOLI'I

Hawaii's largest nut grower, Mauna Loa Macadamias, has a visitors center nearby. Continue south up Highway 11, passing mm4 and Ikaika Street, and turn left on Macadamia Road. The 2.5-mile drive in may be the trip's highlight on a country lane through 2,000 acres of fragrant orchards that are bordered by towering Norfolk pines. You can munch free samples, including an ingenious variety of sweetened versions.

56. HONOLI'I BEACH PARK   SURF

WHAT'S BEST: Where have all the children gone? Hey brah, they're riding the tubes at the east side's hottest surf scene.

PARKING: Go north from Hilo on Hwy. 19. Pass a scenic point and mm4, and turn right on Nahala St. Then go left on Kahoa, which reaches the park entrance after a short distance.

SURF: On nice weekends, surfmobiles will line this quiet street at **Honoli'i Beach Park**, and you may have better luck driving by the park entrance and parking closer to the old scenic bridge that spans the jungly cove. A long flight of stairs leads to a well used rest room and pavilion that is set a little above the black sand beach. Walk left on the sand, past heliotropes and palms, to the stream mouth, where many of the surfers enter. Bodyboarders and board surfers ride the offshore tiers, which are normally larger during the winter. A shore break combines with a north-side point break to give surfers a choice. *Be Aware*: A rip current heads out to sea and then circles to the left.

From the shore is an appealing view toward Hilo, looking into the bay from outside the breakwater. During big surf, crowds gather at the guardrail on the street, a natural grandstand to watch the show. Drooling surfers began climbing down the cliffs in the 1960s, creating a groundswell that resulted in a county park being established in 1970.

Mauna Kea

THE SHADOW OF MAUNA KEA AT SUNSET FROM THE SUMMIT

You might say Mauna Kea is as close to heaven as you can get on earth. For the native Hawaiians it is Wakea's Mountain, sired by the god who is the expanse of the sky—The Famous Summit of the Land. Lake Waiau, near the summit, is the umbilicus, or piko, connecting all generations of people on all the islands to the heavens. For scientists from all over the world, the summit is the eye to the heavens where a dozen powerful telescopes explore the far reaches of the universe.

At 13,796, Mauna Kea is not only the highest peak in the Pacific, but, when measured from its base on the ocean floor, the highest in the world—close to twice as high as Mount Everest. Although born of fire, by the billions of tons of magma that has surfaced from the earth's core, Mauna Kea was in the Pleistocene era capped by 300 feet of solid ice. Permafrost remnants still lie beneath its soils. A trip around the mountain takes you from forests inundated with up to 200 inches of annual rainfall to deserts, lucky to get 10 inches. With all these extremes in elevation, temperature, and moistures it should come as no surprise that a circumnavigation of Mauna Kea is akin to a spin around the globe, taking in some 11 of the world's 13 climatic zones.

On the windward side, Onomea Scenic Drive is in a rain forest, where you can roam the Hawaii Tropical Botanical Gardens and take the historic Donkey Trail to a wild bay. You can get delightfully lost in the garden for hours. Just up the road is Akaka Falls State Park, in the lush upcountry. An easy loop trail that takes in Akaka as well as Kahuna Falls is cut through a tangle of greenery and towering trees that will have you looking for dinosaurs. Then follow the falls' water to the sea to Kolekole Beach Park, set in a gorge with a cascade and pool alongside crashing waves.

Umauma Falls is north of Akaka on the Hamakua Coast. Here the high shoulders of Mauna Kea supported the island's sugar cane fields during the1800s and well into the 1900s. Above the fields are forests reserves, a thicket of greenery sliced by dozens of streams. The falls are a sight that will impress even Yosemite veterans. The beat goes on as you continue north on the Hamakua Coast, passing verdant cliffs. Side trips over one-lane bridges and tight turns on the Old Mamalahoa Highway allow you to put the dripping flora at arm's length.

The coast yawns open to a huge gulch at Laupahoehoe. You can drop down to see one of the most ruggedly scenic beach parks in the islands. Notoriously large waves lash against a lava point created by one of Mauna Kea's last eruptions, and a garden of trees decorates a flat bench set below sea cliffs. The scenic beauty is fittingly dramatic for a point best known for the tragic loss of school children and teachers that took place when a tsunami struck on April Fool's Day of 1946. Stay awhile at Laupahoehoe and you'll never forget it.

On the northeast slopes of Mauna Kea are gulches carved not by lava, or even rain, but primarily by ice during the mountain's glacial period. A number of bumpy roads lead up to forest reserves in this area, but the best place to explore is Kalopa Native Forest State Park—one the Big Island's underrated-attractions. Pick from nature strolls and forests treks in this groomed arboretum, which is set within 500 acres of forest. Another forest reserve, Ahualoa, will bring about the adventurer among hikers particularly attracted to these forests. The Ahualoa reserve takes in some of Mauna Kea's north slopes, which are the pastoral lands of the Parker Ranch, rolling grasslands dotted with eucalyptus and conifers lying at the foot of Waimea's Kohala Mountains.

Mana Road, near Waimea, takes a 45-mile contour around Mauna Kea, ending at Saddle Road. At this north end, even passenger vehicles can drive in for miles. Hikes are available toward the green pu'us and, a few miles later, the arid gulches that fall from the summit. Compare this rural greenery to the high plains on the south side of Mauna Kea, accessible from Saddle Road. That dry, lava-scoured zone shared with Mauna Loa gets 15 inches of rain in a good year.

HAWAII TROPICAL BOTANICAL GARDENS, AKAKA FALLS TRAIL

MAUNA KEA FROM SADDLE ROAD

At an elevation of just 6,000 feet, the Kilohana trailhead is an opportunity to explore the native forests that thrive in this harsh environment. Expeditionary trails rent skyward from Kilohana, but birders and strollers can sample the interesting lowlands of this remote region. A hike here will serve to acclimatize visitors headed for higher altitudes, as will the short hike to Puʻu Huluhulu, which is square in the saddle between the world's highest peaks. The short hike to this native tree sanctuary will take you a long way towards appreciating the geography of the Big Island.

If you head up Mauna Kea Observatory Road, a.k.a. John A. Burns Highway, from the saddle, you pass the southern entrance to Mana Road, called Keanakolu Road on this end. During good weather, passenger cars can get in quite a distance on this old cowboy trail that leads to the lush Hakalau National Wildlife Refuge. It's tough to see all of the Big Island on a week's vacation, but local hikers can dedicate days to exploring these hinterlands.

The road is excellent to the Onizuka Center for International Astronomy, which is set amid a half-dozen puʻus at the 9,000-foot level. You'll have great views and learn more than you can handle about Mauna Kea. But it's well worth the effort it takes to get the final few miles to the top, where you will learn in breathtaking moments what words could never impart.

NASA INFRARED TELESCOPE

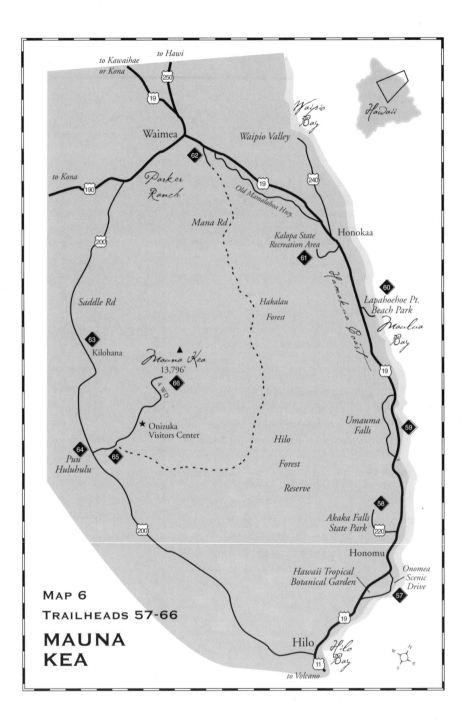

to Hawi

to Kawaihae
or Kona

250

19

Waipio
Bay

Hawaii

Waimea

Waipio Valley

62

Parker
Ranch

Old Mamalahoa Hwy.

19

240

to Kona

190

Mana Rd.

Kalopa State
Recreation Area

Honokaa

200

61

Hamakua Coast

60

Lapahoehoe Pt.
Beach Park

Saddle Rd

Hakalau

Forest

Maulua
Bay

63

Kilohana

Mauna Kea
13,796'

66

4 WD

19

★ Onizuka
Visitors Center

Umauma
Falls

59

Hilo

64

Puu
Huluhulu

65

Forest

Reserve

58

Akaka Falls
State Park

220

200

Honomu

Onomea
Scenic
Drive

MAP 6

TRAILHEADS 57-66

Hawaii Tropical
Botanical Garden

57

MAUNA
KEA

Hilo

Hilo
Bay

N
W E
S

19

11

to Volcano

MAUNA KEA

TRAILHEADS

TH : TRAILHEAD
HIKE : HIKES AND STROLLS
SNORKEL : SNORKELING, SWIMMING
SURF : BOARD, BODYBOARD, BODYSURF
MM : MILE MARKER; CORRESPONDS TO HIGHWAY SIGNS
MAKAI : TOWARD THE OCEAN
MAUKA : INLAND, TOWARD THE MOUNTAINS

57-66

ALL HIKING DISTANCES IN PARENTHESES ARE ROUND TRIP.
ELEVATION GAINS OF 100 FEET OR MORE ARE NOTED. SEE
RESOURCE LINKS FOR CONTACTS AND TELEPHONE NUMBERS.

57. ONOMEA SCENIC DRIVE   HIKE

WHAT'S BEST: Along a lush, four-mile scenic byway are the Big Island's best tropical garden and a short hike to two wild coves. Anyone with a green thumb will want to put a gold star on the map and spend the afternoon.

PARKING: *From Hilo*: Take Hwy. 19 north past mm7 and veer. makai on the scenic route, toward Onomea Bay. Continue 1.75 miles to the Hawaii Tropical Botanical Gardens. *Notes:* An admission is charged. For the Donkey Trail to the beach walk, without visiting the garden, park just past the garden offices. *From Kona:* Head south on Hwy. 19 toward Hilo and veer left onto the scenic road near mm11 in Pepe'ekeo. Follow Old Mamalahoa Hwy. about 2.25 mi.

HIKE: Hawaii Tropical Botanical Gardens (1.25 mi., 150 ft.); Donkey Trail to Onomea Bay and Turtle Cove (1 mi., 150 ft.)

The experience begins at the **Hawaii Tropical Botanical Garden** as you descend a 500-foot boardwalk through a streamside Eden, under the welcoming limbs of monkeypods, mangos, and tree ferns. Make sure you have enough time to fully appreciate all the wandering paths that are a work of love by the garden's ambitious staff. And don't let the rain be a deterrent, as they issue big umbrellas at the top of the boardwalk. You'll get a trail guide, but the gardens are just the right size to wander aimlessly, turning here and there until you've seen it all. Begun in 1978 by Dan and Pauline Lutkenhouse, the nonprofit gardens have blossomed into Hawaii's finest.

The garden is home to more than 2,000 different species, including a plethora of palms, gingers, heliconias, as well as some native endangered flowers, which have been given a new lease on life. The palm jungle trail ends at a waterfall that makes three drops to pools before cascading under a footbridge. The Lily Lake koi pond would inspire Monet, and kids will squawk when they see the big shamrock macaws at the bird aviary. Near the lower end of the garden, a path fronts a wild seascape. To the left is Onomea Bay, and Turtle Cove is to the right. Sit in a few different places and you'll be surprised how much botanical detail—sights, sounds, smells—starts to emerge.

The **Donkey Trail** may not have a sign at the trailhead. It descends a slippery root network under a cathedral of Alexandra palms. Alongside is Onomea Stream, the garden boundary. At rough **Onomea Bay** a finger of land protrudes straight ahead. Across the bay at the point is where the Onomea Sea Arch collapsed in 1956. Go right across the stream and follow a fenced public easement to **Turtle Cove**, a.k.a. Kukilu Bay. If you're in a hurry, the Donkey Trail is a way to see these two coves and take a peek into the gardens while you're at it. The Donkey Trail is so named for the beasts that would haul sugar down to the bay in the late 1800s. The Kahili'i fishing village, the historical use of these twin gulches, was mostly wiped out by the big wave of 1946.

58. AKAKA FALLS STATE PARK HIKE, SNORKEL, SURF

WHAT'S BEST: The Big Island's famous tropical waterfall is easily accessible. A nearby beach park with a cascade and natural swimming pool is seldom visited.

PARKING: Pass mm14 while heading south on Hwy.19 toward Hilo. Look for signs to and turn mauka on Hwy. 220, Akaka Falls Rd. Follow the signs uphill for 3.75 mi. to a large paved parking lot. *Note:* Leave car free of valuables.

HIKE: Akaka and Kahuna Falls loop (.5-mi., 125 ft.); Kolekole Beach Park (.25-mi.)

Akaka Falls State Park is on the tour-bus circuit and if you hit the trail at midday you might feel like you should be wearing a cowbell. Still, **Akaka and Kahuna Falls** deliver the scenic goods, and the lush green trail is well worth the effort. The path makes an oval around 65 acres alongside Kolekole Stream, passing a who's-who among tropical flora—bamboo, plumeria, ferns, ti, bird of paradise, and red ginger to name a few. All crowd the trunks of large trees. You'll cross the stream and reach the Kahuna Falls overlook, which bursts from the greenery of a side canyon to make its 125-foot fall in two pitches. Then continue up the path, passing an enormous banyan, and you'll reach the railed viewing area for Akaka Falls. Meaning "split" or "crack," the 440-foot free-fall of water demonstrates the later stage of the Mauna Kea volcano, when the rolling slopes are eaten away by runoff, and gorges work themselves inland. The final leg of the loop crosses a footbridge and passes philodendrons with leaves as big as card tables.

Kolekole Beach Park is one of the only inlets along cliffs of the Hamakua Coast. The entrance is hard to spot: Going north on Highway 19 from the Akaka Falls turnoff,

HAWAII TROPICAL BOTANICAL GARDENS, AKAKA FALLS

look to your left immediately at the beginning of a highway bridge. You'll see the county sign for the park. The left-turn can be dangerous in traffic, so you may want to locate it on the way by and hang a U-turn. When coming south on Highway 19, you pass mm15, cross the bridge, and make an immediate right turn. The .25-mile scenic road down the gulch, part of the Old Mamalahoa Highway, passes huge monkeypods. The park's calling-card is a cascade and swimming pool that gets frosted by foam during high surf. If you just came from Akaka Falls, then you may have beaten some of the water down here, as this is where Kolekole Stream ends. A pebble-and-rock beach fronts the rough shore way beneath the highway bridge.

More Stuff: A half-dozen stand-alone forest reserves lie mauka the highway on the Hamakua Coast—above rolling cane fields and below the more-arid shoulders of Mauna Kea. One of the easiest to see is the Kaiwiki Forest Reserve, accessible via Chin Chuck Road. From Highway 19, between mm15 and mm16, turn inland at the pedestrian overpass. Over its 3-mile run to an elevation of 2,000 feet, Chin Chuck Road is no problem for passenger vehicles.

Surf: Although boulders and surf are a dangerous combination, you'll find experienced bodyboarders riding the shore break at **Kolekole Beach Park**. If conditions are right, the ride ends in the park's pool. The better bet for surfers, both boogie and board, is **Hakalau Bay**, the next gulch north. To get there, the best way is to continue north from Kolekole on the old highway—a mini-Hana Highway that crosses several bridges before coming to sleepy Wailea. The road joins Highway 19, at a pedestrian overpass. Cross over the highway and take the .25-mile road down to the bay. Due to private property restrictions, you may have to walk the short distance through a green canyon. A stream cascades over bedrock to a coarse, black-boulder beach.

59. UMAUMA FALLS   HIKE

What's Best: A trio of short hikes lead to a botanical garden, a streamside rain forest, and to an Oscar-winning overlook of a triple-tiered waterfall.

Parking: From Hwy. 19 north of Hilo turn mauka at mm16 on Leopolino Rd. *For World Botanical Gardens office and hike:* Turn right on Old Mamalahoa Hwy. and look for garden offices on your right. *For Stream Rain Forest and Umauma Overlook:* Continue .25-mi past garden office and look for the trailhead on the mauka side, marked by two concrete driveways. *Notes:* All hikes are subject to an admission fee. Offices are closed Sundays.

Scenic route: If you are coming south on Hwy. 19, turn mauka just before reaching mm19 in Ninole. The Old Mamalahoa Hwy. passes jungly Waikaumalo County Park and then takes a lush, 3.5-mile saunter the back way to the garden offices, crossing several streams. If continuing north, remain on this scenic roadway after your visit.

UMAUMA FALLS

Hike: World Botanical Gardens (up to .5-mi.); Stream Rain Forest to Mauna Kea view (1.25 mi., 225 ft.); Umauma Falls Overlook (1 mi., 375 ft.)

Opened in 1995, the **World Botanical Gardens** needs a decade or more of growing to live up to its name, but for now you can admire an ambitious undertaking. Some 300 acres are now home to about 5,000 species. In the lower garden, which they call the Rainbow Walk, you'll find a hedge maze and a Japanese garden, as well as a host of fledgling flowers and shrubs, arranged by species. A drive of about two miles takes you through the upper section of the garden planted with young fruit and nut trees, as well as native Hawaiian species. Part of the price of admission, the road heads uphill across from the garden offices through former cane fields. A sign after .6-mile directs you to turn right to the Umauma Falls Overlook. For the hike along the **Stream Rain Forest to Mauna Kea view**, take the left-bearing concrete drive, called the Rainforest Trail. With Honopueo Stream tumbling nosily by, the paved path curves by ginger, orchids, heliconia, and flowering shrubs that will have flower freaks pointing. After .25-mile, the concrete path ends, but the road continues to a view of the big mountain

To walk to the **Umauma Falls Overlook**, head up the right-bearing concrete drive at the trailhead. You may encounter an auto or two, since most people drive to the overlook as part of the garden tour. After a vigorous walk, you come to the big view, with its railing and potted palms. Umauma could be the cover shot for Glamour Falls magazine. The top falls, set at eye-level up the jungle gorge, tumbles to an upper pool, which flows to a second falls, usually in two ribbons, which flow to a middle pool, and, finally, to the third fall, the climatic act of a satisfying show. *More Stuff:* Brain-diminished trailblazers can attempt to hike, slip, and swim to Umauma Falls by driving about .25-mile past the Rainforest Trail and parking before crossing the narrow bridge. Flash floods can be lethal and you should not attempt this adventure in the rain.

60.   LAUPAHOEHOE BEACH PARK   HIKE

WHAT'S BEST: No hiking trails, surfing waves, or swimming beaches are to be found, but this wild point resonates with scenic beauty and the somber memory of the school children who lost their lives here in the great wave of 1946.

PARKING: Drive south from Honoka'a on Hwy. 19. About .75-mi. after mm28, turn makai at a signed road to Laupahoehoe Point. A one-lane paved road curves a scenic mile to a developed lot at the county park.

HIKE: Laupahoehoe Point Beach Park (up to .75-mi.)

To the right at **Laupahoehoe Point Beach Park** is a beefy wharf and boat launch. On the hill above the ramp is the memorial to the 32 people who were killed, including 21 school children, by a tsunami on the morning of April Fool's Day, 1946. A 35-footer struck, bringing boulders and rocks churning in whitewater. One school teacher, Marsue McGinnis survived by scrambling to the top of the schoolhouse, which became a raft, and then debris that she was able to clutch until she was rescued at sea that evening. One of her four rescuers was Dr. Leabert Fernandez, a man with whom she had scheduled a first date that night. Needless to say, they later married. Rescue efforts were stymied because virtually every craft on the coast had been smashed to bits. "The Day the Sea Went Berserk," locals have named it.

Gardeners groom the spacious lawn dotted with ironwoods and palms that sprawl along the inshore of this wildly beautiful seacoast. The lava stacks and tide pools that fan out to form the point are courtesy of an afterthought eruption of Mauna Kea that sent a zillion cubic yards of pahoehoe down the gulch and into the sea. "Leaf of Lava," the ancients called the new point. Taro grown inland complimented the fishing village, and Laupahoehoe was a respite for traveling kings for centuries.

61.   KALOPA NATIVE FOREST STATE PARK   HIKE

WHAT'S BEST: Aficionados of native Hawaiian trees, here before the Polynesians arrived, will be engrossed by this large forest reserve. Everyone else will enjoy a woodsy hike in a pretty park.

PARKING: *From Kona:* Take Hwy. 19 through Waimea and south, passing the Hwy. 240 junction to Honoka'a and mm42. Turn mauka on signed Kalopa Rd. Following signs, continue to the state park, which is about 2.5 mi. from the highway. *From Hilo:* Head north on Hwy. 19, pass mm39, and turn mauka at Papalele Rd. and a sign for Kalopa. Follow signs up to the state park.

HIKE: Nature Trail and Arboretum Rain Forest (1 mi., 125 ft.); Forest Reserve to: Blue Gum Lane loop (1.5 mi., 200 ft.) or Kalopa Gulch Loop (2.75 mi., 475 ft.)

A hundred, well-kept acres of the **Kalopa Native Forest State Park** adjoin 500 additional acres of the Kalopa Forest Reserve, a union that will satisfy both exercise trekkers and aimless strollers. For the **Nature Trail** and **Arboretum Rain Forest**, pass the campground and keep right as you enter the park. Kalopa's central grounds have immediate curbside appeal, with rolling lawns under towering ohia and koa trees, some with diameters of 4 feet. Showy hibiscus add colorful accents, amid several fern varieties. The **Arboretum Rain Forest** is to the left across the lawn as you face downhill looking at the cabins. Koa is the star of the show, standing at nearly 100 feet after being planted from seed in 1978. About 90 percent of the plants that were on Hawaii before the Polynesian migration grow nowhere else but on Hawaii. To preserve these species, those which grow at 2,000 feet and above, is the main mission of the state park, which was opened in 1967. The **Nature Trail** begins to the right.

For **both Kalopa Forest Reserve** hikes, park near where the road forks left into the campground—look on the left for a Robusta Lane sign that may be obscured by brush. Carry rain gear, as you may get some of the 100 inches that nourish these forests each year. After .25-mile the Robusta path hits the Gulch Rim Trail, where you go right, following the lip of the gulch uphill. Surprisingly, the 200-foot deep gulch owes its formation not primarily to erosion, but to the melting of the glacial ice cap that topped Mauna Kea during the Pleistocene era. **For the Blue Gum Lane loop**, turn right after less than .5-mile on the gulch trail. You cut across .5-mile of some of the reserve's planted trees, which include blue gum eucalyptus, ironwoods, and paperback, with a few silk oak thrown in for good measure. The trail joins the Old Road above the campground; turn right on the road to complete the loop.

For the **Kalopa Gulch Loop**, continue past the Blue Gum Trail, ascending for the next .75 mile, and veering right along the Hanaipoe Gulch to the fenced, top boundary of the forest. You'll pass the Silk Oak Lane on which you could hang a right to loop back on the Old Road to the trailhead. Keep your bird eyes peeled for the 'io, the Hawaiian hawk, and the auku'u, a heron. At the fence line, go right for .25-mile to join the Old Road and turn right to descend for 1.25 miles to the trailhead. The route goes through much of the non-native tree plantings, an erosion control project of the CCC in the 1930s.

More Stuff: If you take a liking to these upland forests, try the Ahualoa Forest Reserve, several hundred acres located near Kalopa. The easiest way to get there is to go north on Highway 19 from Kalopa, past mm42 and the turnoff to Honoka'a. Then turn mauka on Pikake Street. Follow the road uphill, veering left after .25-mile. The one-lane paved road turns to graded-gravel after 1.25 miles and makes a zigzag. The road continues on a gradual uphill and comes to a T-intersection. Turn right and look for unmarked access trails on the left. This area is a trailblazer's special.

LAUPAHOEHOE POINT PARK, HAMAKUA COAST

62.   MANA ROAD-WAIMEA

HIKE

WHAT'S BEST: The old cattle trail contours the pastures several thousand feet above the ocean, in the shadow Mauna Kea which rises an astonishing 10,000 feet higher. Hike in the hoof prints of the paniolos, the Hawaiian cowboys.

PARKING: Take Hwy. 19 east of Waimea, heading toward Hilo. Pass the Hawaiian Homelands office on your left near mm55, and then turn mauka, on Mana Rd. Go left at a T-intersection. Pavement ends after 1.75-mi. *Notes:* Mana Rd. continues for 45 miles to the Mauna Kea Observatory Rd. See TH65. This trailhead covers the first 15 miles, which in decent weather can be driven by intrepid passenger vehicles. If weather blows in during your trip, sound the bugle and retreat. Set your trip odometer when leaving the highway. Even if you're game, Mana Road becomes a bona fide 4WD about midway.

HIKE: Mana Puʻus (up to 3 mi., 300 ft.); Hanaipoe Gulch (up to 5 mi., 850 ft.)

Until a corporate transition took place in recent years, Parker Ranch was the largest privately held cattle ranch in the United States, a quarter-million acres, right here on the Big Island of Hawaii. In the early 1800s, the paniolos were roping doggies, 50 years before their American counterparts. **Mana Road** was the cattle trail, circling around Mauna Kea and across the saddle to Mauna Loa on the Puʻu Oʻo Trail, and then down to ships in Hilo harbor. Mana Road begins at nearly 3,000 feet, over the gentle green contours of the saddle between Mauna Kea and the Kohala Mountains. About 3 miles from the highway you'll reach the first of Mana Road's many unlocked but closed cattle gates. Make sure they're secured after you pass through. To walk the rolling pastures upslope toward the **Mana Road Puʻus**, continue until crossing a cattle guard, after 5 miles into the drive. Roadside fences will be absent and you'll be able to see a trio inland; from right to left they are Puʻu Io, Puʻu Makahalau, and Puʻu Kale, forming a triangle. Now pastoral hillocks, they once spewed Mauna Kea's boiling lava. Look mauka after 6 miles for a dirt tract, or pick your own route.

Okay, giddyup. At 6.3 miles into the drive you'll pass a water tank and power line, on a nice red-dirt route. The pastoral scene continues for another 1.5 miles as you go by

MANA ROAD UNLOCKED GATE

an old farmhouse and reach a hunter's station, about 8 miles into the drive. Wiliwili trees dot rocky slopes, whitish now rather than reddish. After two more gates and some rutted road—14 miles in —you'll reach **Hanaipoe Gulch**. You're standing at 5,000 feet when Mana Road crosses the gulch, and Kalopa Gulch is close by—both of which were carved by the melting ice caps of Mauna Kea eons ago. Two jeep trails lead up the gulch for about 6 miles, to join a goat road that encircles the volcano. Though the terrain is hardly flat as you begin your walk, the grade is tolerable and you can pick your way up. On the mountain slopes above are more than a dozen former lava vents, strewn on the steeper, arid cliffs that jut toward the 13,796-foot summit. Pick your own turnaround. You'll get a faraway vibe after climbing a few hundred feet. *Be Aware*: Have your knapsack prepared and keep a weather-eye peeled.

63.   KILOHANA   HIKE

WHAT'S BEST: If you came to Hawaii for a hike into the hinterlands of Mauna Kea, here's your chance. This road climbs from forest to the highest escarpments. Casual hikers can explore down lower in the birdland forest.

PARKING: From Kona or Waimea, take Hwy. 190 to mm6.25, and turn onto Saddle Rd., Hwy. 200. Pass mm44, and, .5-mi. later, turn mauka toward the Kilohana hunter checking station that sits just above the highway.

HIKE: Pu'u La'au Road (from .25-mi. to 32 mi.)

From an elevation of 5,600 feet at the Kilohana hunter's station, **Pu'u La'au Road**, a.k.a. Skyline Road, climbs gradually, then steeply, on the upper shoulders of Mauna Kea. You can do a drive 'n' hike of greatly varying distances. In good weather, most passenger cars can make it the first 4.25 miles to the ranger station that sits near Pu'u La'au. On the other hand, this lower section of cinder road has the best hike, through the Kaohe Forest Reserve, a dryland Mamane-Iliahi forest that is habitat for native birds. (Birders should watch for the endangered Palila.) So, maybe driving in a mile or two and then walking is the best option.

At the ranger station, the road forks. The left fork, called the Mauna Kea Access Road, takes a hairball, 32-mile circumnavigation of the peak, winding up near Hale Pohaku at the Onizuka Visitors Center. Even in a chunky SUV, the route takes about 5 hours, climbing 3,000 feet. Trekking trailblazers who drive to the old ranger cabin can get a taste of this trail, but prepare for both blazing sun and snow. The road skirts the lower boundary of the scraggly Mauna Kea Forest Reserve.

The right fork at the old ranger cabin heads seriously up, and eventually climbs almost 5,000 feet over a ragged 12 miles. This right fork will give you some exercise, plus spectacular views of Mauna Loa, Hualalai, and Maui on the downward leg. About a mile from the ranger cabin, the road forks; the right fork climbs to about 10,000 feet. The left fork bears toward the observatory stations at Pu'u Pohaku, near the summit.

64. PU'U HULUHULU   HIKE

WHAT'S BEST: It's not just fun to pronounce. This mini-hike in the middle of the saddle offers spectacular vistas and is a smart way to acclimatize to the altitude if you're heading up either Mauna Loa or Mauna Kea.

PARKING: From Kona or Waimea, take Hwy. 190 to mm6.25, and turn onto Saddle Rd., Hwy. 200. Continue to mm28, and, .75-mi. later, pull off to the right at a dirt parking lot and hunter checking station. The trailhead is directly across from the Mauna Kea Observatory Road, a.k.a., John A. Burns Hwy.

HIKE: Pu'u Huluhulu (.75-mi., 200 ft.)

A ten-minute traverse takes you atop Pu'u Huluhulu, a bump almost dead center in the lava-scoured Humu'ula Saddle between the Big Island's big mountains. With its summit above the lava flows of 1843 and 1935, and also beyond the chomping teeth of range cattle, Pu'u Huluhulu has grown into a native tree sanctuary. On top are a picnic area and a few mamane and wiliwili trees, along with other flora. Take the time to do a slow 360-degree spin on this place of geographical significance.

65. MANA ROAD-HUMU'ULA SADDLE   HIKE

WHAT'S BEST: Lush forests reside below Mauna Kea at 7,000 feet, with blue water views and chilly trade winds. If you want a slice of wild nature, here it is. But you'll need a sense of adventure to get there.

PARKING: From either Hilo or Kona, head to the middle of Saddle Rd., Hwy. 200. At mm27.75, turn mauka on John A. Burns Hwy., which is also the Mauna Kea Observatory Rd. Continue 2 mi. and veer right on an unpaved, public road where a sign reads "4-Wheel Drive Recommended."

HIKE: Hakalau National Wildlife Refuge (up to 3 mi., 650 ft.); Dr. David Douglas Monument (.75-mi., 275 ft.)

Mana Road, which is called Keanakolu Road on this side of the mountain, circles for 45 miles around Mauna Kea to Waimea. Passenger cars creeping along in lower gears can navigate all but the middle 5 miles of the unpaved cattle road, *if* wind, rain, or fog are not present, and no big rain storms have created serious ruts or mud. Four-wheel drive vehicles are preferable. The hikes begin 17 miles in from the turnoff, so plan for

3 hours of round-trip driving. The road swerves and dips through the pu'us around the Pu'u O'o Ranch for the first half-dozen miles, but roughly maintains a 6,800-foot elevation. After 16 miles, the road dips down a grade, and you'll find a gate for the **Hakalau National Wildlife Refuge**. Some 7,000 of the refuge's 32,000 acres are open to the public, while the rest are reserved for a half-dozen or more endangered species of birds. Downslope is the Laupahoehoe Natural Area Reserve, 8,000 acres of dense ohia and koa rain forest, thick with ferny undergrowth and washed by several streams.

The **Dr. David Douglas Monument** is about a mile beyond the refuge road, at 17.75 miles in on the dirt road. The famous, yet unfortunate, botanist after whom the Douglas fir is named was inspecting the forest plantings when he fell into a pit, dug to trap wayward cattle. Sadly, the pit was occupied already by a frustrated bull. Some say triple-D was pushed into the pit by escaped Aussie convict Ned Gurney. No sign marks the trailhead. Go downhill across tree-fringed pasturelands to a gate in the Humu'ula Forest Reserve. The monument, erected in 1934, is a short distance after the gate.

66.   MAUNA KEA SUMMIT   HIKE

WHAT'S BEST: What can you say about the top of the world? Scientists and spiritualists can join hands on the sacred summit. Mauna Kea is a high-impact experience that requires some planning, but not too much effort.

PARKING: From either Hilo or Kona, head to the middle of Saddle Rd., Hwy. 200. At mm27.75, turn mauka on John A. Burns Hwy., which is also the Mauna Koa Observatory Rd. Continue 2,500 ft. over 6 mi. on this excellent road to the Onizuka Center for International Astronomy, the visitors center.

Driving Notes: All visitors must stop for 30 to 45 minutes to acclimatize to high altitudes at the visitors center, which sits just below 9,300 ft. The road continues from the center, climbing more than 4,000 ft. over 8 mi. to the summit trail and observatories. The first 5 mi. is unpaved washboard, with grades up to 15 percent. The last 3 miles is paved again. Four-wheel drive is highly recommended—and new regulations may require it. A fleet of companies with 12-passenger tour vans will take you up for varying prices. Among the best, cheapest, and most flexible is Arnott's Lodge; they will also pick you up at the visitors center, if you choose to drive that far. One disadvantage to taking a tour is that they are not allowed visit Lake Waiau and the Mauna Kea Ice Age Natural Area. And, of course, tours maintain their schedule not yours. So, consider renting a four-wheel drive vehicle for the day, which will be cheaper anyway for 2 passengers or more. See *To Four-Wheel or Not To Four-Wheel?* on page 214.

HIKE: Onizuka Center (up to .75-mi.); Mauna Kea Summit and observatories (.75-mi., 225 ft.); Lake Waiau and Mauna Kea Ice (.75-mi., 200 ft.)

Be Aware: Bring warm clothes, as low temps are common. Drink plenty of water before and during your trip. The summit is arid, with clear skies 325 days a year, but it does get snow and high winds. The likelihood of getting sick is perhaps overstated, but you are bound to feel the lack of oxygen from reduced air pressure. Slooooooow down.

Perched at 9,000-plus feet and surrounded by a handful of pu'us, the **Onizuka Center for International Astronomy** is a destination unto itself. Inside you'll find interpretive displays and interactive computers. The volunteer staff is very knowledgeable, although a crush of visitors can leave them with little time for extended queries. Every evening a stargazing telescope is set up, and on weekends, the staff leads a tour to the top—transportation not included. It's all free. The center honors Hawaii's favorite son, Ellison Onizuka, an astronaut killed in the Challenger Space Shuttle disaster of 1986.

The center is where you change into warm clothes and get used to the thin air. At the summit atmospheric pressure is 40 percent less than at sea level. If you want to spend your acclimatizing time walking around, head toward the far end of the parking lot, where the short Hale Pohaku Trail leads to a some rare silversword plants—only two remain, after six plants died when visitors ignored "don't touch" signs. Longer walks in the area lead to the tops of several pu'us, all visible from the center's outside patio. The tallest, at 9,394 feet, is Pu'u Kalepeamoa, which you can get to by crossing the road and veering right, downhill. *Note:* Center hours are from 9 a.m. to 10 p.m. daily. *More Stuff:* Trekkers who want to say they walked all the way to the top of Mauna Kea, by God, can take the summit trail that begins near the center. It leads 16 miles and over 4,000 feet to the top, some of it on the road.

If you're taking a tour to the **Mauna Kea Summit**, be sure to ask if you are allotted the 20 or 30 minutes that it takes to do the hike. If not, consider getting another tour. If you are travelling independently, set your trip odometer, stick it in gear, and proceed. *Note:* You will pass through the Mauna Kea Ice Age on the way. After 7 miles, keep right as the road makes a hairpin right. Chug another mile up a switchback and then keep right again where another road drops down to the Keck and NASA observatories. Just after this junction, park on the left, near the University of Hawaii and United Kingdom buildings. The trail to the summit is over the guardrail, across the street.

MAUNA KEA OBSERVATORIES (L TO R), SUBARU, KECK I, KECK II, NASA INFRARED TELESCOPE

The red-cinder summit trail crosses a little saddle and makes the short climb to Mauna Kea's summit, also called Ka Piko Kaulana o Ka Aina, "The Famous Summit of the Land." A shrine at the top is for Hawaiians to worship at this sacred spot, also known at Wakea's Mountain, the mountain begat by the god of all the heavens. Long before physicists developed modern unified-field theories, the Hawaiians believed all things, living or not, were imbued with a common life force, called mana, that is present everywhere in the here and now. Mauna Kea was not simply heavenly, it *was* heaven. In recent years, Hawaiian groups and their supporters have begun to seek limits to the ever-expanding telescope emplacements on the mountain's crater rims,

MAUNA KEA TRAIL AND SUMMIT

which now number over a dozen, and are heading toward 20. The view from the top is fabulous to the nth degree. Sometimes, a layer of clouds hangs several thousand feet below, making Mauna Loa, Hualalai, and Maui appear like islands in the sky.

Although the **observatories** of Mauna Kea are for working scientists and are not tourist attractions, you are free to roam around. A few observatories will let you inside to take a peek. Try the University of Hawaii telescope at the parking area, from behind which you can also get a view of the 10 or more telescopes that encircle the mountain.

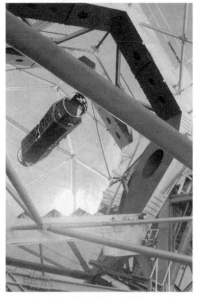

INSIDE KECK I OBSERVATORY

Just up the hill, the Gemini Telescope will wow you with its gigantic retractable roof. To make a driving loop, get in the car heading down and turn right after 100 feet. Proceed to the Keck Observatory, which has two white domes connected by a long building. Enter the left-side dome, where, between 9 a.m. and 4 p.m., you can duck inside to a public alcove to see the intricate and massive workings of the telescope. The shiny dome to the right of the Keck is the NASA Infrared Telescope. Then drive to the right of the Keck to circle around the detour road which takes you by the flat-topped Subaru Telescope, one of the world largest optical telescopes. It is able to observe squeaks of light up to 15 billion light years into the universe. The road continues, passing the Maxwell Telescope and then one operated by the California Institute of Technology.

The 4,000-acre **Mauna Ice Age Natural Area Reserve** boundary is just 1.5 miles up the dirt road from the Onizuka Center. In the recent geologic past, perhaps only 8,000 years ago, a 300-foot thick, 25-square-mile cap of ice covered Mauna Kea, extending down it slopes to within a few thousand feet of sea level. The heart of the reserve is between 6 and 7 miles as you drive up, where you'll see a paved turnout on the right. This area is some-times called Moon Valley, since it was used to simulate the moon's landscape before the Apollo missions—and woo-woo theorists proclaim that photos taken on the moon were actually shot here. Yeah, here and outside of Vegas.

One trail to **Lake Waiau** begins across the street from the turnout. Although it's a short hike, conserve your energy. Resting at the base of Pu'u Poliahu, the milky green lake is thought to be the third highest in the U.S., at 13,020 feet. It's about 10 feet deep, set in a cinder crater and devoid of vegetation. The lake's main claim to fame, however, is that it is fed not by springs or rainfall, but by a gradually melting permafrost beneath Mauna Kea's desert slopes—truly a vestige of the Ice Age. For the ancient Hawaiians, Lake Waiau was the "umbilical cord to the heavens," where birth offerings were made. For certain ceremonies, would-be ali'i would scale Mauna Kea as a test of courage and skill, and bring the sacred water down to coastal villages. Natural resources, such as the lake, were valued as actual embodiments of the gods. The harrowing trek to the summit was also made for more prosaic reasons. Sort of nearby is the Keanakakoi Crater, which was a quarry for basalt that was used for adzes and weapons. Volcanic glass, a black rock very similar to the obsidian, was also gathered in this area—and nowhere else in the Pacific universe that was ancient Hawaii. The old quarry is 700 feet in elevation down from the lake, on the Humu'ula Trail.

BIG ISLAND
Driving Tours

BIG ISLAND DRIVING TOURS

About twice the size of the other Hawaiian Islands combined, the Big Island doesn't surrender its charms to a leisurely day trip. Circling just the perimeter roads is nearly a 300-mile jaunt that only Indy wannabes can make in less than 7 hours without pit stops. The Big Island is like visiting five islands in one, literally. Driving from Hilo to Kona, or from Kohala to Kau, has all the impact of an inter-island flight. Even jaundiced suburbanites can discover the joy of driving. Although traffic is often congested in a 15-mile segment around Kailua-Kona, and to a lesser extent for a few miles south of Hilo, most of the driving will call forth fantasy car commercials. Getting off the scenic highways onto numerous country lanes and byways will be pleasantly lonely. The following three driving tours are designed as day trips for persons staying in the Kona-Kohala area. On all the driving tours, you can cross-reference the trailhead sections for more details.

TOUR ONE: PARKER RANCHLANDS & KOHALA VALLEYS

WHAT'S BEST: The Kohala valleys surrender the scenic wonders most sought by many Hawaii visitors—green chasms laced with waterfalls that open to remote beaches. The high pastures of Parker Ranch around Waimea are soothing to the eyes, and a spittin' image to parts of California's Napa-and-Sonoma wine country. Shoppers and snoopers will love the sugar-town storefronts of Hawi and Kapaʻau, on the north Kohala coast, ideal places to settle in for lunch. Then drive back through sunny western Kohala, with the opportunity to duck in at several history parks and beaches.

DRIVING TIME FROM KONA: 3.5 to 7 hours, depending on stops (165 miles). **ROADS:** Paved state highways. **BEST DAYS:** Any day is okay. Use caution on Hwy. 190, where lack of shoulders and speeding drivers pose hazards. **START TIME:** Start early to avoid the cloud layer that often rises to Waimea later in the day. If you encounter foul weather in Waimea, bail out. Go west and find a sunny beach in South Kohala.

START EARLY FROM KAILUA-KONA, TAKE HWY. 190, PALANI RD., TOWARD WAIMEA

Highway 190—also called the Mamalahoa Highway or Hawaii Belt Road—climbs to about 3,000 feet and opens up to expansive seaward looks toward the south Kohala Coast. On the mauka side, you'll have a sunrise panorama of the Kohala Mountains, Mauna Kea, and Hualalai Volcano. Much of the 38-mile run on Highway 190 is over lava flows from 1859 and earlier, where ohia grasslands are springing to life. A few miles from town (the mile markers click down) you'll enter some of Parker Ranch's quarter-million acres of green pastures. Just a mile from town, on the left, is Puʻuopelu, "the meeting place," John Palmer Parker II's attractive French Provenical homestead. Built in 1862, the homestead houses Impressionist and Chinese art—worth a drive-by, even though it may not be open in the early morning. Next door to Puʻuopelu is Mana Hale, the 150-year-old home of patriarch John Parker Palmer.

IN WAIMEA, GO RIGHT, OR EAST ON HWY. 19. CONTINUE FOR SEVERAL MILES. JUST BEFORE MM52, VEER RIGHT ON OLD MAMALAHOA HWY. (Tour will double back to Waimea)

The old highway, now a country lane, curves on a 10-mile contour through choice ranchlands with blue-water views. At a downhill S-turn that is 3.75 miles from the main highway, look on the right for a reminder that you're on a volcano. Dripping ferns mark the entranceway to a cavern, the result of a collapsed lava tube of an old Mauna Kea eruption. Then you'll pass large eucalyptus groves and the lush Ahualoa Forest Reserve, before the old road rejoins the highway.

MIDMORNING. TURN RIGHT ON HWY. 19. THEN TURN LEFT, NEAR MM42, ON HWY. 240 TOWARD HONOKA'A AND WAIPIO VALLEY

Honoka'a, whose several blocks of storefronts are designated as an official "Main Street USA" town, is a good place to snag another cup of coffee before continuing on. Paniolos made this an Old West town in the cattle heyday, a bawdy image that was furthered by thousands of Marines during WWII who were stationed at nearby Camp Tarawa. Highway 240 passes bucolic fields and ironwood groves before ending at Waipio Valley Lookout. On a nice day, you may be tempted to blow off the driving tour and walk down there. Upon leaving the lookout, you have the option of veering left on Kukuihaele Road, a 2-mile scenic byway that passes the old social hall and sugar shacks.

BACKTRACK ON HWY 240 TO HONOKA'A AND HWY. 19. TURN RIGHT AND RETURN TO WAIMEA

Waimea, which is also called Kamuela to avoid postal confusion with Kauai's town of the same name, had its origins as a company town for Parker Ranch. John Palmer Parker was one of those guys with brains, pluck, and the luck of being in the right place in the right time. After arriving in 1809 from Massachusetts, he jumped ship. Not long afterwards, he married a Hawaiian chiefess and became acquainted with Kamehameha the Great. Parker was handy with a gun and horse, and he was able to help the king in subduing the wild cattle that were ruining the Hawaiians' agricultural lands. This arrangement netted Palmer a small plot of land, that was parlayed in the following years to a ranch larger than any in America.

CAVERN, OLD MAMALAHOA HIGHWAY, PU'UOPELU

'Road' to Waipio, Church Row

Although lacking a central charm, Waimea has several spots of interest. As you enter town, after mm56, pull off to the right on Church Row. You'll find several historic churches, including Buddhist, Baptist, and congregational— a calabash that is Hawaii. Imiola Congregational, at the end of the row, was built in 1855 and features koa and other hardwoods from floor to ceiling. Continuing on the highway, on the left is the shopping center that houses the Parker Ranch Museum, a collection of memorabilia that will delight horse buffs.

AT THE SHOPPING CENTER, TURN RIGHT ON HWY. 19 TOWARD HAWI AND KAWAIHAE

On the left after making this turn you'll see the Waimea Visitors Center—the best in this area—and also the Waimea Nature Park, which has a streamside stroll of the Hawaiian Cultural Garden.

ABOUT 2 MI. FROM WAIMEA, VEER RIGHT ON HWY. 250 TOWARD HAWI ON KOHALA MOUNTAIN RD

SIDE TRIP: Highway 19 continues left at the above junction. Immediately to the left on Highway 19—look for a tall rock wall—is the Kamuela Museum. After many decades, this family operation has changed hands, and may not be open. If it is, you gotta see it. The family has a remarkable collection that reflects their heritage, which includes both John Parker and the Hawaiian ali'i. Son Albert Kehaulani Solomon presides over his parent's collection, which is the embodiment of eclectic.

Highway 250 twists downhill for 20-plus miles through the pastoral Kohala Mountains, with distant sea views that disappear when you enter lovely tunnels of trees, mostly eucalyptus and ironwoods. Those green hills you'll see inland midway on the drive are part of the Pu'u Umi Natural Area Reserve, million-year-old volcanic vents that became the island's first land.

NOON & LUNCH. REACH HAWI AT JUNCTION WITH HWY. 270

The historic sugar mill town of Hawi is a block or so to either side of the junction; Kapa'au, is 2 miles to the east, or right. In Hawi, people flock with good reason to the

POLOLU BEACH, KAMEHAMEHA STATUE IN KAPA'AU

Bamboo Restaurant, but don't overlook the counter at Aunty's Place or the to-go treats at the Kohala Health Foods, both of which are across the street from the Bamboo. In Kapa'au, check out Jen's Kohala Café, across the street the Kohala Town Center, and the Nambu Courtyard, a couple doors down from Jen's. You may regret having only one mouth to devote to lunch in north Kohala. These towns combine to make the one of the Big Island's better runs of shops and galleries. In Hawi, the Bamboo has a gift gallery to explore, and, nearby, As Hawi Turns is crammed with island delights, including locally made crafts. Don't overlook Hawi's back alleys, where you'll fine quirky stuff at the Ungeneral Store.

Window shoppers won't be finished after Hawi. In Kapa'au stop to see the Kamehameha Statue, the famous painted-bronze likeness that was lost at sea near the Falkland Islands on its voyage from Italy, where it was crafted. A new statue had already been re-commissioned for Honolulu when an enterprising sea captain arrived with the original, which he had fished from the drink. The eight-foot, six-inch original giant became an extra, and was erected in Kohala, where the king was born and reared. Across the street from the statue is the Kohala Book Shop, the state's largest used-book collection and the best selection of titles you'll find anywhere on Hawaii and the South Pacific.

AFTERNOON. CONTINUE EAST, TOWARD THE END OF THE ROAD AND POLOLU VAL-LEY LOOKOUT ON HWY. 270

The road east of Kapa'au, about 7 miles long, enters lush tropical forests with a few one-lane bridges. You'll pass the funky Makapala Filipino Camp and the colorful Wo Tong Society Building along the way, both reminders of the island's smorgasbord of cultural heritage. The lazy highway comes to an end where a guardrail marks the Pololu Valley Lookout, a stunning sight.

BACKTRACK ON HWY. 270 TOWARD HAWI. CONTINUE TO KAWAIHAE

Along the 28-mile run from Pololu Valley to the coast at Kawaihae is a transition from rain forest to a grassland desert. The changeover is gradual, since in-between are green former cane fields and pockets of forest. On the way are potential stops at three of Hawaii's best living-history parks. At mm19 is the Old Coast Guard Road to the trailhead for the Kamehameha Birthplace and Mo'okini Heiau. This side trip involves a short coastal hike. Then, well marked to the south near mm14, is Lapakahi State Historical Park, with a drive-up interpretive center. Finally, right at Kawaihae is a national historic park, Pu'ukohola Heiau, a massive structure where Kamehameha finally achieved dominion over all of the Big Island.

SUNSET. AT THE JUNCTION WITH HWY. 19, TURN SOUTH TOWARD KONA

The vast lava fields of South Kohala are never more pleasing to the eye that when the big red Kona sun is rolling into the Pacific. At the north end of this homeward leg you'll have the view inland of the island's memorable ridgeline, with the Kohala Mountains and Mauna Kea rising steeply, and Hualalai and Mauna Loa looming like far off lands. On a highway that is wide and straight, you can kick back and cruise control over a seemingly extraterrestrial landscape. People longing to do magic hour with bare feet on sand will have several easy opportunities. By stopping at after-work time, you'll also avoid the pesky car snarl from the airport south into Kailua. Hapuna Beach State Park is a good choice at the north end of the drive. Midway, Anaeho'omalu Bay will be a quieter curve of sand. Or try Honokohau Harbor or Old Airport Beach State Park. Both are quick pull-offs with plenty of seating available for the sunset show.

TOUR TWO: COFFEE COUNTRY AND KEALAKEKUA BAY

WHAT'S BEST: World-renowned Kona coffee will fuel this half-day trip of tasting rooms, along a green corridor as rich in history as it is in agricultural bounty. With spring in your step, stroll Holualoa, the artist's enclave in the hills. Then drop down to visit Old Hawaiian-style towns of Kealakekua and Captain Cook, with their heritage stores, quirky shops, living museums, and botanical gardens—and coffee tasting. Then, teeth chattering, head down to dramatic Kealakekua Bay, for ocean time (more coffee) and a visit to a national historic park. As a finale, plan for a late-day snorkel and a tropical picnic dinner.

TOUR TIME FROM KAILUA-KONA: 2.5 to 5 hours, depending on stopover time (72 miles). **ROADS**: Paved highways and rural roads, in small towns with moderate traffic. Among the 600 growers in Kona, some 50 have coffee farms and tasting rooms. Keep your eyes peeled for your own discoveries. **BEST DAYS**: Holualoa's streets roll up on Sundays. Try Saturday or any weekday other than Monday, when some attractions are closed. **START TIME**: Since this tour includes stops at businesses and museums, beginning around 10 a.m. will give them a chance to be open.

START MID-MORNING. GO SOUTH FROM KAILUA-KONA ON HWY. 11, PAST HENRY DR., AND TURN MAUKA ON HUALALAI RD.

Hualalai Road ascends about 1,000 feet through 3 miles of gardenscape, before reaching Holualoa. Now an artist's enclave, this rich agricultural zone was home to pre-contact Hawaiian farms. Later, a string of family-owned stores were built. They bartered coffee and other farm products with the passing ships that put in at the small harbors of the Kona Coast. During the late 1800s the sugar industry established its only Kona stronghold here, but it was soon eclipsed by coffee. Don't expect anything too spiffy or commercial. It's easy to miss things driving by. Just before Hualalai reaches the highway, is Blue Sky Coffee Country where you can sip and pick up a bag of beans.

TURN LEFT AT THE JUNCTION OF HUALALAI RD. AND MAMALAHOA HWY. 180. CONTINUE FOR ABOUT 3 MI.

Much of Holualoa's attractions are strung along the road in this direction, including the galleries and old heritage stores. Earlier stores were manned by Europeans, later by Hawaiians and Chinese, and finally by Japanese. About a dozen of the stores still stand along this 3-mile stretch. Among them are the M. Onizuka Store in Keopu, begun in 1933 by the family of Hawaii's beloved astronaut, and K. Komo, which is still open after 80-plus years of operation. Open 24/7, these were mom & pop places, with families living in the back with the pigs, chickens, and gardens. Goods-laden customers would use one of a store's donkeys, called Kona Nightingales, to haul stuff up the mountain, that day's version of "paper-or-plastic?"

The Kona Arts Center is mauka after you make the turn, just north of Holualoa School. Bright pink, you can't miss it. Up the road, on the mauka side past the library, is perhaps the best gallery in the area, Ululani, which features works of resident painter and author Herb Kane. Then, a little farther on the mauka side past the post office, is Holualoa Gallery, another pay-off stop with paintings, glasswork, and Raku ceramics. Studio 7, featuring pottery and a garden room, is on the other side of the road, as is Holualoa Ukulele Gallery, known for fine locally made ukuleles and other collectibles. Nearby is Paul's Place, a mom-and-pop mercantile.

HOLUALOA

Before the junction with Highway 11 you'll have opportunity to bust your mouth on salty-sweet crack seed at Doris' Place, and to take a taste and tour at the estate orchards of the Holualoa Kona Coffee Company, pleasantly set on the hillside.

Although you won't know it from road signs on Highway 11, Kainaliu is the first set of old-style storefronts you'll pass. Look for the Deco Aloha Theater, still playing after all these years. Some two-dozen heritage buildings are scattered on both sides of the road over the next dozen miles, 7 of which are still running after 50 or more years. Fabric lovers will want to stop in to see the collection at H. Kimura, which is located on the makai side just as you get into Kealakekua, just down the highway from Kainaliu.

The oldest structure is the H. N. Greenwell Store, which opened in 1875 and has housed the Kona Historical Society since 1976. Look on the right before mm112, as you're leaving Kealakekua. Henry Nicholas Greenwell brought his gold fortune from California in the late 1800s, and became sort of the father of Kona coffee in 1873, when his Kona brew took home a medal in Vienna. Staffed by helpful docents, the historical society is a good place for a primer on local lore, and features displays, photos, and an excellent book collection. A short walk down the hill from the historical society is Greenwell Farms, where you can sample some java and tour some of the 35-acre orchard and low-tech roasting facility that started it all.

South of these places on the highway, you'll pass Napoʻopoʻo Road, one route down to the bay. Just past Napoʻopoʻo Road (makai at mm110) is one the Big Island's memorable family outings, at the Kona Living History Farm. Although not guaranteed to be open, you'll want to pull into the 7-acre re-creation of the Japanese immigrant coffee and macadamia farm that thrived for about 20 years, beginning in 1925. It's nationally recognized as a historical attraction.

Then, a must stop for anyone interested in Polynesian agricultural life, is Amy B. H. Greenwell Ethnobotanical Garden, located on the mauka side, also near mm110 in

KONA HISTORICAL SOCIETY, DRYING COFFEE BEANS

Captain Cook. Some 15 acres are landscaped in terraces, with the 30 or so plants that the Hawaiian voyagers brought with them. Above the gardens is an example of the Kona Field System, where forests with trees like koa and hau were used in the making of canoes and dwellings.

Past Captain Cook (oops, did you miss the venerable, funky Manago Hotel on the makai side of the highway?) the road enters Honaunau, where shops are less frequent and you'll have views down to the bay. For a highly scenic coffee stop, pull in before mm107 on the makai side at the red Royal Kona Coffee. They have an outside deck, set up with many Kona coffee varieties. Also on the makai side, about a half-mile after Royal Kona, is Super J's, a home-kitchen where you can pick up an authentic plate dinner for later consumption. Look closely, since it's easy to pass by. For a more fruit-and-veggie cuisine, try the Bong Brothers, also on the makai side, after passing mm106. The bros. business is housed in the former T. Kudo Store, circa 1922. Nearby, watch for Coffees 'N Epicuria, with more tasting, but also lots of stuff that will end your quest for gifts. Another hot tip: Just past Epicuria, at Middle Ke'ei Road, is the Kona Coast Macadamia Factory. This low-key place offers deals on big bags of reject nuts, about one-third retail when available, along with fancier varieties.

NEAR MM104, TURN MAKAI ON HWY. 160 TOWARD PU'UHONUA O HONAUNAU NATIONAL PARK. AFTER ABOUT 1 MI., TURN RIGHT ON PAINTED CHURCH RD.

SIDE TRIP: If you continue straight for a few miles, instead of turning right on Highway 160, you'll reach Kealia Ranch Store, home to lots of reasonably priced arts and giftware, as well as the addictive Mauna Kea Icecap, a creamy shave ice concoction. Look for the old ranch buildings on the makai side at mm101.

On wide Highway 160 you leave the Kona commerce behind, beginning a 1,500-foot descent to the Big Island's remarkable bay. Painted Church Road is the scenic route down, where, shortly after making the turn you can stop to see the route's namesake. Established in 1898 as St. Benedict's Catholic Church, it became the Painted Church after the artistic Father John Berchman Velge adorned its wooden walls with tropical-

PAINTED CHURCH, MANINI BEACH PARK

KEALEKEKUA BAY, CREATORS OF MAUNA KEA ICECAP AT KEALIA RANCH STORE

themed Christian murals. The spacious grounds feature breadfruit, Norfolk pines, a garden, as well as a spiritually inspiring view. Speaking of which, check out the panorama at Bay View Farm's tasting room, which is a half-mile past the Painted Church, on the makai side. A coffee gazebo overlooks the farm's rolling orchard and mill, and serves up a big view of Kealakekua Bay along with some choice Kona brew. This place doesn't get crowds, and you'll probably get a chance to chat with owners Roz and Andy. (Nothing like Kona coffee to get the chatter humming.)

CONTINUE, TURN MAKAI ON MIDDLE KE‘EI RD, THEN KEEP LEFT ON NAPO‘OPO‘O RD.

Try to save room for one last shot, since partway down on Napo‘opo‘o Road is Ueshima Coffee Company and the Kona Pacific Farmers Cooperative—a large facility standing alone at a bend in the road. Unless your teeth are floating, stop in to sample Ueshima's top-of-the-line brew, which may well win your taste test. The company processes its own beans (their estate is up on Holualoa Road) and also roasts the bagged bean offerings of some 300 local growers.

CONTINUE DOWN NAPO‘OPO‘O TO A STOP SIGN. TURN RIGHT, CONTINUE A SHORT DISTANCE TO THE KEALAKEKUA BAY HISTORICAL PARK

Across from the stop sign is Napo‘opo‘o Wharf, where you can get out to wave watch and see novice kayakers try to deal with putting in kayaks for the paddle to the Cook Monument. The beach park, just a block to the right, is known for Hikiau Heiau, where the ancients were celebrating the fertility season of Makahiki when Captain Cook's ship sailed into the bay in 1779. The beach isn't much to look at, but the snorkeling is good and the concrete bulkhead is a grandstand to watch the after-school bodyboarders.

BACKTRACK FROM THE PARK, TURN RIGHT ON MANINI BEACH RD.

This little side loop passes an undeveloped park with an exquisite view across the bay toward Kealakekua's famous cliffs. You'll see the white obelisk that is the Cook Monument near the point—not to be confused with the similar-looking lighthouse that is farther west on the point. Coco palms and ironwoods shade picnic tables, providing a perfect place for everyone to get out of the car and kick back.

LOOP OUT TO PU'UHONUA RD. AND TURN RIGHT. AFTER ABOUT 3 MILES, ENTER PU'UHONUA O HONAUNAU NATIONAL HISTORIC PARK

The single-lane paved road along the bayshore crosses an a'a lava field where Kamehameha won a decisive victory at the Battle of Mokuohai, strengthening his reputation as a would-be king. The road widens just before reaching Pu'uhonua O Honaunau National Historic Park. One of the Hawaiian Island's best snorkeling spots is just to the right, before the park's entrance station. Two Step is the local name for the lava benches that lead to the waters of Honaunau Bay. One dip in Two Step and you'll be hooked. Thus refreshed, loop around on the one-way road, and head into the park. Inside are the remains of a former place of refuge, where miscreants and vanquished warriors could sojourn for short periods to escape more severe punishment. Queen Ka'ahumanu, Kamehameha's favorite wife, once did a night here, and you can bet there were two sides to that story. The pretty site was also an enclave for royalty, and features the largest stone wall you'll find in Hawaii.

By now, the sun should be setting in the Pacific, a sight to behold at the Pu'uhonua Beach Park—a spot tourists overlook but a locals' favorite. To get there, take the un-paved road that is to the left at the lower end of the large parking lot. After a short distance you'll reach a line of palms strung along a strip of sand and a lava reef. A coastal trail leads south from the park. Or, take a stroll out to the reef to catch a peek at a turtle, dolphin, or whale, if you're lucky.

FROM PARK ENTRANCE TURN RIGHT ON HWY. 160, WHICH IS KEALA O KEAWE RD. THEN TURN LEFT AT THE JUNCTION WITH HWY. 11 TO RETURN TO KAILUA-KONA

TOUR THREE-HILO HERITAGE COAST

WHAT'S BEST: You won't see the heart and soul of the Big Island until taking a trip to green Hilo. On the way, the Hamakua Coast is cleaved by dozens of stream valleys choked with flora. Tucked away are heritage sugar towns, with blue-water views on open slopes. Hilo's historic old town is host to a huge farm-ers market with exotic fruits and flowers, and an imagination-defying selection of ethnic clothing, jewelry, musical instruments and crafts.

TOUR TIME FROM KAILUA-KONA: 7 to 11 hours, depending on stops and side trips (215 miles). **ROADS:** High speed scenic highways and paved scenic byways. **BEST DAYS:** Try Saturday or Wednesday to see the Hilo Farmers Market. Although the entire market is covered and many other attractions are indoors, bring an umbrella if you have one. Rain walks are part of Hilo, so don't let weather deter your trip. **START TIME:** Arriving in Hilo between 8 a.m. and 9 a.m. is optimum to catch the market on the upswing, which calls for a 6 a.m. departure. In so doing, you leave Kona in no traffic and catch Mauna Kea at sunrise, up high in Waimea.

START VERY EARLY MORNING. TAKE HWY. 19 NORTH FROM KAILUA-KONA TO KAWAIHAE AND TURN MAUKA TOWARD WAIMEA. *Note:* Highway 190 is an alternate, high-country route to Waimea. Highway 19, on the other hand, takes about the same time and is a safer road.

In Waimea you can take a rest stop at the Parker Ranch Shopping Center. Snag breakfast in a bag at a S———k's, or frequent a local joint by driving 11 more miles to Tex's in Honoka'a. It's just off the highway to the left near mm42 on Highway 240. Throw diet to the wind and try the sugary-hot malasada balls. Side-trips and scenic routes are built into the tour's homeward leg, so enjoy the morning and cruise Highway 19 for the remaining 40 miles to downtown Hilo.

MORNING. ARRIVE HILO

With mile-markers winding down to zero, you'll cross the Wailuku River on the steel (singing) bridge. Turn right on Waianuenue Street, and then immediately turn left on Kamehameha Avenue. You'll see a public parking lot that extends for several blocks. To avoid congestions later, you're better off parking and walking a block or two. The market and a walking tour of historic Hilo are described in Trailhead 44 on page 145.

NOON. LUNCH IN HILO

You'll find a number of eateries along main drag and side streets, ranging from the gourmet Café Pesto to rice plates and a burger spa. A better option, particularly in fair weather, is to gather goodies at the market or a snag a take-out plate lunch, and head to one of two parks, both less than a mile away off Kamehameha Avenue. One option is Waiakea Fishpond, at Wailoa River State Recreation, the island's largest lake. Huge trees dot a large lawn sprinkled with picnic tables. The better choice for a noon break is Moku Olu at Queen Liluokalani Gardens. A footbridge leads from near the Japanese-style gardens across to the tiny island, with its palm-lined shore and portrait-quality view across the bay to Hilo. Regardless of your lunch choice, take a swing by this park before leaving Hilo. (See TH47 on page 150 for directions.)

HISTORIC HILO, LILUOKALANI GARDENS

HAWAII TROPICAL BOTANICAL GARDENS, GEPHART'S HAWAIIAN ARTIFACTS

After lunch, you have some choices to make. The scenic route back to Kailua takes about 3 hours; with side trips, you can figure up to 5 hours. So, add those times to what your watch reads as you wistfully contemplate your immediate fate on Moku Olu. If you have time, one sightseeing option is an hour-long trip to see the beach parks that run along the south side of Hilo Bay, outside the breakwater. These are described beginning on page 153. Another choice is to check out touristy Rainbow Falls and Boiling Pots, which are a couple miles above Hilo on the Wailuku River State Park. A third choice, if you have at least two hours to burn, is to head down to the Puna coast, a beautiful region that most tourists miss. That region is described in trailheads 49 through 55. Okay, mull it over. Or don't mull it over, and forget all of the above by sticking with the program, which continues below.

TAKE HWY. 19 NORTH FROM HILO. PASS A SCENIC POINT AND MM4, TURN MAKAI ON NAHALA ST., AND THEN GO LEFT ON KAHOA

This scenic detour passes Honoli'i Beach Park where the east-side surf scene amps up on sunny weekends. You get a great view of it from the stairs that lead down to the beach. Then continue on this side road, past the beach park and over the one-lane bridge. Kahoa Street reaches Kulana Street and then rejoins the highway.

CONTINUE NORTH ON HWY. 19 PAST MM7 AND VEER RIGHT ON THE SCENIC ROUTE, TOWARD ONOMEA BAY.

The Onomea Scenic Drive is a verdant 4 miles that passes through the Hawaii Tropical Botanical Gardens—the Big Island's best. Not far after beginning the drive, look on the right for the modest digs of Hawaiian Artifacts, where artisan Paul Gephart can offer you some bargain-priced hardwood treasures, including rare replicas of ancient weaponry. The botanical gardens are a mile or so farther. Then continue on the old highway and you'll rejoin the main road.

CONTINUE NORTH ON HWY. 19

SIDE TRIP (30 TO 60 MIN.): TO AKAKA FALLS AND HONOMU. AT MM13 TURN MAUKA ON HWY. 220 A 4-mile mauka drive gets you to the short path to Akaka Falls State Park. When tour buses arrive, you may have to elbow your way down the short, paved trail to the 440-foot ribbon of white water. But the green amphitheater is striking, backed by a dense arboretum of tropical trees. Honomu, the little town near the highway, has an appealing historic block that includes a temple and old shops, frequented by locals and not all cutsied up. Check out the homemade buns, plate lunches and made to order shave ice specialties at Aloha Akaka. In the 1940s this quiet village had a raucous air and was known as "Little Chicago." *Note:* After rejoining the highway from Akaka Falls, look for a sneaky left-turn just before reaching the bridge and mm15. This turn takes you down to Kolekole Park where you can snake along the old highway toward Hakalau Bay and come back out to the main highway before mm16.

CONTINUE ON HWY. 19. TURN MAUKA AT MM16 ON LEOPOLINO RD.

Here's another choice 4-mile run of the Old Mamalahoa Highway, twisting through an all-star assortment of tropical greenery over several narrow bridges. You'll pass the World Botanical Gardens, which have some growing to do, but provide entree to the queen bee among scenic cascades, Umauma Falls. The falls are a bit off the main road, as described in TH59 on page 172. Near the end of this segment, the old highway passes the streamside flora of Waikaumalo Park.

CONTINUE ON HWY. 19

Along the green margins of the makai side of the road, near mm24, is the former mill camp of Papaʻaloa, a chance to take a quiet swing by sugar shacks arranged around a central area. Nearby the camp dwellings is the old mercantile, still in business, the Papaʻaloa Store. Then, just a mile farther, past mm25 on mauka side of Highway 19, is Laupahoehoe Train Museum, where you can take a walking tour of the old town. Long before there were roads on the Hamakua Coast, railroad tracks and bridges spanned the deep gulches, carrying freight cars that were filled with donkey-loads of cane destined to satisfy America's sweet tooth. The train museum's grounds include a schoolhouse, former jail and police station, and post office. The railway served 21 stops on the way to Hilo. An authentic mini-train—diesel engine, freight car, and the caboose—are retired on the grounds.

SIDE TRIP (30 MIN.): TO LAUPAHOEHOE POINT BEACH PARK. TURN MAKAI PAST MM27. You'll reap a healthy interest in fond memories by investing a half-hour of your life on a mile-long trip to the Laupahoehoe Point Beach Park. A poignant memorial to the school children and teachers who lost their lives in the giant tsunami on April Fools Day, 1946 is set beside lovely grounds and crashing waves.

CONTINUE ON HWY. 19

KALOPA NATIVE FOREST STATE PARK

The green gulches you see mauka the highway were carved mostly by the ice cap that covered Mauna Kea eons ago. A number of unpaved tracts lurch mauka through the former cane fields to forest reserves that ring the mountain. On the makai side, near mm36, is Pa'auilo, a former plantation town. The field manager's home and workers camp sit above the abandoned mill site. A landing is way farther down, at sea level. If you want to learn more, ask and get an earful at Earl's Snack Shop, which is just mauka the highway, next to the post office.

SIDE TRIP (30 TO 60 MIN.): TO KALOPA NATIVE FOREST STATE PARK. PASS MM39, AND TURN MAUKA AT PAPALELE RD. TURN RIGHT ON KALOPA RD., FOLLOW SIGNS UP TO THE PARK. A 5-mile round-trip ride takes you to the upcountry forest reserve and the groomed grounds of Kalopa Native Forest State Park. Birders, botanists, and campers will award high marks. You won't have to be a tree-hugger to enjoy a stroll around the luscious gardens that surround the park's cabins, set at a refreshing elevation of 2,000 feet. Then roll back down the hill, keeping left on country-road options that will rejoin the highway, slightly north of the road you came up on.

SIDE TRIP (45 TO 60 MIN.): TO WAIPIO VALLEY LOOKOUT. AT MM42, VEER RIGHT ON HWY. 240 TOWARD HONOKA'A. If you won't otherwise see Waipio Valley, it's worth a family squabble to extend the tour to the lookout that would have King Kong pounding his chest. Pick up a tall beverage or ice cream cone in Honoka'a to soothe the 9-mile scenic ride to the end of the road. Waipio is a classic green fissure that gives way to a long beach, once the playground of kings.

CONTINUE ON HWY. 19. PASS MM42 AND PIKAKE ST. NEAR MM43 TURN MAUKA ON MAUNA LOA RD. THEN TURN RIGHT IMMEDIATELY ON OLD MAMALAHOA HWY.

A mellow 11-mile segment of the Old Mamalahoa Highway runs mauka the new road and then rejoins it just east of Waimea. You'll swerve through open ranch country, rolling hills with copses of eucalyptus and cypress trees. This bypass doesn't add much time but, if you're up to your eyeballs with scenic stuff, just stay on Highway 19.

FROM WAIMEA, TAKE EITHER HWY. 190 TO KAILUA, OR STAY ON HWY. 19 TO KAWAIHAE AND THEN GO SOUTH TOWARD KAILUA.

Strategies FOR VISITING THE BIG ISLAND

You can get anywhere on the island in one day, but in some cases it will be a long day of driving with little time for hikes and stops. You'll need an active week to be able to see most of the best stuff. With two weeks, you won't have to choose which featured attractions will have to be postponed until the next trip. A visit of three weeks or more is required to take a thorough gander. Depending on the type of visit you'd like to have, you can choose from among four different strategies for where to stay and for how long.

DESCENDING MAUNA LOA OBSERVATORY ROAD

KONA BEACH HOG

Stay your whole visit in Kailua-Kona or Kohala resorts, choosing from among the modest to the swank. This option takes advantage of beaches and snorkeling. You can easily spend a week exploring beaches from Miloli'i north to Hapuna. On alternating days, take day trips to Hawaii Volcanoes National Park, Mauna Kea, Hilo, Mauna Loa, and Waipio Valley. This may be the best strategy if you only have one week. *Downside:* You won't see much of Hilo and the Puna coast, the island's green windward side, and you will spend a longer time driving.

KONA-HILO YIN-YANG

Stay about half the time in Kona and half the time in Hilo. While in Kona, focus on the Kohala beaches, Kealakekua Bay, North Kohala, and South Point. While in Hilo, see Hamakua and Waipio, Mauna Loa and Mauna Kea, Hawaii Volcanoes, and the Puna coast. As a variant on the yin-yang, rob a day or two from Hilo and stay in Volcano, which is one mile from Hawaii Volcanoes National Park. Seeing sunrises and sunsets at the park is a big plus. You can pull off this strategy during a week's stay, but it is perfect for a 10-day stay, or longer. *Downside:* The west side is normally sunnier and has better beaches.

ISLAND HOPPER

Stay at several spots on a trip around the island. You'll enjoy mornings and evenings in different locales, and spend less time driving. For example, if you have 14 nights, spend the first 3 in Kona, the next 2 in Volcano, then 4 in Hilo, 1 or 2 nights in Waimea, and the last 3 or 4 back in Kona. Island hoppers will also want to consider Wood Valley and Hawi. This strategy makes most sense for longer visits and people who aren't all about beaches. *Downside:* This is a lot of check-ins and checkouts. Two-night minimums are less hectic.

CAMP & INN HOPPER

The Big Island is ideally set up to circle around, spending some nights staying in rustic cabins and campgrounds, and then going modestly upscale in tasteful inns and B&Bs. Money-wise, you can do this for the price of a mid-level resort, or even less. See *Camping and Rustic Lodging* map, for these options. Look at *Where to Stay* to cherry pick among the top inns and B&Bs. *Downside:* Why does there always have to be a downside?

BIG ISLAND *Biking*

KEʻEI VILLAGE

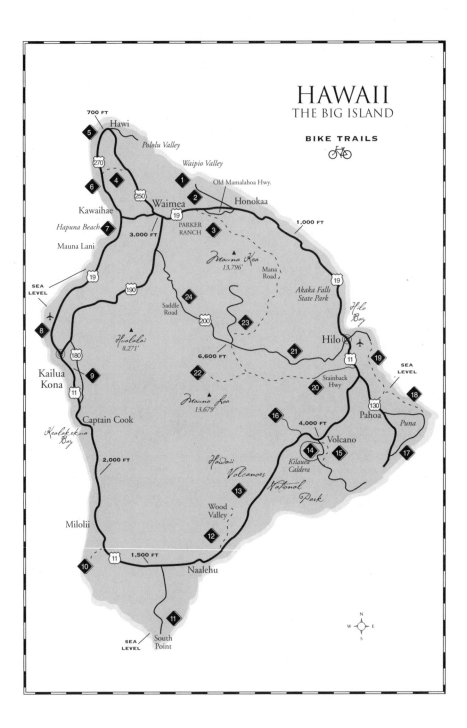

HAWAII
THE BIG ISLAND

BIKE TRAILS

700 FT

Hawi

5

Pololu Valley

270

Waipio Valley

6

4

250

1

Waimea

2

Old Mamalahoa Hwy.

Honokaa

Kawaihae

19

1,000 FT

Hapuna Beach

7

3,000 FT

PARKER RANCH

3

Mauna Lani

Mauna Kea
13,796'

Mana Road

Akaka Falls State Park

SEA LEVEL

19

190

24

Saddle Road

200

23

Hilo Bay

8

Hualalai
8,271'

6,600 FT

21

Hilo

11

19

180

9

22

Stainback Hwy

SEA LEVEL

Kailua Kona

11

Mauna Loa
13,679'

20

18

Captain Cook

Kealakekua Bay

16

4,000 FT

Pahoa

130

Puna

2,000 FT

Hawaii Volcanoes

14

Volcano

15

17

Kilauea Caldera

National Park

13

Milolii

Wood Valley

12

11

1,500 FT

10

Naalehu

11

SEA LEVEL

South Point

N
W · E
S

BIG ISLAND BIKING

Strap a mountain bike to the car and you'll be ready for island routes that will suit a wide-range of bicycling skills. Included are four-wheel drive roads, forested single-tracks, and coastal paths. Or forget the car, and lash the camping gear to the pedaling machine. The Big Island is well suited for hardcore cyclists who can handle some elevation and weather extremes. Cycling among campgrounds, B&Bs, and rustic lodging is very possible for adventure riders who want to muscle-power around the island.

CONSULT THE BIKE MAP FOR LOCATIONS OF THE RIDES LISTED BELOW. IN PARENTHESES ARE THE RIDE'S TOTAL LENGTH, ELEVATION GAIN, THE TYPE OF RIDE, AND THE TYPE OF RIDING SURFACE. PARKING DIRECTIONS ARE GIVEN LAST.

1. WAIPIO VALLEY (5 MI., 500 FT., OUT-AND-BACK, ROUGHLY PAVED)
Rolling down to the famed valley from the lookout is a third option to walking or driving. Ride deep into the valley or head right when you reach the bottom and hit the beach. *Parking:* See TH1, page 31 for driving directions and trail descriptions.

2. MUD LANE (10.75 MI., 2,100 FT. DOWN, CAR-SHUTTLE, UNPAVED ROAD AND SINGLE TRACK)
Ocean views toward Waipio are fantastic as you descend an ironwood-and-eucalyptus forest on a challenging ride. Descend 1.75 miles on a gravel road, and snake down on a twisting single track for another .5-mile—and then keep left at a junction. You'll soon reach Mud Lane, where you go right. Fallen trees and other debris, as well as mud, will test riding skills over the next 2 miles of descent. Then turn right at a junction with the Mauka Cane Haul Road, a paved-potholed road that takes you 5.5 miles to Highway 240. If you miss this junction, Mud Lane continues down for another mile and reaches a private road that takes you to the highway between mm7 and mm8. *Parking:* Take Hwy. 19 east, or toward Hilo, from Waimea. Turn left just before mm52, across from the junction with the Old Mamalahoa Hwy., and park near the golf course. Car-shuttle pick-up is on Hwy. 240, between Honoka'a and Waipio Valley, between mm3 and mm4.

3. MANA ROAD-WAIMEA (UP TO 20 MI., 2,000 FT., OUT-AND-BACK, UNPAVED ROAD)
Pastoral lands with blue-water views are at 3,000 feet, but still about 10,000 feet below looming Mauna Kea. *Parking:* See TH62, page 175 for driving and trail descriptions.

4. PU'UHUE ROAD (5 MI., 1,500 FT. DOWN, CAR-SHUTTLE, DIRT ROAD)
Coast down rolling hills with ocean views, in the heart of cattle country. From Highway 250, a .75-mile paved road leads to a pasture, where you go right past a cattle guard. Maui will rise offshore to enhance the view. Pu'uhue is a downhill thrill that

OLD MAMALAHOA HIGHWAY THROUGH PARKER RANCH

doesn't require a lot of technical skill. *Parking:* Take Hwy. 250 north from Waimea, headed toward Hawi. Look for Puʻuhue Rd. on the left, after mm17. Pick-up at the bottom is on Hwy. 270, headed north from Kawaihae. About .75-mi. after mm17, look mauka for Puʻuhue-Honoipu Rd. A stop sign marks the spot.

5. KING KAMEHAMEHA BIRTHPLACE (5 MI., 150 FT., SEMI-LOOP, UNPAVED ROAD)

This easy coastal pedal along open grassy bluffs takes you by the Kamehameha Birthplace and the Moʻokini Heiau. Using the hiking directions in TH4 as a guide, continue past these two attractions to the Upolu Airport, a fenced landing strip. Pass on the makai side of the airport and then loop around to your right for the return leg. For hardy riders wishing to explore more, the road continues for several miles along the coast to Kepuhu Point, where Hoea Road climbs up to Hawi. *Parking:* Use the driving directions for TH4, page 38.

6. MAHUKONA BEACH KAPAʻA BEACH PARKS (3.75 MI., 300 FT., LOOP, UNPAVED AND PAVED ROAD)

Check out two beach parks that are connected by an old road along a rugged coastline. Lots of village ruins, overgrown by kiawe trees, will be in the area as you make your way north from Mahukona to Kapaʻa. Be sure to hang a left when you reach the paved road to see Kapaʻa Beach Park before pedaling up to the highway to make the return leg. *Parking:* Park near the old mill ruins near the wharf, as described in the *More Stuff* of TH5, page 40.

7. HAPUNA STATE PARK TO MAUNA LANI (6 MI., 200 FT., CAR-SHUTTLE, PAVED AND UNPAVED ROAD)

You start at the state park and take beachside back roads to the grounds of the luxury Mana Lani Resort. From Hapuna, follow Old Puako Road past Beach 69 and keep right on Puako Beach Drive. After 3 miles, you need to head into the last Shoreline Public Access and take a .25-mile connector single-track to Holoholokai Beach Park. Take pavement out from the beach park and keep making rights as you work your way to the resort. *Note:* This ride can be extended for several miles by starting farther north at Spencer Beach Park. From there, take the road south (not the Mau'umae Trail) to the Mauna Kea Hotel. From there, go right on Rockefeller Road and take Kauna'oa Drive to Hapuna. *Parking:* Park near the entrance to Hapuna Beach State Park, as described in TH9, page 52. Pick up is at the Mana Lani, as noted in TH11, page 57.

8. PINETREES AND KEAHOLE PT. (6 MI., LEVEL, OUT-AND-BACK, SAND AND LAVA ROAD)

This is a double out-and-back, as you head north from the beach park to Keahole Point, and then return to head south to Pinetrees. Be prepared to push the wheels through sand sections. This is a wild section of coast leading to historical sites and a popular surfer beach. See TH19 for trail descriptions. *Parking:* Start at the main lot for Wawaloli Beach Park, TH19, page 83.

9. WALUA ROAD (6.5 MI., 600 FT., OUT-AND-BACK, PAVED NEIGHBORHOOD)

Bike path segments connect with a rural neighborhood road that goes through a gardenscape with sea views. Turn around where Walua Road reaches the highway, about 1.5 miles past Kamehameha III Road. *Parking:* Head south on Hwy. 11 from Kailua-Kona and turn mauka on Lako St., just after mm120. Look for the bike path on your right.

10. ROAD TO THE SEA (14 MI., 1,900 FT., OUT-AND-BACK, 4WD ROCKY ROAD)

The bumpy drop to the sea is a Big Island classic, leading to two beaches on a remote section of coast. Bring plenty of water. The ride back up is a leg-burner. You'll see fewer vehicles on weekdays, which is not a good thing if you decide to mooch a ride back up. See the *More Stuff* section of TH30 on page 109 for detailed route descriptions. *Parking:* Head south of Manuka State Park and look mauka for the road at the corner with Shady Grove Farms fruit stand, near mm79.

11. GREEN SANDS BEACH (5 MI., 250 FT., OUT-AND-BACK, ROUGH UNPAVED ROAD)

The blustery and open coastal road to unique Green Sands Beach makes a better bike ride than a hike. Inland are views of Mauna Loa. See TH31, page 118, for a trail description. *Parking:* Take Hwy. 11 south from Kona, pass mm70 and turn right on South Point Rd. Continue 10 mi. and veer left toward Ka Lae.

12. WOOD VALLEY (4.5 MI., 400 FT., LOOP, PAVED AND UNPAVED ROAD)

These flowered rain forests are best seen from the seat of a bicycle. You can take off into the mountains on a network of old cane and forest reserve roads. This place is like an unlisted mountain biking park. *Parking:* See Wood Valley access in Kau Forest Reserve, TH34, page122.

13. AINAPO TRAIL (UP TO 16 MI., 2,800 FT., OUT-AND-BACK, UNPAVED HUNTERS ROAD)

An 8-mile road winds through the pastures of Kapapala Ranch and climbs into indigenous woodlands that are home to the Hawaiian nene and other native birds. Prepare for cool weather and be sure to close gates after passing through. The road ends at the gate for the historic Ainapo Trail. *Parking:* See TH35, Ainapo Trail, for driving directions and more route descriptions.

14. CRATER RIM DRIVE (11 MI., 150 FT., LOOP, MOSTLY PAVED ROAD WITH CARS)

Take the big circle around one of America's most amazing national parks. The trailhead descriptions describe the turnouts and side-trips along the way. Near the beginning of the ride, you can leave the road and take the bike-friendly 2.25-mile section of the Crater Rim Trail. Access is across from the Kilauea Military Camp. *Parking:* Park at the Hawaii Volcanoes National Park Visitors Center, as described in TH36, Kilauea Caldera, page 125.

BEGINNING OF MANA ROAD

15. ESCAPE ROAD (8 MI., 700 FT., OUT-AND-BACK OR LOOP, ROUGH LAVA AND CINDER)

Head partway down the Chain of Craters, enveloped by a lush ohia and tree fern forest. To access Escape Road, go right at the entrance to the Thurston Lava Tube trail and through a gate. You can also access the road outside the park, which will add 1.5 miles to the round-trip ride. The forest gives way to the open lava flows from the 1970s near the end of the ride. You'll come to Mauna Ulu Road, where you can turn right to reach Chain of Craters Road to ride back. *Parking:* See TH36, Kilauea Caldera, page 125. Park at the Thurston Lava Tube lot.

16. MAUNA LOA LOOKOUT (10 MI., 2,600 FT. DOWN, CAR-SHUTTLE, PAVED ROAD)

Make sure the brakes are adjusted and then enjoy the roll down from the 6,700-foot level on the shoulder of Mauna Loa. Views of Kilauea are superb as you pass through lava flows and native forest. *Parking:* See the driving directions for TH39, Mauna Loa Lookout, on page 132.

17. POHOIKI SCENIC COASTAL DRIVE (11 MI., LEVEL, CAR-SHUTTLE, PAVED HIGHWAY)

Ride the bluffs along the Puna coast, as lush a forest as you'll find in the Hawaiian Islands. Traffic is never heavy, but weekdays should be downright sleepy. The road undulates a little, but is basically straight and made for a brisk pedal. *Parking:* See driving directions for Kalapana Lava Bay, TH49, on page 155. Pick-up point is Isaac Hale Beach Park.

18. BEACH ROAD (UP TO 21 MI., LEVEL, OUT-AND-BACK, CINDER AND 4WD DIRT)

This is the best coastal jaunt on the island, through fields of wild orchids and rain forest. Expect to get moist and muddy. Weekdays are best for this route. *Parking:* Head south from Hilo on Hwy. 11 and turn toward Pahoa on Hwy. 130. By-pass Pahoa, keeping left on Hwy. 130. After mm4 turn makai on Kaloli Rd. Continue 4.25 mi. to Beach Road, turn right, and go another 1.25 mi. to road's end.

19. OLD PUNA TRAIL (UP TO 20 MI., 300 FT., OUT-AND-BACK, ROUGH CINDER)

This 1830s tract connects the Puna coast to the Hilo Airport. You'll pass Haena Beach, set in a grove of ironwoods and conifers, and ride through tropical fruit trees and flowers. Weekdays are best, since 4WD fishermen and locals like this route on weekends. It's a tough pedal in places, but improvements are planned to make the ride suitable for beginners. *Parking:* Use the driving directions above, only park when you get to Beach Rd. Go left on Beach Rd., or north, toward Hilo.

20. KULANI TRAILS (UP TO 10 MI., UP TO 900 FT., LOOPS AND OUT-AND-BACK, CINDER ROADS AND SINGLE TRACK)

HAWAII VOLCANOES NATIONAL PARK

Experienced riders will eat up the network of roads and single-track that are part of the Lower Waiakea Forest Reserve. Roots, mud, and tree-debris will keep you on your toes. Ferns and eucalyptus dominate these lush woodlands in this mountain biking haven. Many options available for all levels of rider. *Parking:* Take Hwy. 11 south from Hilo, pass mm4, and turn mauka on Stainback Hwy. Continue 2.5 mi., passing the zoo turnoff. Park at the Waiakea Arboretum on the highway, or turn left, drive in .5-mi., and park at the quarry.

21. WAIAKEA TREE PLANTING ROAD (UP TO 22 MI., 500 FT., OUT-AND-BACK OR CAR SHUTTLE, PACKED LAVA AND CINDER)

While maintaining an undulating contour at an elevation of 3,500 feet, Waiakea Tree Planting Road runs straight over the lava flow of 1852. After 11 miles, the road joins Stainback Highway, coming up from Hilo, making the possibility of a car-shuttle. About midway, the route passes the Waiakea Natural Area Preserve, 640 acres of ohia forest that are rejuvenating after a 1942 flow. Prepare for extreme conditions. *Parking:* Head to Saddle Rd., just west of mm16, which is much closer to the Hilo side. Look for the big turnout on the Mauna Loa side of the road, crossed by a cable.

22. MANA LOA OBSERVATORY (17.5 MI., 4,500 FT. DOWN, CAR-SHUTTLE, POT-HOLE PAVED)

Provided a Good Samaritan will drive you up, this downhill glide looking toward Mauna Kea and Maui is similar to that island's Haleakala ride. Sunrise or sunset will add drama to the panorama, and also avoid the glaring heat over a Marslike terrain of recent a'a flows. Be prepared for cold weather. *Parking:* The observatory road is off the middle of Saddle Rd. See TH43, Mauna Loa Observatory page 138 for directions.

23. MANA ROAD-HUMU'ULA SADDLE (UP TO 45 MI., 4,700 FT. DOWN, CAR-SHUTTLE, UNPAVED CINDER AND DIRT, SOME RUTTED)

A high-elevation ranch road wraps around Mauna Kea, from its arid north slopes, past forest reserves and into the pasturelands of Parker Ranch. It's a roller coaster, with plenty of dips in either direction, though you definitely want to start from this side if you're going to eat the whole thing. Most of the ride is easy, though weather extremes (fog, sun, wind, cold rain) can be a factor. All level riders will enjoy an out-and-back on this end. *Parking:* The route begins on Mauna Kea Observatory Rd., just up from Saddle Rd. See TH65 on page 178 for driving directions and more trail descriptions. Pick up is off Hwy. 19 east of Waimea, as described in TH62 on page 175.

24. KILOHANA (UP TO 30 MI. AND 4,500 FT., OUT-AND-BACK, CINDER-ROCK AND DIRT HUNTER'S ROAD)

Starting at 5,500 feet, Pu'u La'au Road, which is also called Skyline Road, is ready-made for thunder-thighs riders who want to pedal to heaven. These are wild lands, so bring along plenty of water and weather protection. The first part is an easier forest ride that climbs to the ranger station. From there you have options, all of them upward. Kilohana, TH63 on page 177, gives more details. Loose rocks and cinder will be trying going up and require attention on the downhill slide. *Parking:* The trailhead is on the Kona side of Saddle Rd. See TH63 on page 177 for driving directions.

KAPA'A BEACH PARK

Trailblazer
KIDS

Hapuna Beach

In Hawaiian, the word keiki (KAY-kee) means both 'child' and also the green shoot of a new banana plant. Bananas are plants, not trees, and each year a new generation must be nurtured to maturity—just like children in the family. Is there anyplace in the world better suited than the Big Island for keikis to learn while having fun? Volcanoes, dolphin pools, tropical gardens, ancient petroglyphs, tide pools and lagoons, and stargazing are just some of the unforgettable wonders. In addition to the attractions listed below, most of the larger resort hotels have programs especially for kids. Create your own program by selecting from the categories listed below. Remember when you look over each category, trailheads that are close together numerically will be in the same area.

SEE THE VOLCANO HIKES
Halemaumau Crater Overlook, TH36, page 126
Iki Crater-Thurston Lava Tube, TH36 page 128
Pu'u Huluhulu, TH37, page 129
Chain of Craters, bottom, TH37, page 130
Kalapana Lava Bay, TH49, page 155

PETROGLYPHS
Puako Petroglyphs, TH10, page 55
Waikoloa Petroglyph Preserve, TH12, page 60
Kaupulehu Petroglyphs, TH16, page 70
Pu'u Loa Petroglyphs, TH37, page 130

BEACH PARK PICNICS
Keokea Beach Park, TH3, page 37
Holoholokai Beach Park, TH10, page 54
Kekaha Kai Beach Park, TH18, page 73
Pu'uhonua Beach Park, TH27, page 102
Richardson Ocean Park, TH48, page 153
Ahalanui County Park, TH52, page 158
Kolekole Beach Park, TH58, page 170
Laupahoehoe Beach Park, TH60, page 173

MUSEUMS
Eva Parker Woods Museum, TH11, page 57
Onizuka Space Center, TH19, page 84
Hulihe'e Palace, TH22, page 88
Kona Historical Society, DT2, page 190
Volcano Art Center, TH36, page 125
Jaggar Museum, TH36, page 126
Laupahoehoe Train Museum, DT3, page 196
Kamuela Museum, DT1, page 186

KOHALA FOREST RESERVE, DOLPHIN QUEST,
OLD AIRPORT BEACH

KAILUA, VOLCANO, KAHALU'U BEACH PARK

Free Advice and Opinion

FREE ADVICE & OPINION

DISCLAIMER
Think of this book as you would any other piece of outdoor gear. It will help you do what you want to do, but its depends upon you to supply responsible judgment and common sense. The publisher and authors are not responsible for injury, damage, or legal violations that may occur when someone is using this guidebook. Please contact public agencies to familiarize yourself with the most current rules and regulations. Posted signs and changes in trail status determined by public agencies supersede any recommendations in this book. Okay, be careful and go out there and have fun.

HIKING
Never walk downhill with your hands in your pockets ... Wet cowboy bandanas combat the heat... Stay on trails: cliffs, earth cracks, steam vents, loose rocks, collapsed lava tubes, dense foliage, and so forth ... Plan your return time before you start ... Don't get caught in the dark ... Begin mountain hikes early to avoid cloud cover ... Avoid hiking alone, and always let someone know where you're going ... Keep your hiking group together ... Wear sunscreen, hat, and sunglasses ... Lava turns the ground into a grill ... Always take your equipped knapsack on a hike; see *Packlist* ... Flashlights or headlamps are essential gear ...

Carry 2 liters of water per person, per day ... And drink it ... Stash water bottles half-way on out-and-back hikes to avoid having to carry it all ... The Cook Monument hike is a good one for this trick ... Bring your cell phone ... Wear white or bright colors ... Avoid hunter's roads on weekends ... Do not drink stream or pond water ... Don't climb cliffs; rocks are unstable ... If you lose the trail, backtrack immediately ... Don't attempt to make your own loop trail ... It's easier to get lost following rock cairns down a mountain that going up ... Pay attention ...

Don't try to hike out at night if you get lost ... Part of Pele's curse: Don't climb on ancient walls or heiaus ... Use a hiking stick ... Figure out a way to hang snorkeling gear on your knapsack ... Malama i na mea kahiko (Care for things of the past).

VIEWING FLOWING LAVA
All the usuals about sun and footing, plus high winds ... Volcanic fumes contain hydrochloric acid and sulfur dioxide, so don't be downwind ... Stay back about half-mile from the steam plume where lava enters the ocean ... Another reason to stay back is a steam explosion, which sends rocks the size of TVs hurtling through the air ... Stay back 100 yards from lava flowing through vegetated areas ... Methane from burning plants is trapped in underground lava tubes, until it goes kaboom ... Keep your balance at all times when close to flowing lava ... People fall in ... A'a can cut like glass ...The degree of difficulty for lava hikes is triple that of normal hiking on a trail or path ... While you're standing there gawking, that lava stream is moving somewhere, so don't get surrounded by an advancing stream ...

Stay well back from benches along the coast that are at all close to recent flows ... The overhanging benches fall in multi-acre chunks into the surf ... Bring one flashlight per person on night walks to see lava ... A hiking pole will greatly help, especially at night ... Fill up on drinking water and bring plenty with you ... There's no food down there either, usually ... Avoid trekking onto the lava fields in midday ... Stop at the visitors center at Kilauea Caldera to get latest conditions before heading down ... Make a mental offering to Pele before venturing to see the volcano ... And after.

ALTITUDE SICKNESS, A PRIMER BY DR. JOHN BARR

Causes: Can occur above 8,000 feet, due to decreased concentration of oxygen … Rapid ascent and exertion increase your chances of getting sick … *Symptoms:* Generally, a decreased tolerance for physical activity … Minor symptoms include flatus expulsion (yes, farting), sore and dry throat, tunnel vision, and shortness of breath… More severe symptoms include headache, confusion, slurred speech, dizziness and fainting, and difficulty walking … *Prevention and Treatment:* Acclimatize for at least an hour at a high altitude before ascending above 8,000 feet … Drink plenty of fluid before ascending and during your stay … Take aspirin or Tylenol … Move more slowly when at a high altitude … Pressure breathe by inhaling, compressing your diaphragm, then exhaling (you force oxygen to absorb) … Rest or lie down … When symptoms are severe, descend below 5,000 feet immediately.

SNORKELING & SWIMMING

Shore break can knock anybody down … Don't turn your back on waves … Never let children beyond grabbing distance … Bigger surf means increased current … Always float and watch the bottom to see if current is in force … Current will release you offshore … Don't panic and swim against it … Swim with a buddy, or have a buddy watch from the beach … Swim perpendicular to the direction of current … Rip currents go straight offshore through rippled openings in the waves, you can see them from shore … Steep shores mean sudden drop-off and possible undertow … If caught in an undertow, you will pop up on the backside of the wave …

Complex shorelines and surf make for dangerous conditions in Hawaii … If in doubt, stay out … Always ask a lifeguard if one is on duty … Don't step on or grab coral … You'll kill it … To disturb or touch a sea turtle is both impolite and illegal … High waves roll in without high wind or storms … If caught on burning sand in bare feet, scrape off the top few inches to stand on the cooler grains below … Dry your towels by hanging them in rolled-up car windows (also keeps car cooler, hides the inside, and looks "local") … To keep your mask from fogging up you can buy a squirt bottle of defogger, or just spit in it … Fins with heel straps and separate booties mean you have a surf shoe to aid in rocky entries … But booties float your feet …

The entire coast of Hawaii is open to the public … All beaches have public access … Once you get used to snorkeling on clean, pahoehoe lava beaches, you may swear off sand forever … Lack of streams and erosion on the Kona side means gin-clear water. If you want to avoid sharks while swimming, stay out of the water at dawn and dusk, and avoid cloudy, murky water, such as near streams … And, according to local lore, never swim when the wiliwili is blooming … In April.

BIKING

Always wear a helmet … Drink twice as much water in the tropics … Bring water with you in the car … Allow time to adjust to high altitudes … Carry first aid and treat minor scrapes right away … Take extra care not to get lost in remote areas … Bring a spare tube and a repair kit … You ain't had road rash until you fall on a lava road … Bikes are permitted on all highways, and most roads have extra shoulder width … But watch out on Highway 11 south from Honaunau and especially watch out on Highway 190 from Kailua to Waimea: dangerous and no shoulders … Highway 19 north to Kohala has nice wide shoulders.

DRIVING

Drive aloha … Allow turns and merges … Watch for pedestrians and cyclists … Don't leave valuables in the car … Never move valuables to the trunk while at a parking space … Vandals know they shouldn't rip off local cars: Put a bumper sticker in the back window, or a local newspaper; hang beads or a lei from your rearview mirror … Broken glass at a parking space indicates a prior break in … Generally, you are very safe parking on the Big Island … Parking directions for trailheads will indicate a less-safe spot … Road maps left out on the dash say, "I'm a tourist" … Be prepared for Nene Crossings, Banana Virus Areas, and Donkey Zones …

Watch out for speeders on mountain roads … Driving will be your most-dangerous activity, statistically speaking … Highway 11 north of Kona has long turn and merge lanes; don't use them for passing … Set the cruise control and mellow out … Make sure to pull safely off the road when sightseeing … You meet people by asking directions … Drive with your low-beams on … Carry towelettes (baby wipes) for instant refreshment … Carry drinking water and food along for the ride since finding either can be very inconvenient.

TO FOUR-WHEEL OR NOT TO FOUR-WHEEL?

Steep roads to two major attractions require four-wheel drive vehicles: The last 8-miles from the visitors center to the top of Mauna Kea, and the 1.5 miles from the Waipio Valley Lookout to the beach and valley below. To see these attractions (and you should) without driving, you can sign on for a tour to Mauna Kea, and you can walk down to Waipio Valley. You can also rent a four-wheel drive from an appropriate company for a day or two, which will be cheaper than a tour for two or more people. Plenty of other roads require four-wheel capability, but you'll be able to see all other major attractions without having one.

Aside from road quality, the big issue is the policies of car rental agencies. The Big Island is peculiar in that driving on State Highway 200, a.k.a. Saddle Road, is prohibited by most car rental companies, even though it is perfectly passable in a passenger vehicle. This road provides access to the visitors center at Mauna Kea, the highest trailhead at Mauna Loa, as well as several other hiking trails. Therefore, renting a four-wheel drive from one of these agencies doesn't solve the problem.

HERE ARE YOUR CHOICES: 1. Call your insurance company before booking a car to see if you will be covered on this state highway, even though it is restricted by your car rental agency. Full coverage often will pick up the voids in rental car coverage. If you're covered, you can then drive a four-wheel to the top of Mauna Kea and Waipio Valley, as well as the other trails on Saddle Road. 2. Rent a four-wheel drive for the entire trip or specific days from Harper, which allows driving on Saddle Road, to Mauna Kea, and to Waipio Valley. 3. Rent from the limited stock at Aloha Car Sales, which allows driving on Saddle Road, but does not have four-wheel drive vehicles. 4. As suggested above, book a tour to Mauna Kea and walk to Waipio Valley, and forget about the other trailheads on Saddle Road.

Saddle Road is paved all the way, although on the Kona side the surface is not as good as the Hilo side. On the Kona side, people tend to drive down the center of the road, rather than use the actual lanes, since the outside of the road is a hodge-podge of patches. Shoulders don't exist in most places, but speeding drivers are the road's main hazard. Let 'em by.

BIG ISLAND *Calabash*

A CALABASH, OR GOURD, WAS USED IN ANCIENT TIMES AS A WATER VESSEL. IN HAWAII TODAY,
THE CALABASH IS A GROUP OF FRIENDS, LIKE FAMILY, THOUGH NOT BLOOD-RELATED.

VOLCANOES

Hawaiian volcanoes result from billions of tons molten magma roiling into the sea from the Hot Spot, a crack in the earth's crust in the middle of the Pacific. Very fluid magma (see *Lava* below) piles up and eventually breaks the ocean surface and continues to pile up thousands of feet above sea level. These are called "shield" volcanoes, because as seen on the horizon this gentle piling up of lava looks like the profile of a shield. The Hawaiian volcanoes differ from other volcanoes in the Pacific's "Ring of Fire," such at Mt. Fuji and Mt. St. Helens, which are called "composite" or "strato" volcanoes. These are formed by friction between tectonic plates grinding together to melt rocks. Strato volcanoes produce viscous lava and violent eruptions.

Most experts say the Big Island is comprised of five volcanoes whose flows have joined them together—Mauna Loa, Mauna Kea, Hualalai, Kilauea, and Kohala. Others say six volcanoes, and include Ninole, which is on the southeast coast. Another volcano, Loihi, is in its submarine stage, erupting 20 miles offshore Hawaii's southeast coast. Several thousand feet under the surface, its coming-out party is scheduled about 10,000 years from now. Since 1983, about 700 acres of new land have been added to the Big Island by Kilauea's Pu'u O'o eruption.

Recent observations show the swelling of Mauna Loa's surface to be related to subsequent eruptions on Kilauea, indicating that the underground plumbing of Kilauea and Mauna Loa may be related. Three volcanoes are active: Kilauea, which has been erupting since 1983; Mauna Loa, which sent lava to within four miles of Hilo in 1984; and Hualalai, whose most recent eruption was in the early 1800s. All these volcanoes don't erupt from a single crater, but along rift zones that themselves have a series of cones or vents that release lava. On Hawaii there are many dozens of these vents, each called a pu'u (poo-oo).

The life of a Hawaiian Volcano has six stages, most of which are occurring today on the Big Island. Loihi is in the submarine stage, and headed toward the second, emergent stage, when steam blows sky-high but no dry land is present. The third stage is the shield building, when frequent eruptions occur on rift zones, such as is occurring on Mauna Loa and Kilauea. The fourth stage, only recently discovered, is the giant landslide phase, when up to one-third of a shield volcano can slide into the sea. Scientists speculate Kilauea has this to look forward to. Mauna Kea is an example of the fifth stage, the capping phase, when viscous lava covers and stops flows. The erosional stage comes next, as evidenced in Kohala, where streams carve valleys and canyons, and ocean waves produce sea cliffs. A renewed volcanism phase can follow, like on Maui's Haleakala, where activity can begin again after eons of dormancy. The final destiny for Hawaiian volcanoes is the atoll stage. Moving northwest along with the earth's crust, the volcanoes wear down to sea level and coral reefs grow, forming a low island with a lagoon in the middle. An example is the Kure Atoll that is 1,500 miles northwest of the Big Island.

LAVA

Magma, the molten rock that is at the core and below the crust of the earth, is called lava when it reaches the surface. Magma that cools beneath the earth's surface is called igneous rock, such as basalt and granite. Worldwide, Hawaiian names are used to classify lava into two types, which are very different looking but have basically the same chemical composition. Hawaiian lava is more than half silicon and aluminum oxides, about one-quarter iron and magnesium oxides, and also has small amounts sodium and potassium. The result is usually a dark red or brown color, although fresh-cooled lava is often black, with a gleaming, oily surface.

Hawaiian lava also contains lots of gas that is driven into the atmosphere during cooling. Most of the gas is harmless: Two-thirds is steam, or water. About 13 percent of the trapped gas is carbon dioxide, and some 8 percent is nitrogen. The stuff that kills you is the 9 percent sulfur dioxide and the 1 percent carbon monoxide. The markedly different physical characteristics between the two types of lava result from gas content and cooling rate. Surface temperatures of lava range from about 1,800- to 2,200-degrees Fahrenheit. Toss a rock on hot lava and it will melt. The two types of lava are:

A'A (*ah-ah*) erupts and cools in rough, jagged piles. Walking across this stuff is a nightmare. (Remember: "Oh-oh, it's a'a.") A'a lava contains more gas and cools faster. It flows in jumbled, clinking, and crumbling piles, and has no sheen on its surface.

PAHOEHOE (*pa-hoy-hoy*) erupts and cools in smooth streams and ribbony waves. Although collapsed lava tubes can be a hazard, walking over these surfaces is generally safe and easy. (Remember: "Oh boy, it's pahoehoe.") Pahoehoe contains less gas and cools more slowly. It flows in ropy sheets and bulging drips, looking like thick cake batter. The surface of fast-moving pahoehoe streams often cools and hardens while a subsurface stream continues. When the eruption stops, or shifts in direction, the subsurface stream drains, leaving a hollow tube, or long cave. The ceiling of tubes near the surface will often collapse. The entire mass of Hawaii is riddled with tubes and cracks.

TSUNAMI

Often mistakenly called tidal waves, the deadly tsunamis have no relation to waves that are generated by the rise and fall of the tide, or with hurricane-generated high seas that come ashore with great force. "Tsunami," a Japanese word meaning "harbor wave," refers to a series of waves traveling across the ocean with very long wavelengths, up to 100 miles between crests. In the open sea, a tsunami wouldn't upset your drink, since the wave's height is a few feet or less. When approaching shallow waters near land, the wave's speed decreases and its size drastically increases, rearing up to an ugly 30- to 50-foot wall of water that carries boulders and sea debris with it in a destructive assault on the coastline.

Oceanographers say tsunamis are the result of a sudden rise or fall of the earth's crust on the ocean floor, such as an earthquake, landslide, or volcanic eruption. Hilo is known as the tsunami capital of the world, with 13 of the monsters coming ashore in the 20th century. In 1946 and 1960, behemoth waves wiped out coastal communities and killed more than a hundred people. The 1960 wave, generated by an earthquake in Chili, traveled 10,000 miles to Japan at 500 miles an hour, and struck with enough force to kill 150 people. In Hawaii, these tragedies have led to the establishment of a detection and warning system, as well as new coastal building codes, that safeguard against fatalities.

Unfortunately, regional tsunamis can be generated by local earthquakes, of which the Big Island has a hundred or more yearly. Most quakes don't make waves, but the ones that do strike before a warning can be issued. In November of 1975, an earthquake dropped a miles-long section of coastal bluff some 10 feet at Hawaii Volcanoes National Park, generating a wave that swept 32 campers into the sea, two of whom didn't make it back. Don't put this high on your things to worry about, but if you do experience a trembler at the beach, head to high ground pronto.

ANCHIALINE PONDS

To nature's subtleties that are peculiar to the Big Island, add anchialine ponds, which you'll find primarily on the North Kona-South Kohala coast, as well as on the Puna coast. What these coastlines have in common is a lack of streams, since the land is so new that rain has not yet eroded the surface into valleys. The mauka showers percolate down through the porous lava slopes of Mauna Loa, creating a vast aquifer that sits at about sea level under the mountain.

At coastal depressions, this fresh water daylights, creating little ponds that were crucial for survival for the ancients, used for drinking water, agriculture, and raising fish. At some locales, such as the fishponds at the Mauna Lani, canals with fish gates were dug to enhance nature's handiwork. At many other places, like the ponds near the Hilton at Anaeho'omalu, the ponds are unaltered. The ponds are always brackish, more so at high tide when underground sea water intrudes, and less so farther ashore and after heavy rains, when freshwater percolates in greater volume. So, don't bother looking for inlets or outlets for these little lakes. There are none, above ground anyway.

PETROGLYPHS

Of the 150 known petroglyph sites in the state, most are on the Big Island—due to its size, availability of smooth pahoehoe lava on which most pictures are etched, and the fact that foliage has not had time to overgrow the fields. The rock carvings, called ki'i pohaku in Hawaiian, are a combination of a newspaper, diary, and mural. The etchings span centuries. A few are a mystery, made by artisans before the Polynesian migrations. Most depict events during the 1,000- to 1,500-year period before Western culture arrived in the late 1700s. But many are post-contact, depicting such things as whalers and horseback riders.

Petroglyphs are best viewed during the morning and late afternoon hours, when slanting light casts shadows that highlight the indentations in the rock. Photographers should stand with the sun at their backs. Many ki'i pohaku are in remote locations, but several fields are marked and easily accessed. Some of the best are the Puako Petroglyphs at Holoholokai Beach Park, the Kulia Petroglyphs at the Mana Lani, the Waikoloa Petroglyph Preserve, the Kaupulehu Petroglyphs at the Kona Village, and the Pu'u Loa Petroglyphs off Chain of Craters Road. One vast site harder to get to is the Pu'u Ki Petroglyph field in Ocean View. (All sites are referenced in the index.)

When viewing a field, note that the oldest drawings are usually clustered in the center, and the most recent efforts are on the periphery. The exact story told by many of these etchings will never be known, but others, such as sails, fishermen, paddlers, and surfers are less obscure. Circles with dots are thought to commemorate the birth of boys, while semi-circles with dots denote girls' births. Avoid stepping on petroglyphs.

KAMEHAMEHA THE GREAT

A fair number of history's heavy hitters have earned the title "great," but if you lined them all up in some kind of pageant that measured composite skills, the smart money would be on Hawaii's

Kamehameha to be a favorite to take home the top prize. To clone a replica of this man, the first ruling monarch of the Hawaiian Islands, start with a religious leader with the clout of the Pope or Dali Lama, add the political savvy and charisma of JFK or MLK, throw in the quick hands and wit of Muhammad Ali, blend the athletic gift for winning and timing possessed by Joe Montana—and then pump it all up to a package with the size to push around Shaquille O'Neal, that is, north of seven-feet and around 400 pounds. This is the guy, Kamehameha the Great, whose bodily gifts were matched by a peculiar convergence of historical events.

Intrigue clouded his birth. He had been slated as a future king by his uncle, the Big Island's Chief Kalaniopu'u, but another chief in Hilo had other plans, and had vowed to slay the infant. To save the baby's life, Kamehameha's mother was secreted away to a forlorn, windswept spot in north Kohala. The birth took place in 1758, a date later confirmed by the passing of Haley's Comet. Kamehameha spent his youth in hiding but hardly in hardship, since much of his time was spent frolicking on his surfboard and with the wahines of Waipio Valley.

His training for leadership began early also. A famous warrior from Napo'opo'o in Kealakekua Bay, named Kekuhaupio, was enlisted to train the boy. Even as a youth he towered over his five-foot-eight mentor, but it would be years before he matched his teacher's skills. Kamehameha learned the Hawaiian martial art of the lua, and as a teenager he was a one-man army—able to catch spears thrown at him and artfully deploy his ikoi, a type of bolo that would bring down a running man. He mastered the wrestling art of "bone-breaking," for which the lua is renowned. The Hawaiians had no metal weapons or complex armaments, but they may have been the most fearsome hand-to-hand combatants the world has ever seen. Their skills were matched by tremendous size: Bone records indicate some ancient warriors were closer to eight feet than seven. In his day, Kamehameha was a standout. As a graduation test, he had to jump off an outrigger with a pointed stick and kill a large tiger shark.

At age 20, he and Keuhaupio were on the fringes of a great battle in Maui, the battle of the Sand Hills, at which the Big Island's army ignored the advice of the kahunas and were killed in great numbers. Kamehameha and his mentor defeated a small army of Maui warriors in the nearby village of Olowalu. Then, as they retreated from this foray, offshore they sighted the towering white sails of the *Endeavor*, the ship of British Captain James Cook. Coincidentally, Cook had returned to the islands after making the first contact with Hawaii a year earlier, 300 miles north in Kauai. Kamehameha and Keuhaupio decided to approach and board this alien vessel.

Three days later, as the people of the Big Island lamented the loss of their young warrior to this bizarre visitation, Kamehameha and his mentor appeared. The young warrior, beaming, was stuffed into a red British officer's jacket. Far from being fearful, Kamehameha had seen at once that the apparition that was Western contact was an opportunity for his future. He had seen steel and iron, and to a Hawaiian warrior these were like assault rifles.

In the next few months, Cook was to land in Kealakekua Bay during the peace-and-fertility festival of Makahiki. The British captain was heralded as the god Lono—only to be bludgeoned to death on the bay's shores just weeks later in a scuffle over a stolen dory. Western ships would not return to the islands for six years.

In 1780, based on his exploits thus far—and his ability to move the mammoth, ceremonial Pohaku Naha stone—Kamehameha was commissioned with custody of the war god, Kukailimoku, by his uncle, Chief Kalaniopu'u. The chief's son, Kiwalao, received land. Though ultimately wise, the chief's decision stirred enmity, both between his son and Kamehameha, and among other island chiefs. This bad-blood rose to a full-scale battle when the Chief Kalaniopu'u died. In 1782, Kiwalao and other chiefs, met Kamehameha and his forces, along with Keuhaupio, in the Battle of Mokuohai, near Napo'opo'o. Using superior knowledge of the terrain, Kamehameha prevailed against a larger force and his legend ramped up a notch. He was 24.

By 1785, Western ships had begun stopping in the islands to provision for trading journeys to China. Conflicts arose, one of which resulted in the massacre of scores of villagers on Maui in 1790. As revenge, and also for his own personal gain, Kamehameha's warriors captured a vessel, the *Fair American*, offshore the Big Island. Conscripting two of the ship's officers as aides, Kamehameha sailed the *Fair American* to Maui. Using the ship's cannon, he routed the forces of the Maui Chief Kahekili's son, Kalanikupule, in the famous battle of the Iao Valley. The bodies of fallen warriors were said to dam the stream and turn its waters red.

A year later, upon the advice of his kahunas, Kamehameha built Pu'ukohola Heiau in Kawaihae, laboring alongside the workers to complete the task. Then, Kamehameha's cousin from the Hilo side Keoua, was invited to an opening ceremony. Keoua also had been groomed as a youth to be king, by the same branch of the family who conspired to kill Kamehameha at birth. Upon Keoua's arrival, a skirmish ensued—perhaps a planned subterfuge—and the cousin was killed. Although later that year he had to defend the island from invaders from Maui and Oahu, Kamehameha's control over the Big Island was now unquestioned.

Kamehameha did not attack Maui until 1794, after the death of its Chief Kahekili, a man who claimed to be Kamehemeha's father. (The intrigue among the ali'i is Shakespearean.) The following year, his forces took Oahu. A year later, in 1796, a huge storm thwarted his invasion of Kauai. To prepare for another invasion that would bring all of Hawaii under his rule, Kamehameha and his sprawling retinue went to Lahaina on Maui, where a fleet of 1,000 war canoes was constructed, and where the young leader also reacquainted himself with life's pleasures, such as surfing and cavorting. Once again using conscripted Westerners, he built himself a brick palace. Showing his humility, he labored in his gardens alongside the commoners.

In 1804, another attempt to invade Kauai failed, this time due to disease brought by Europeans that depleted his army. By this time, Honolulu, the only deep-water port in the islands, was frequented by Western ships, and Kamehameha moved the capital to that village in order to better control trading. Not a squealing pig was traded for a single nail without the great man's approval. In 1810, Kamehameha and Kauai's Chief Kaumuali'i entered into a treaty that gained Kamehameha control over all the islands as the first Hawaiian monarch. Both men could see that the Hawaiian people were dying in great numbers due to new diseases, and that the Western sailing ships were arriving in great numbers.

In 1812, the 44-year-old king returned to his Big Island home, and made Kailua the capital of Hawaii. He appointed governors for all the islands' major land areas, and supervised the sandalwood trade with ships bound for China. (The fragrant sandalwood was Hawaii's first cash crop, but the forests were denuded within a decade.) Kamehameha's heir, Liholiho was educated in Kona, and his youngest boy, later Kamehameha III, was born in 1814. In nearby villages, Kamehameha built huge fishponds that were a marvel to Western visitors.

In May of 1819, the great king died, and his remains were spirited away to a location that remains a mystery to this day. Liholiho became Kamehameha II, and, at the urging of his mother, Queen Keopuolani, and Kamehameha's favorite wife Queen Kaʻahumanu, he immediately abolished the kapu system that had treated women unfairly. Liholiho struggled with not only trying to fill his father's huge sandals, but also with the onslaught of Western culture. Change came in the same year of his father's death, in the form of missionaries and whaling ships. While on a trip to London to further educate himself on these matters, Kamehameha II died in 1824.

The rule of the islands was left to Kamehameha III, then only 11 years old. The queen mothers stood watch over the boy until he matured into Hawaii's longest-ruling monarch. He died in 1854. The native population diminished from some 800,000 people to around 60,000 during the 70 years of European and American contact. In an effort to adapt, the royal family embraced Western religion, and established the best school system west of the Rocky Mountains. The literacy rate was among the nation's highest after only a few years, although the Hawaiians previously had no written language. The Hawaiian nation was able to withstand the raucous whalers and traders, but the emergence of the sugar cane industry in the late 1800s, to make a long story short, was to do in the monarchy. Hawaii was annexed as an U.S. Territory in 1893.

PELE

If the Big Island is this planet's giant wedding cake, then Madame Pele, the Goddess of Volcanoes, is the bride standing on top—all by her lonesome. She is the maternal goddess of lust, impetuousness, and violence to be respected and feared—Pele, the "woman who devours the land," while at the same time adding new land to the earth.

Legends say Pele's first Hawaiian home was the little island of Niʻihau off the northwest coast of Kauai, but the volcano goddesses' sister, Namakaokahi, the goddess of the sea, was angry and caused her to move. Over the millennia, move she did, first to Kauai, then Diamond Head Oahu, followed by Molokai and then Maui. But each time the sea goddess put a damper on things, causing Pele to move—until she found her present home, in the Halemaumau Crater in the Kilauea Volcano on the Big Island. Here she resides with her fiery sisters, each called Hiʻiaka. From the look of things, both scientists and kahunas agree that Pele isn't going anywhere for a long time. (The ancient legend of Pele's travels mirrors the geophysical observations made by contemporary science.)

There are many legends and curses surrounding the volcano goddess. Tourists think they're quaint stories. Locals think differently. In 1801, Kamehameha the Great, who was not known for being hen-pecked by any of his 20-plus wives, went to his knees with offerings to save a Kona village from a Hualalai eruption. Prayer answered. In 1881, same story with Princess Ruth Keʻelikolani, who traveled from Honolulu to Hilo to divert a Mauna Loa flow. In 1960, the Cape Kumukahi Lighthouse survived an east-rift eruption days after the keeper gave food to a hungry, lone woman (a typical Pele incarnation). The nearby village of Kapoho, which had turned the woman away, was destroyed. On March 30 of 1984, many observers saw a fireball shoot across the sky between Kilauea and Mauna Loa, a white streak that the ancients call a popoahi, which Pele issues to announce an eruption. Following the popoahi came the first dual blast from these two volcanoes in more than 130 years. Today, Pele is revered at yearly fetes, including the Merrie Monarch and Aloha festivals, as well as by daily offerings left at Halemaumau Crater.

Pele's existence will never be proven, but you cannot be on the Big Island for long without feeling her presence. Sometimes, she does appear, taking different forms, such as that of a shapely young woman with coils of dark hair, or, more commonly, a gin-swilling gray-haired tutu (old woman), often walking lonely trails on the mountains or seacoast. If you see someone who meets that description, play it safe and be nice. If you see her hitchhiking, pick her up.

Scores of tourist scoff at the notion of Pele, and break the curse against taking lava rocks, or na pohaku, home for souvenirs. Ha, ha, they think, only to be inundated with a run of bad luck. Should this happen to you, or any of your loved ones, know that Pele may forgive you. Each month, on the first Wednesday at high noon, a ceremony is held on the grounds of the Outrigger Waikoloa Beach resort, where, in an area called a Hoaka Ho'omalu, the rocks are placed in a shrine, called an ahu paepae. You can ship your ill-gotten souvenir to the resort (which gathers all such stones from around the island) and it will be added to the shrine and returned to Pele via a piko, or navel, which travels to the surrounding mountains. Laugh if you dare.

COFFEE

Kona coffee worshipers can thank Kamehameha's interpreter, Don Francisco de Paula y Marin, who planted the first scraggly tree nearly 200 years ago. Homage must also be paid to Reverend Samuel Ruggles whose arabica-bean orchards took hold in 1828, and to Henry Nicholas Greenwell, whose Kona blend took a medal in Vienna in 1873. But to give credit where credit is due, 600 small-time growers and small companies that comprise today's market also must be honored. When the world coffee market crashed in 1899, coffee orchards were sold off in 3- to 5-acre parcels, many to Japanese and later to Hawaiians, Chinese, Filipinos, and growers from the mainland. The backbone of today's Kona coffee industry remains this calabash of smaller growers.

In the spring, coffee trees (technically bushes) issue white flowers called Kona snow, which aromatically reveal the tree's relation to the gardenia flower. The flowers give way to red berries, called cherries, that are picked by hand. It takes seven pounds of cherries to make one pound of ground coffee. Top pickers can snare about 300 pounds of cherries a day, or, if you do the math, several cherries per second over the course of an 8-hour day. After being picked, the cherries are rolled and washed, separating the beans from their red husk and a whitish pulp that is underneath it. Then, most beans are dried the old-fashioned way, by spreading them out in the sun for about a week and raking periodically. Roller dryers are also used. The dried beans are called parchment.

Not yet roasted, the beans are sorted into grades. About one-fifth make the top grade, Kona Extra Fancy, which has two flat seeds. About a third of the parchment is bagged as Kona Fancy, and another third as Kona Number One, the third-best grade. Ten percent of the coffee is Kona Prime (apparently there is no Kona Krummy), while five percent is Kona Peaberry, a bean that has only one seed. Many of the beans are sold on the world market prior to roasting. Roasters are like vintners, using their eyes, nose, and even ears to achieve the perfect roasts. Lighter roasted coffee—which contains the most caffeine—is allowed to make one 'pop' during the roasting. The darker roasts, like Italian, French, and espresso, 'pop' twice.

Kona coffee is grown along a 20-mile stretch of the coast, at an elevation of 800 to 2,000 feet, on lands that during ancient times produced breadfruit, bananas, sugar cane, and taro. Worldwide, demand far outstrips supply. Like wine, Kona coffee taste can vary from year to year. The large number of growers also results in a varying product. To find the perfect cup, take the coffee tour described in *Driving Tours*, or see the growers listed in *Resource Links*. Don't bother to buy a Kona blend coffee, as the distinctive smoothness and flavor will be lost.

ORCHIDS AND EXOTICS

Drive to the green slopes of Puna and you'll understand why the Big Island's nickname is the Orchid Isle. Most of the world's supply of this flower, as well as other tropical flowers, is flown out daily from the Hilo Airport. This region can also take credit for 95% of the state's papayas, and nearly three-quarters of the bananas. Virtually all of the ginger grown in the United States, about 8 million pounds per year, also comes from the lush slopes of Puna. Also grown in abundance are guava, anthuriums, carnations, roses, and protea. The Big Island is the nation's exotic fruit-and-flower basket.

Many flower growers, situated around Pahoa, are set up to receive visitors. A drive around the upper slopes of Puna will also reveal large papaya and other fruit orchards. Orchids can be seen growing along the coast of Puna. (See the Beach Road bike tour, number 18, on page 205 for driving directions.) A convenient place to see scads of orchid varieties is at the Akatsuka Orchard Gardens, near Volcano. To get there from Hilo, take Highway 11 to .5-mile past mm22. Volcano Orchid Farms is located between mm20 and mm21.

MACADAMIA NUTS

You can't chomp a big, meaty mac nut without thinking of Hawaii, but the snack treats are a native of Australia and were not harvested here in any great volume until the late 1950s. The nuts were named to honor an Australian doctor, John Macadam, but it was a Massachusetts man, Baron Ferdinand von Muller, who first planted a tree in Honolulu in 1921. To Muller's chagrin, nut quality varied hugely from tree to tree, and from year to year. It took botanists from the University of Hawaii 20 years to study some 60,000 different trees and come up with today's variety. Unlike coffee, small growers account for only fraction of the island's macadamia production. Big companies like Castle & Cooke (Dole) and C. Brewer and Company got into growing the subtropical trees, which can reach a height of 40 feet. Brewer's Mauna Loa brand orchards cover more than 2,000 acres outside of Hilo. Smaller growers harvest nuts along the Kona coast.

Trees may produce a nut after about 5 years, but it takes 15 years until large quantities can be harvested—at four or five different times through the year. The nuts have a leathery outer husk that covers a thin smooth shell that is known as a tough nut to crack. In the old days, orchard workers would lay boards over the round, in-shell nuts and drive over them in cars. Nowadays, mechanized rollers are used, as you can see at the Mauna Loa Macadamia Visitors Center. Most of Hawaii's sweet meats are produced on the east side, where 130-plus inches of rain, porous soil, and the right combination of sun and clouds combine to make nut heaven. But you'll find plenty of acres of orchard in southern Kona, and you can crack your own at the Kona Coast Macadamia Factory, just south of Captain Cook.

Climate

RAINFALL, AVERAGE INCHES PER YEAR

Kailua-Kona 40

South Kohala 20

Kawaihae 10

Hawi 42

Honoka'a 125

Hilo 150

Puna coast 100

Hawaii Volcanoes Park 85

Wood Valley 90

Na'alehu 45

Manuka State Park 55

Mauna Kea summit 10

LAVA FLOW RISK

Lava flows from eruptions occur slowly and are not an immediate threat. Vog, or volcanic smog, is most prevalent in South Kona, and occurs occasionally in North Kona and Waimea. Taking into account all locations on the island, vog density exceeds healthful standard set by the Environmental Protection Agency about 20 days per year.

1 = HIGHEST LAVA RISK, 9 = LOWEST LAVA RISK

Kailua-Kona 3-4

South Kona, Kau 2

Hawaii Volcanoes Park 1

Puna 1-2

Hilo 3

Hamakua 8

Waimea-North Kohala 9

South Kohala 3-4

Mauna Kea 7

Mauna Loa 2

TEMPERATURES

OCEAN

Low, late February to March : 73 degrees Fahrenheit
High, late September to October: 80 degrees Fahrenheit

AIR

Average high temperatures on the Big Island, at sea level range from a low of 78 degrees in January to a high of 85 degrees. In Waimea, daytime temps are normally in the mid-60s to low-70s. At Hawaii Volcanoes National Park (4,000 feet in elevation), 60 degrees is an average high, with nighttime temps dropping to the 50s and high 40s. Atop Mauna Kea, expect temperatures in the high 40s to low 50s, with a potential to drop below freezing at night. Mauna Loa is generally 10 degrees warmer.

WIND

Trade Winds occur about 300 days a year, hitting the east side of the island with speeds hovering around 20 mph. The winds are more prevalent in the summer. The winds normally are stronger as the day progresses, and then die down at night. Kona winds, buffeting the west side of the island, bring warmer air and occur mostly in the winter and spring.

POPULATION

Nearly 150,000 people live on the Big Island, about double the number since 1970 and some 12 percent of the state's total population of 1.2 million. (With an area of 4,030 square miles, the Big Island has almost two-thirds of the state's landmass.)

PACKLIST

If your closet is lacking any of the items, consider picking them up once you arrive. All the surf-and-sun stuff and Alohawear is readily available at budget prices. Don't overpack. Leave room in your suitcase for the Kona coffee and macadamia nuts.

ONE-WEEK VACATION
Shoes
>Slippers (a.k.a. zoris, go-aheads, thongs, slappers, flip-flops)
>Plane & hotel shoes (clean athletic shoes, sandal pumps, or boat shoes)
>Hiking shoes (light weight hikers or cross-trainers)
>Surf shoe (optional, Teva or bootie-style)

Khaki pants plus Aloha shirt for plane, hotels. Women can bring a sundress or go with slacks and top.
Swimming suit
Sarong to wrap around waist (women)
Two or three pairs shorts
4 or 5 short sleeve tops (quick-dry polypropylene preferred)
1 or 2 long sleeve tops (mountain hikers bring 2 for layering, polypro)
Gore-Tex shell, or equivalent, rain jacket
Fleece vest, lightweight (optional)
Sun hat, sunglasses
Gloves (optional, for warmth on Mauna Kea and Mauna Loa, and to protect hands on lava hikes.)
Retractable hiking pole
Mask, fins, snorkel (consider booty-style fins with straps on the heel, since the booties will aid in rocky entries)
Umbrella (optional, but the retractable model tucks into a knapsack and provides instant shelter for rain forest strolls)
Knapsack (most everything below can be picked up in Kona or Hilo)
>Antibiotic ointment
>Band Aids
>Camera
>Cell phone (won't work everywhere, but good for emergencies)
>Energy bars, emergency food
>Flashlight or headlamp (one for each person, if planning
>>nighttime, lava-viewing hikes)
>Handkerchief/bandana
>Mosquito repellant
>Small bottle hydrogen peroxide
>Sunscreen, lip balm
>Swiss Army Knife (be sure not to include in your carry-on)
>Water bottles
>Water purification tablets or pump
>Whistle

Resource Links

RESOURCE LINKS

All area codes are 808 unless otherwise noted

AIRPORTS
Hilo International, 934-5838, Kona International, 329-3423

AIRLINES
American, 800-433-7300
Aloha, 800-652-6541, 935-5771
Continental, 800-523-3273
Delta, 800-221-1212
Hawaiian, 800-367-5320
United, 800-241-6522

CAR RENTALS
Alamo, 800-327-9633, 836-3000
Avis, 800-367-3367, 840-2847
Aloha Car Sales, 935-9958
AA Aloha Cars-R-Us (quotes for all companies), 800-665-7989
Budget, 800-527-700
Dollar, 800-367-7006, 329-2744
Harper Car and Truck (4WD), 800-852-9993, 969-1478
Island Safari RV Rentals, 800-406-4555
National, 800-227-0891
Thrifty, 800-367-5238, 329-1339

BUSES AND SHUTTLES
Mass Transit Agency (public) 961-8343
Speedishuttle, 329-5433

BLUE HAWAIIAN HELICOPTERS
Features the quiet Eco-Star, tours all over the Big Island, and departs from both the Hilo Airport and on the Kona side at Waikaloa. This is as close as you can get to the eruption at Pu'u O'o, as well as the green valleys of Kohala. Blue Hawaiian may not be the cheapest, but this is something you don't want to skimp on. You get luxurious, well-maintained flying machines, as well as first-class narratives from the pilots. 800-786-2583, 961-5600, Hilo, 886-1768, Waikaloa.

PUBLIC PROPERTY

COUNTY
Beach Parks and Camping, Hilo, 961-8311,
 Kona, 887-3014, 327-3560
Aquatics, 961-8694
Culture & Arts, 961-8706
Information, 961-8223
Recreation Programs, 961-8740

VOLCANO TRACKING
http://hvo.wr.usgs.gov/
http://volcano.und.edu/vw.html
http://www.soest.hawaii.edu/
 GG/HCV/kilauea.html
http://virtual11.pgd.hawaii.edu/goes/
http://www.nps/gov/havo/

STATE

State Parks (Department of Land and Natural Resources), 974-6200, 587-0300
Na Ala Hele Trail System (Division of Forestry and Wildlife), 974-4221, 933-4343,
Hapuna Beach State Park, 882-7995
Lapakahi State Historical Park, 882-6207, 889-5566
Mo'okini Heiau, 591-1170

NATIONAL

Hawaii Volcanoes National Park, 985-6000
   Hawaiian Volcano Observatory, 985-6049
   Volcano House (private), 967-7321
   Volcano Art Center (nonprofit) 967-7565
Hakalau National Wildlife Refuge, 933-6915
Kaloko-Honokohau National Historic Park, 329-6881
Pu'uhonua o Honaunau National Historic Park, 328-2288, 328-2326
Pu'ukohola Heiau National Historic Site, 882-7218

VISITOR INFORMATION

Big Island Visitors Bureau, 800-648-2441, Hilo, 961-5797, Kona, 886-1655
Bus schedules, 961-8744
Destination Kona Coast, 322-6809, 327-9373
Destination Hilo, 935-5294
Governor's State Information Office, 327-4953
Hawaii Attractions Association, Honolulu, 596-7733
Hawaii Tourism Authority, Honolulu, 973-2255
Mauna Kea Management Office, University of Hawaii, Hilo, 944-0734
Mauna Kea Observatories, 969-4894, Roads, 974-4203
   Keck Observatory, 935-8693
Mauna Loa Observatory, Hilo, 933-6965
Waimea Visitors Center, 885-6707
Waiola Center (includes state parks), 933-4390, 933-0416
Weather, island-wide, 961-5582, Hilo, 935-8555

MUSEUMS, CULTURAL EVENTS

Amy Greenwell Ethnobotanical Garden,
   Captain Cook, 323-3318
East Hawaii Cultural Center, 329-3441
Hawaii Kupuna Hula, Kona, 322-1812
Hula Halai Na Lei O Kaholoku, 883-9005
Hulihe'e Palace, Kona, 329-1877, 329-9555
Jaggar, Thomas A. Museum, Volcano, 985-6000
Kamuela Museum, 885-4724
Kaupulehu Cultural Center, 323-8520
Kealakowa'a Heiau, Kona, 329-7286
Kona Coffee Cultural Festival, 800-648-2441
Kona Coffee Living History Farm, 323-2006
Kona Historical Society, 323-3222
Lapakahi State Historical Park, 882-6207
Laupahoehoe Train Museum, 962-6300

Museums, cultural events, cont'd—

Lyman House Museum, Hilo, 935-5021
Mokupapapa Discovery Center for Hawaii's Reefs, Hilo, 933-8195
Moʻokini Heiau, 591-1170
Na Mea Hawaii Hula Kahiko, Volcano, 967-8222
Onizuka Space Center, Kona, 329-3441
Onizuka Center for International Astronomy, Hilo, 961-2180,
   Mauna Kea, 935-7606, 969-4892
Pacific Tsunami Museum, Hilo, 935-0926
Parker Ranch Historic Homes, 885-5433, 885-0554
Parker Ranch Visitors Center, 885-7655
Volcano Art Center, 967-8222, 967-7565
Waiola Center, 933-0416

SUPPLEMENTAL MAPS

*Free maps are widely available in shopping centers, on the plane, and from the visitors bureau.
National park maps are included with the price of admission. This book's maps and directions are
enough for you to get around the island, but having a street map and detailed, all-purpose map is a
good idea.*

Map of Hawaii, The Big Island. University of Hawaii Press. James A. Bier, cartographer. Full
Color Topographic, 2840 Kolowalu Street, Honolulu, HI, 96822. *Best all-purpose map.
Indexes place names and shows unpaved roads. Be sure to get the 2002 copyright, since over-inking
on earlier versions make them almost unreadable. Widely available at mainland and Hawaii
stores.*
Island of Hawaii Recreation Map. Department of Land and Natural Resources, 974-6200,
587-0300. *Available free. Shows hunter's forest reserves, state hiking trails, and public lands.*
The Ready Mapbook of West Hawaii, East Hawaii. Odyssey Publishing, 888-729-1074, 935-
0092. *Best street maps. In book form, one for each side of the island. The choice if you plan of
doing a lot of exploring by car. Does not include Saddle Road, however.*
A Guide to Public Parks. County of Hawaii, Department of Parks & Recreation, 961-8311.
*Includes current facility information and is useful in planning your trip. But beach parks are hard
to miss and the map itself is so-so.*
Big Island Mountain Biking. Big Island Mountain Biking Association, 961-4452 *Not a 'must-
have,' but cyclists may wish to request this free map.*
Map of the Neighbor Islands, Hawaii, Maui & Kauai, Compass Maps, 800-441-6277 *Fold-up
street map. Needs update. Includes neighbor islands.*
USGS Topos, 800-ASK-USGS. *Set of 3 topographical maps covers the island at a 1:100,000
scale. Shows roads and trails, but place names are not marked well enough for all-purpose use.*

REFERENCE BOOKS

*Also contact public agencies, visitor information, and organizations.
They will provide a wealth of information at no cost.*

Alexander, William D., *A Brief History of the Hawaiian People*, 1899
Bushnell, O. A., and Daws, Gavin *The Illustrated Atlas
of Hawaii*, 1970-91
Desha, Stephen L., *Kamehameha and His Warrior Kekuhaupio*, 2000
Ellis, William, *The Journal of William Ellis*, 1963
Ii, John Papa, *Fragments of Hawaiian History*, 1959

James, Van, *Ancient Sites of Hawaii*, 1995
Judd, Henry P., *The Hawaiian Language*, 1982
Kamakau, Samuel M., *The Ruling Chiefs of Hawaii*, 1961
Kane, Herb Kawainui, *Ancient Hawaii*, 1997
Moon, Jan, *Living With Nature In Hawaii*, 1971-89
Pratt, H. Douglas, *A Pocket Guide to Hawaii's Trees and Shrubs*, 2002
Wright, Thomas L., Editor, *The Early Serial Publications of the Hawaiian Volcano Observatory*, 1988

NEWSPAPERS, NEWSLETTERS

Big Island Gold (visitors guide), 326-6077
Hawaii Herald Tribune, 935-6621
Hawaii Island Journal, 328-1880
Kau Calendar, 928-9811
Ka Wai Ola OHA, 800-468-4644
North Hawaii News, 885-0507
This Week Big Island (visitors guide), 329-5466
Volcano Art Center Gazette, 967-8222
Waimea Gazette, 885-6472
West Hawaii Today, 329-9311

PRESERVATION AND CULTURAL GROUPS

Hawaii Natural History Association, Volcano, 985-6051, 985-6050
Hilo-Hamakua Heritage Coast, 966-5416
Hilo Main Street Program, 935-8850
Kahikolu Congregational Church, 328-8110
Kaupulehu Cultural Center, 325-8520, 325-8467
Kona Historical Society, 323-3222
Mauna Kea Management, University of Hawaii, Hilo, 944-0734
Mokuaikaua Church, Kona, 329-1589
Paniolo Preservation Society, 887-6059
Pulama Ia Kona Heritage Council, 323-3222
Queen Liliuokalani Trust, 935-9381, 329-7336, 329-0503
ReefTeach, 329-2861
Waimea Outdoor Circle, 885-5210
Waimea Preservation Association, 885-6707

GARDENS AND ORCHARDS

Akatsuka Orchid Gardens, Volcano, 967-8234
Hawaii State Bonsai Repository, Hilo, 982-9880
Hawaii Tropical Botanical Garden, Hilo, 964-5233
Hilo Farmers Market, 933-1000
Kona Coast Macadamia, 328-8141, 800-242-6887
Mauna Loa Macadamias Visitors Center, Hilo, 888-628-6556
Nani Mau Gardens, Hilo, 959-3500
Panaewa Rainforest Zoo (county), Hilo, 959-7224, 959-9233
Sadie Seymour Botanical Gardens, Kona, 329-7286
World Botanical Gardens, Hilo, 963-5427

KONA COFFEE
Auntie Loraine's, 322-1675
Bay View Farm, 800-662-5880, 328-9658
Captain Cook Coffee, 322-3501
Coffees 'n' Epicuria, 866-707-8688
Greenwell Farms, 888-592-5662
Heavenly Hawaiian, 322-7720
Kona Blue Sky Coffee, 322-1700
Ueshima Coffee Company, 888-822-5662

CULTURAL GIFT STORES AND GALLERIES
Alapaki's, Keauhou, 322-2007
As Hawi Turns, 889-5023
Basically Books, Hilo, 800-903-6377, 961-0144
Cook's Discoveries, Waimea, 885-3633
Eva Parker Woods Cottage, Mauna Lani, 885-6622
The Gallery at Bamboo, Hawi, 889-1441
Hawaiian Artifacts, Hamakua Coast, 964-1729
Hawaii Tropical Garden, Hamakua Coast, 964-5253
Hawaiian Force, Hilo, 934-7171
Holualoa Gallery, 322-8484
Holualoa Ukulele Gallery, 324-4100
Honoka'a Artworks, 775-8255
Kealia Ranch Store, Honaunau, 328-8744
Kohala Book Shop, Kapa'au, 889-6400
Parker Ranch Store, 885-5669
Paul's Place, Holualoa, 324-4702
Rankin Gallery, Kapa'au, 889-6849
Star Light Crystals, Hawi, 884-5444
Ululani Gallery, Holualoa, 322-7733
Upcountry Connection Gallery, Waimea, 885-0623
Volcano Art Center, 967-8222, 967-7565
Waipio Valley Artworks, Honoka'a, 800-492-4746, 775-0958
Woodshop Gallery-Café, Akaka Falls, 877-479-7995

OUTFITTERS, TOURS, AND RECREATIONAL GROUPS

HIKE/DRIVE
Arnott's Lodge & Hiking Adventures, 969-7097
Mauna Kea Summit Adventures, 322-2366, 888-322-2366
Hawaii Ecotourism Association, 877-300-7058, 956-2866
Hawaii Forest & Trail, 331-8505, 800-464-1993
Hawaiian Walkways, 800-457-7759
Kona Historical Society, 323-3222
Waipio Valley Shuttle, 775-7121

BIKES

Big Island Mountain Bike Association, 961-4452
Dave's Bikes, 329-4522
Hawaiian Pedals, 329-2294
Kona Coast Cycling Tours, 877-592-2453, 327-1133
Mauna Kea Mountain Bikes, 888-682-8687
Paniolo Adventures, 889-5354
PATH (People's Advocacy for Trails Hawaii-bikes),
    326-9495, 327-9429
Red Sail Sports, 886-2876
Top of Waipio, 885-7759

SNORKEL, BOAT RIDES, WATER SPORTS

Adventures in Paradise, 866-824-2337
Big Island Divers, 800-488-6068, 329-6068
Big Island Water Sports Snuba, 326-7446
Body Glove Cruises, 800-551-8911, 326-7122
Captain Zodiac, 329-3199
Dolphin Quest (kids, Hilton), 886-7825
Dolphin Discoveries, 322-8000
Fair Wind (Cook Monument), 322-2788
Flumin' Da Ditch Ride, Hawi, 889-6922
Hawaiiana Boat Rentals, 322-8006
Kamanu Charters (catamaran), 329-2021
Kohala Divers, Kawaihae, 882-7774
Kona Boat Rentals, 326-9155
Kona Honu Divers, Kailua, 324-4668
Manta Ray Dives of Hawaii, 325-1687
Planet Ocean Watersports, Hilo, 935-7277
Red Sail Sports, 886-2876
Sea Quest Raft & Snorkel,
    Keauhou, 329-RAFT
South Kona Snorkeling, 328-1609

SURF

Ocean Eco Tours, 324-7873
Surf Kids, Keauhou, 324-0442

HORSES

Ainahou Ranch, Waimea, 985-7373
Dahana Ranch, Waimea, 885-0057
Kapapala Ranch, Volcano, 968-6585
Kealia Ranch, Honaunau, 328-8744
Kohala Na'alapa Stables, 889-0022
Mauna Kea Beach Stables, 885-4288
Paniolo Adventures, Waimea, 889-5354
Waipio on Horseback, 775-7291
Waipio Ridge Stables, 877-757-1414

GOLF

Kohala
Hapuna Golf Course, 880-3000
Hilton Waikoloa Seaside, 886-1234
Big Island Country Club, 325-5044
Francis H. I'i Brown North and
    South Courses, 885-6655
Waikoloa Beach Course, 886-6060
Waikoloa Kings' Course, 886-7888
Waimea Country Club, 885-8777

Kona/Keauou
Kona Country Club, 322-2595
Makalei Hawaii Club, 325-6625

Hilo
Hilo Municipal Course, 959-7711
Naniloa Country Club, 935-3000

Honokaa
Hamakua Country Club, 775-7244

Punaluu/Volcano/South Point
Discovery Harbor, 929-7353
Sea Mountain Golf
    Course, 928-6222
Volcano Country Club, 967-7331

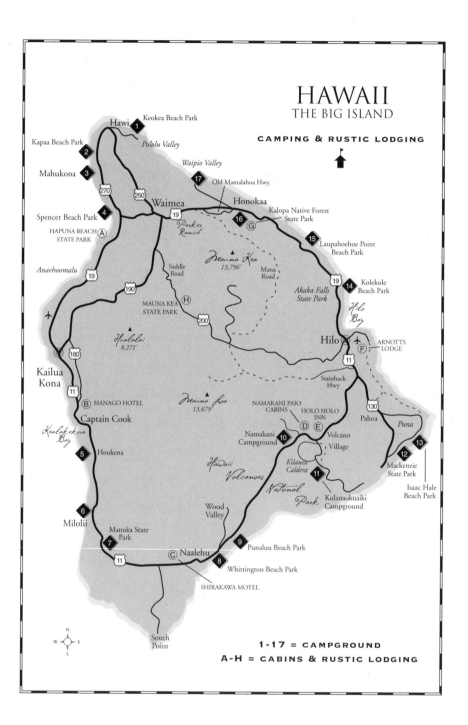

HAWAII
THE BIG ISLAND

CAMPING & RUSTIC LODGING

Keokea Beach Park
Hawi ①
Pololu Valley
Kapaa Beach Park
② Waipio Valley
Mahukona ③
⑰ Old Mamalahoa Hwy.
Honokaa
270 250 Waimea
Spencer Beach Park ④ 19 ⑯ Kalopa Native Forest
Parker State Park
HAPUNA BEACH Ⓐ Ranch Ⓖ
STATE PARK
⑮ Laupahoehoe Point
Beach Park
Anaehoomalu Saddle Mauna Kea
19 Road 13,796' Mana
Road Akaka Falls 19 ⑭ Kolekole
190 State Park Beach Park
MAUNA KEA Ⓗ Hilo
STATE PARK 200 Bay
Hualalai Hilo Ⓧ
8,271' Ⓕ ARNOTTS
LODGE
⑪
Kailua Stainback
Kona Hwy
11
Ⓑ MANAGO HOTEL 130
Mauna Loa NAMAKANI PAIO
Captain Cook 13,679' CABINS HOLO HOLO Pahoa
INN Puna
Kealakekua Namakani Ⓓ Ⓔ
Bay Campground ⑩ Volcano ⑫ ⑬
⑤ Hookena Village Mackenzie
Kilauea State Park
Caldera Isaac Hale
Hawaii ⑪ Beach Park
⑥ Volcanoes
Milolii Kulanaokuaiki
Wood National Park Campground
Valley
Manuka State ⑨ Punaluu Beach Park
⑦ Park Ⓒ Naalehu
11 ⑧ Whittington Beach Park
SHIRAKAWA MOTEL
N
W E South
S Point **1-17 = CAMPGROUND**
A-H = CABINS & RUSTIC LODGING

Camping & Rustic Lodging

SPENCER BEACH PARK

The Big Island has the state's best camping, with beach and forest sites spread around the island. You'll also find cabins and rustic lodging, priced at less than $50. When planning your trip, also take a look at *Where to Stay* for budget-priced hotels, as well as reasonably priced inns and B&Bs, where you can stay as a treat between campouts.

Duffel Bag Campsite:
Most of what you need for a night's camping will fit into a duffel bag, checked with the rest of your airplane luggage: a backpacking tent, lightweight sleeping bags, kitchen set, and cook stove that takes readily available fuel. One stop at a super market will complete your camp set: a Styrofoam cooler, picnic dinnerware, stove fuel, and gallon water jugs.

See the *Camping Map* for locations of campgrounds and cabins. Call ahead for reservations where necessary and to inquire about specific amenities. Thumbnail descriptions follow each listing, but you can read the trailhead descriptions to get a better handle on the area. Use the *Trailhead Directory* in the front of the book for a quick reference to page numbers.

CONTACTS AND PERMITS

All area codes are 808

Hawaii County: Department of Parks and Recreation, 101 Pauahi Street, Suite 6, Hilo, HI, 96720. Phone: 961-8311, Fax: 961-8411. County fees are $5 a night, per adult.

State of Hawaii: Department of Land and Natural Resources, Division of State Parks, P. O. Box 936, Hilo, HI, 96721. Phone: 974-4343, 974-6200, Wailoa Center, 933-0416, Honolulu, 587-0300. No fees for campgrounds.

National: Hawaii Volcanoes National Park, P.O. Box 52, Hawaii National Park, HI, 96718. Phone: 985-6000, 985-6017. Two no-fee, no reservation campgrounds are within the park.

CAMPGROUNDS

1. Keokea Beach Park (county) – Set on a remote bay, with good access of Pololu Valley. Pavilion, lawn, showers, drinking water. Popular with neighboring Filipino community, particularly on weekends. Directions are in TH3, Polulu Valley.
2. Kapaʻa Beach Park (county) – Beautifully situated on a rugged coastline. More remote-feeling than most coastal camping. Basic rest rooms and pavilion. No drinking water or picnic area. See TH5, Mahukona, for directions.
3. Mahukona Beach Park (county) – Nice lawn camping with good snorkeling nearby. Large pavilion with tables. Shower, but no drinking water. Doesn't get a lot of local use, but fairly popular among travelers. See TH5, Mahukona.
4. Spencer Beach Park (county) – Beautiful stone pavilion, drinking water, indoor showers. Shaded large camping area next to swimming beach and a short walk to excellent snorkeling beach. Gets a lot of use. See TH7, Puʻukohola Heiau.
5. Hoʻokena Beach Park (county) – 'Cozy' beachside camping at this popular park, the closest to Kailua-Kona. Rest rooms, showers, picnic tables. See TH28 for directions.
6. Miloliʻi Beach Park (county) – Not many tourists spend the night in Miloliʻi, and the campground feels more like a day-use area. You'll have more privacy on weekdays. May feel too 'local' for some. See TH29 for directions.
7. Manuka State Park (state) – Beautiful native forest, midway between Kona and Hawaii Volcanoes. Set at about 2,000 feet, cooler but not cold. One of the more woodsy, quiet camping experiences available. See TH30 for directions.
8. Whittington Beach Park (county) – Remotely located, this is one of the least used county parks, in spite of its scenic charms. Rest rooms, showers, and pavilion, but no drinking water. Directions are in TH32.
9. Punaluʻu Beach Park (county) – Set on a hillside next to the Big Island's most popular black sand beach. Wind can be a factor. Locals like the pavilion for parties, particularly on weekends. See TH33 for directions.

10. Namakani Paio Campground (national) – Located 3 miles west of the entrance to Hawaii Volcanoes National Park on Highway 11. Nice lawn surrounded by lush forest. Full facilities. Can be damp and chilly, set at 4,000-feet. No fees or reservations required. Fairly popular among tourists.

11. Kulanaokuaiki Campground (national) – Located within Hawaii Volcanoes National Park, on Hilina Pali Road. Will be warmer and drier (at 2,700 feet) than Namakani Paio, but also in an arid setting. Usually quiet and more private than most Big Island campsites. Nice views and new tent pads. Rest room and fire grates. No fees or reservations required, although you need to pay the park admission.

12. Mackenzie State Recreation Area (state) – Set within a huge coastal ironwood grove along the lush Puna coast. Has picnic area, pavilion, and rest rooms, but no drinking water. Frequented by fishermen, mostly on weekends, and not many tourists. Some spillover from Isaac Hale Beach Park. See TH50 for the driving directions.

13. Isaac Hale Beach Park (county) – Not the greatest facilities. Gets a lot of locals use, particularly on weekends. Some permanent blue-tarp campers. Ahalunai hot pool is nearby. See TH51 for a description.

14. Kolekole Beach Park (county) – In a lovely jungle gorge, fairly close to Hilo and very near Akaka Falls State Park. Nice lawn with pavilion, picnic facilities, and showers. Gets local action, particularly on weekends, due to proximity to Hilo. See TH58, Akaka Falls, for directions.

15. Laupahoehoe Point Beach Park (county) – Beautiful, well-kept coastal setting. Nice lawn area with plenty of trees and full facilities. On weekend evenings, locals like the gather at the park, but the place usually is not overcrowded with campers. Details are given in TH60.

16. Kalopa State Park (state) – Among the best sites, set around a large meadow in a native forest. Full facilities. Can be damp and chilly, at 2,000 feet. Usually uncrowded and quiet. Also has cabins, which are listed below. Directions are in TH61.

17. Waipio Valley (private, 842-8211) – A several-site, unimproved campground managed by Kamehameha Schools is located on the beach in Waipio Valley. Access is via walking or 4WD vehicle.

NAMAKANI PAIO CAMPGROUND

CABINS AND RUSTIC LODGING

A. Hapuna Beach State Park (state) – About a half-dozen A-frames are nicely spaced on an arid hillside above the island's most-popular beach. A large communal cooking pavilion is nearby. Great location for exploring Kona and Kohala. Cabins rent for about $40.

B. Manago Hotel (private, 323-2642) – Basic but hardly rustic, the Manago is a Big Island classic. Views of Kealakekua Bay. Easy Kona access from Captain Cook. Japanese restaurant attached, and stores of the town are nearby. Deluxe rooms for $50 and under.

C. Shirakawa Motel (private, 929-7462) – South Island's version of the Manago, located in jungle greenery on the outskirts of Na'alehu. Clean, quiet rooms for under $40.

D. Namakani Paio Cabins (private, 967-7321) – Ten cabins next to the campground, 3 miles west from the Hawaii Volcanoes National Park entrance. Communal rest rooms and showers. Bedding is included, but it gets chilly, so bring an extra blanket. About $40 gets you a cabin. Operated by Volcano House Hotel. (Getting a good deal on one of their standard hotel rooms costs more, but may be a better value.)

E. Holo Holo Inn (private, 967-7950) – To call the modest Holo an Inn is generous, but they're located in Volcano near the park, and have clean rooms with showers. Dorm rooms are under $20, and private doubles are $40.

F. Arnott's Lodge and Hiking Adventures (private, 969-7097) – Enterprising Aussie Doug Arnott has tent spaces for $9 and private rooms for around $50— with lots of options in between. Just ask. Walking distance to good beaches in Hilo. Shuttle service from the airport, plus cross-island excursions. You're bound to meet interesting people, many of them Euro-style and student travelers. A television series could be set in and around this quirky place. See TH48; Arnott's is on Apapane Street.

G. Kalopa Native Forest State Park – Large cabins on the manicured grounds of the park, set at 2,000 feet. Surrounded by 500 acres of native forest. Can be chilly and damp, but these cabins are a find. Cabins range from $30 to $50 a night. See TH61.

H. Mauna Kea State Park – A rather forlorn location, off Saddle Road at 6,000 feet, and next to a military training area. Still, spending the night between Mauna Loa and Mauna Kea is a memorable experience. Cabins may not be open, since the state's plans for them have been uncertain. Prices hover around $40.

KALOPA NATIVE FOREST STATE PARK

Where to Stay

HILTON WAIKOLOA VILLAGE,
FAIRMONT ORCHID HAWAII,
SHIPMAN HOUSE,
MAUNA LANI,
HALE OHIA

All listings are recommended but **bold** type indicates a preferred lodging. Give them a call to inquire about amenities and location, and anything else that is important to you. Listings range from large destination resorts to single-room lodgings in private homes. In all cases, be sure to ask if you're getting the lowest rate. You'll find that most people in Hawaii will have time to talk to you. Also see *Camping & Cabins*, page 235, for economy lodging; and *Strategies For Visiting The Big Island*, page198, for tips on booking your stay. For island-wide bed & breakfast referrals, try Hawaii's Best Bed & Breakfast, 800-262-9912. Area codes are 808, unless otherwise listed.

(P) = PRICEY, $200 AND WAY UP
(M) = MODERATE, $100 TO $200
(C) = CHEAP, UNDER $100

KONA COAST

Kailua-Kona is the island's most-developed coast, with a 4-mile run of moderately priced resorts and condominiums situated mostly along Ali'i Drive. Captain Cook, Holualoa, and Kealakekua are a few miles from downtown Kailua and lodgings are set among vintage storefronts or in rural area. You're guaranteed sunshine, and excellent snorkeling is nearby, but Kona doesn't have big beaches. Kohala's beaches are nearby.

ROYAL KONA RESORT

Areca Palms, (B&B) Captain Cook (C-M), 800-545-4390, 323-2276
Black Bamboo Hawaii (agent, B&Bs, homes) Kealakekua (M-P) 800-527-7789
Cedar House B&B, Captain Cook (C) 328-8829, 328-1006
Granma's Cabin, mauka Kailua (C) 325-5438
A Hale Lanai (cottage), Holualoa (M) 530-583-6062
Hawaiian Bay Beach (B&B), Kealakekua (M) 604-462-8315
Holualoa Inn (breakfast) (M) 324-1121, 800-392-1812
  Spectacular view, private, in the rural hills above Kona.
Keauhou Beach Resort (M-P) 800-462-6262
  Next to Kona's most popular snorkeling lagoon, mid-range to high rates.
Keauhou Surf and Raquet Club (M-P) 925-552-9980
King Kamehameha Hotel, Kailua (M-P) 923-4511, 800-367-6060
Knutson & Associates (agent, condos) Kailua (M) 329-6311, 800-800-6202
Kona Bali Kai Resort (condos) (M-P) 329-9381
Kona Magic Sands (condos) (C-M) 800-622-5348
Kona Surf Hotel, Kailua (C-M) 322-3411
Kona Tiki Hotel (breakfast) (C) 329-1425
  Oceanfront, unpretentious, great value, book way ahead.
The Lilikoi Vine, Kona mauka, (B&B) (C) 325-9856
Manago Hotel, Captain Cook (C) 323-2642
  A Big Island classic, some rooms with views of Kealakekua Bay, family owned since 1917, a real deal.

Nancy's Hideaway, Kona mauka (B&B) (M) 866-125
Rainbow Plantation (rooms, cottages) Kealakekua (C)
   323-2393, 800-494-2829
Royal Kona Resort (M), 329-3111
Sea Village (condos) (M) 326-7434
Tara Cottage, Kealakekua (M) 328-9607, 800-527-7789
Tommy Tinker's Pink House, Captain Cook (M) 889-5584

SOUTH KOHALA

Hawaii's best beaches and its luxury resorts lie in green oases along the coast of this 25-mile stretch of barren lava flows. You'll also find several wild beaches. These swank destination resorts are exquisitely beautiful. You can visit this area on easy day drives from Kona or Hawi-Waimea. All listings are oceanfront.

MAUNA LANI

Fairmont Orchid Hawaii (P) 885-2000, 800-845-9905
Four Seasons Resort Hualalai (P) 325-8000
   Pamper yourself in understated luxury.
Hawaii Vacation Rentals (agent, Puako) (C-P) 882-7000, 800-332-7081
Hilton Waikoloa Village (P) 886-1234, 800-445-8767
   Opulent family fun. Waterslides, monorail, Dolphin Quest program, hop on a motorboat to your room.
Kona Village Resort (P) 325-5555, 800-367-5290
Mauna Kea Beach Hotel (P) 882-7222, 800-882-6060
Mauna Lani Resort (P) 885-6622, 800-367-2323
   La creme de la creme.
Outrigger Waikoloa Beach (M-P) 886-6789, 800-922-5533

HAWI-WAIMEA

At nearly 3,000 feet in elevation, Waimea, a.k.a. Kamuela, is set in rolling pasturelands. You're able to drop down easily to the beaches of Kohala and Waipio Valley, and also to the Hilo-Hamakua Coast. Cool weather rolls through Waimea, which is in a saddle between Mauna Kea and the Kohala Mountains. Hawi is in rural north Kohala, with easy access to Pololu Valley and not far from the beaches of South Kohala. Obviously, you won't get oceanfront at either location.

Cabin in the Treeline, mauka Hawi (C-M) 884-5105
Waimea Country Lodge (M) 885-4100
Kamuela Inn (Waimea) (C-M) 885-4243, 800-555-8968
   Set off the road, nicely appointed rooms belie moderate rates.
Kohala Guest House, Kapa'au (C-M) 889-5606
Hale O Kohala (home), Kawaihae (M) 822-7022

Hawi, Waimea accommodations cont'd—

Tom Sherman House, Kapa'au (C-M) 889-0553

Whale Watchers (guest house), Hawi (C-M) 889-5756

HILO-HAMAKUA

They're aren't many accommodations on the lush Hamakua Coast, nor in Hilo, relative to Kona. Banyan Drive hotels are underrated, and the Shipman House is one of the best places in the Hawaiian Islands. This is the green side of the island, with easy access to Waipio, Mauna Kea, and Hawaii Volcanoes National Park. The Puna coastline has excellent snorkeling, and Hilo's beach parks are a pleasant surprise. Hilo is known for its rainfall, but it comes in downpours, followed by tropical sunshine.

Shipman House (B&B), Hilo (M) 934-8002, 800-627-8447
> *Jack London stayed here, one of the state's premier historic accommodations; lavish breakfast.*

Arnott's Lodge (hostel, rooms) (C) 969-7097
> *For the adventure travel set, great rates and location. Organized group tours to volcano and Mauna Kea.*

Hale Kukui Orchard Retreat (cottages), Honoka'a (M) 775-7130, 800-444-7130

Hawaii Naniloa Hotel (M), Hilo 969-3333, 800-367-5360

Hilo Hawaiian Hotel (M) 935-9361
> *Oceanfront resort hotel value.*

Holme's Sweet Home (B&B), Hilo (C) 961-9089

Hotel Honoka'a Club (dorm, rooms) (C) 775-0678, 800-808-0678

Inn at Kulaniapia Falls (M) 966-6373, 888-838-6373

Luana Ola B&B Cottages, Honoka'a (M) 775-1150, 800-357-7727

Old Hawaii B&B, Hilo (C) 961-2816, 877-961-2816

Palms Cliff House (B&B) Honomu (M-P) 963-6076

Waipio Ridge Vacation Rental (cottage), Honoka'a (M) 775-0603

BREAKFAST AT SHIPMAN HOUSE

VOLCANO

Within a mile of the national park, Volcano is a quiet burg with has several excellent B&Bs, fabulous Kilauea Lodge and also several fun choices for dinner. Birds flock to the ohia and fern forest, set at a chilly 4,000 feet. You get to enjoy evenings and mornings at the park, at see it at its most beautiful and quiet. A night or three in Volcano is highly recommended.

Hale Ohia Cottages (B&B) (M) 800-455-3803, 967-7986
> *Lots of intriguing options on these historic beautifully groomed grounds.*

Kilauea Lodge (includes breakfast) (M) 967-7366
> *Great to come home to after a day at the volcano; ambiance matches excellent cuisine.*

Carson's Volcano Cottage (B&B) (M) 967-7683

Guesthouse at Volcano (cottages, B&B) (C-M) 967-7775

Holo Holo Inn (C) 967-7950

Kilauea Military Camp (retired, active military and guests) (C) 967-8333

Volcano House (historic hotel in park) (C-M) 967-7321

My Island Bed & Breakfast (C-M) 967-7216, 967-7110

KAU-WOOD VALLEY

Not many people stay is this section of the Big Island, in spite of several excellent lodging choices. A rain forest is close by, and you have access to the coast at several places—although snorkeling is generally not good. You're within range to visit Hawaii Volcanoes National Park, as well as South Point, Wood Valley rain forest, and Miloli'i.

Becky's Bed & Breakfast, Na'alehu (C) 929-9690, 866-422-3259
The Big Island Cottage, Wood Valley (C-M) 888-256-4206
Bougainvillea B&B, Ocean View (C) 929-7089, 800-688-1763
Macadamia Meadows Farm B&B (C-M) 929-8097, 888-929-8118
Pahala Plantation Cottages (C-P) 928-9811
SeaMountain at Punalu'u (condos) (M) 928-8301, 800-488-8301
   Great oceanfront value near Black Sand Beach.
Shirakawa Motel, Na'alehu (C) 929-7462
South Point Bed & Breakfast (C-M) 939-9049
Wood Valley Temple & Retreat (C-M) 928-8539
   Peace and contemplation in a rain forest.

KILAUEA LODGE, WOOD VALLEY TEMPLE
HALE OHIA COTTAGE

Where to eat

Whether you hunger for Pacific gourmet or island-style grinds, pupus or a full-on luau, you can end the quest at one of these Big Island winners. Call ahead to see if they suit your tastes. Not all serve dinner. All area codes are 808.

(C) CHEAP OR TAKE-OUT (LESS THAN $10)

(M) MODERATE, FAMILY ($10 TO $20)

(P) PRICEY, SPECIAL OCCASION ($20 AND UP)

KAILUA
Ba-le Sandwiches & Bakery (C) 327-1212
Don's Chinese Kitchen (C) 329-3770
Keauhou Beach Resort (M-P) 322-3441
   Immersed in outdoor tropical atmosphere. Dining by the lagoon.
Kona Inn Restaurant (M-P) 329-4455
   Great food since Don Ho was a keiki. Peacock chairs,
   view of Kailua Harbor. Watch the sunset.
Ocean View Inn (C) 329-9998
   An old marlin fisherman's watering hole. 'Behind the Green
   Door' you'll find a menu out of the 1950s.
Royal Kona Resort (luau) (P) 329-3111
Sam Choy's (P) 326-1545

KEALAKEKUA-CAPTAIN COOK
Evie's Natural Foods, Kainaliu (C) 322-0739
Manago Hotel, Captain Cook (C) 323-2642
   Try the pork chops and potato-mac salad. A taste of Old Hawaii.
Super J's, Honaunau (C) 328-9566
   Aunty and the keikis prepare authentic Hawaiian take out plates.
Teshima's, Kainaliu (C) 322-9140
   Japanese food is a magnet for locals.

KOHALA

Aunty's Place, Hawi (C-M) 889-0899
Bamboo Restaurant, Hawi (M) 889-5555
  Just look for the crowds, everyone's favorite.
Jen's Kohala Café, Kapa'au (C) 889-0099
Kawaihae Harbor Grill (C-M) 882-1368
  A real find in South Kohala, on the water.
King's Shops Food Court (C-M)
Kohala Health Foods, Hawi (C) 889-0277
Nambu Courtyard, Kapa'au (C) 889-5546
  Lots of homemade goodies.

HILO-HAMAKUA

Akaka Noodle Shop, Honomu (C) 963-6071
  Homemade buns and lotsa talk story at this
  Hawaiian hangout. Handcranked shave ice made to order.
Cafe 100, (M-P), 935-8683
Cafe Pesto (M-P), 969-6640
Don's Grill, Hilo (C-M) 935-9099
  Neighborhood eatery. Spirited service and great value.
Miyo's, Hilo (C-M) 935-2273
  Romance on the moonlit pond without paying through the nose.
Naung Mai Thai Kitchen (C-M) 934-7540
Paolo's Bistro, Pahoa (M-P) 965-7033
What's Shakin', Pepe'ekeo (C) 964-3080

VOLCANO-SOUTH POINT

Kilauea Lodge, Volcano (M-P) 967-7366
  Fireside gourmet cuisine where you can bring along a healthy appetite.
Kilauea Military Camp, Volcanoes National Park (C)
  A cafeteria style smorgie and bowling alley burgers cater to student travelers.
Lava Rock Café, Volcano (M) 967-8626
  Family friendly, and a lengthy menu for all tastes. Great homemade soups.
Na'alehu Fruit Stand (café) (C) 929-9009
  Famous macadamia nut shortbread cookies, banana-walnut poundcake, local oranges, guava, mangoes.
Shady Grove Farms (fruit stand), Ocean View (C) 939-9817
Volcano House, Volcanoes National Park (P) 967-7321

WAIMEA-HONOKA'A

Don's Pake Kitchen (C) 885-2025
Daniel Thiebaut (P), 887-2200
Hawaiian Style Café (C) 885-4295
Kamuela Deli, Waimea (C) 885-4147
Tex Drive-in & Restaurant, Honoka'a
  (C) 775-0598
Merriman's Restaurant (P) 885-6822
  Enjoy a special evening at this gourmet hideaway.
Paniolo Country Inn (M-P) 885-4377

Hawaiian Glossary

VOLCANO ART CENTER

The Hawaiian language was first written by Big Island missionaries in the 1820s, who transcribed phonetically. *Hawaiian Grammar*, which is now out of print, was published by Lorrin Andrews in 1854. Only 12 letters were needed—A, E, I, O, U, plus the consonants, H, K, L, M, N, P, and W. Note that there is no B. and S. in Hawaiian.

Hawaiian can be thought of as a dialect of the Polynesian language; others include Samoan, Tahitian, Marquesan, and Maori. The original home of the Polynesians was India, and after a long period of migrations they reached the South Pacific, as their language transformed with their travel

Vowels may follow each other, but consonants stand alone. A "W" is sometimes pronounced as a "V," when in the middle of a word. Words always end in a vowel. The funny apostrophe (') between some vowels is called an okina. It creates a glottal stop in the word; for instance, in "ahupua'a," the ending is pronounced "ah-ah." Among all words, stress is usually placed on the second to the last syllable, unless the word only has two syllables, in which cast the last is stressed. Today, an increasing number of schools in Hawaii are centered around teaching the language, as well as the time-honored crafts, dance, and legends.

a'a – sharp, broken lava
ahupua'a – a division of land from the mountains to the sea around which a
    village lived; watershed
aina – land, country
aka'aka – to laugh
akua – god, deity
akua ki – image of a god
ala – path, way, or trail
ali'i – chief or chiefess descended from original chiefs or nobles
aloha – hello or goodbye, welcome or farewell, love and best wishes
aumakua – ancestral spirit, personal or family god
hale – house
hana – work
haole – foreigner, sometimes Caucasian
hau – breeze, dew; a king of tree
heiau – temple, church, worship ground
hilo – twisting, braiding
hoaloha – a friend
hoku – a star
holua – a sled, or sliding place
honi – to touch, taste, kiss
hono – bay
honu – a turtle
huhu – angry, offended
hui – group, meeting
hukilau – group net fishing
hula – dance that enacts
    the stories that
    become myths
huli huli – barbecue
iki – small, little
ipo – sweetheart, darling
ka'a – cart or car
kahuna – teacher, expert, priest

KING KAMEHAMEHA'S KONA BEACH HOTEL LUAU CEREMONY

kai – the sea

kama'aina – native born, or longtime resident

kanaka – the people

kane – man

kapa – tapa, bark cloth

kapu – forbidden, no trespassing

kapuna – older, wise person

keiki – child, or young banana plant

keiki pond - beach or swimming area for children

ki'i – image, statue

ki'i pohaku – etchings made in rock, petroglyphs

kiawe –the algaroba tree from South America, has long thorns

kipuka – a portion of native forest surrounded by a lava flow

koa – largest of the native forest trees

kona – leeward

kokua – help

kopa'a – sugar

Ku – god of war

kukui – a type of tree; lamp or torch

lanai – deck, porch, patio

laulau – fish, pork, sweet potatoes, and taro leaves in steamed pouch

lei – garland of flowers, vines, or beads worn around the neck

lolo – dumb

lomi lomi – a traditional massage

Lono – god of peace and fertility

luau – feast

mahalo – thank you

mahina – lunar month

makahiki – fall celebration of return of peace and fertility; a year

makai – toward the sea

mana – spiritual power in all things

mauka – toward the mountain, inland

mauna – mountain

Mele Kalikimaka – Merry Christmas

menehune – dwarf person; legendary first settlers

moana – ocean

moku – island

nalu – surf breaking on the beach

nani – pretty, beautiful

nene – Hawaiian goose

niu - coconut

o'ne – sand

ohana – family

ohia – mountain apple, lehua blossom bearer

oluolu – please

opala - rubbish

pahoehoe – smooth, undulating lava

pali – cliff, precipice

paniolo – Hawaiian cowboy

Pele – the goddess of volcanoes

peleleu – a large, double canoe

piko – umbilical cord or, figuratively, a blood relation

pohaku – stone

poi – pasty food made from taro

pono – good, blessed; in balance with nature

pu'u – hill or cinder cone

pu'uhonua – a place of refuge

puka – a hole

pupu – snack or hors d'oeuvres

tsunami – tidal wave (Japanese)

tutu – grandmother, old woman, term of   endearment

ula - red

ulu – the breadfruit tree

wahine – woman, girl

wai – fresh water

wailuku – breaking waves, destructive water

wiki – fast, quickly

Index

Notes

FOR PUBLISHER-DIRECT SAVINGS TO INDIVIDUALS AND GROUPS, AND FOR BOOK TRADE ORDERS, PLEASE CONTACT:

DIAMOND VALLEY COMPANY
89 Lower Manzanita Drive
Markleeville, CA 96120

Phone-fax: 530-694-2740
www.trailblazertravelbooks.com
trailblazer@gbis.com

All titles are also available through major book distributors, stores, and websites. Please contact the publisher with comments and suggestions. We value your readership.

DIAMOND VALLEY COMPANY'S TRAILBLAZER TRAVEL BOOK SERIES:

ALPINE SIERRA TRAILBLAZER
Where to Hike, Ski, Bike, Pack, Paddle, Fish
from Lake Tahoe to Yosemite
ISBN 0-9670072-6-7

KAUAI TRAILBLAZER
Where to Hike, Snorkel, Bike,
Paddle, Surf
ISBN 0-9670072-1-6

GOLDEN GATE TRAILBLAZER
Where to Hike, Stroll, Bike, Jog, Roll
in San Francisco and Marin
ISBN 0-9670072-2-4

MAUI TRAILBLAZER
Where to Hike, Snorkel, Paddle,
Surf, Drive
ISBN 0-9670072-4-0

HAWAII THE BIG ISLAND TRAILBLAZER
Where to Hike, Snorkel, Bike, Surf, Drive
ISBN 0-9670072-5-9